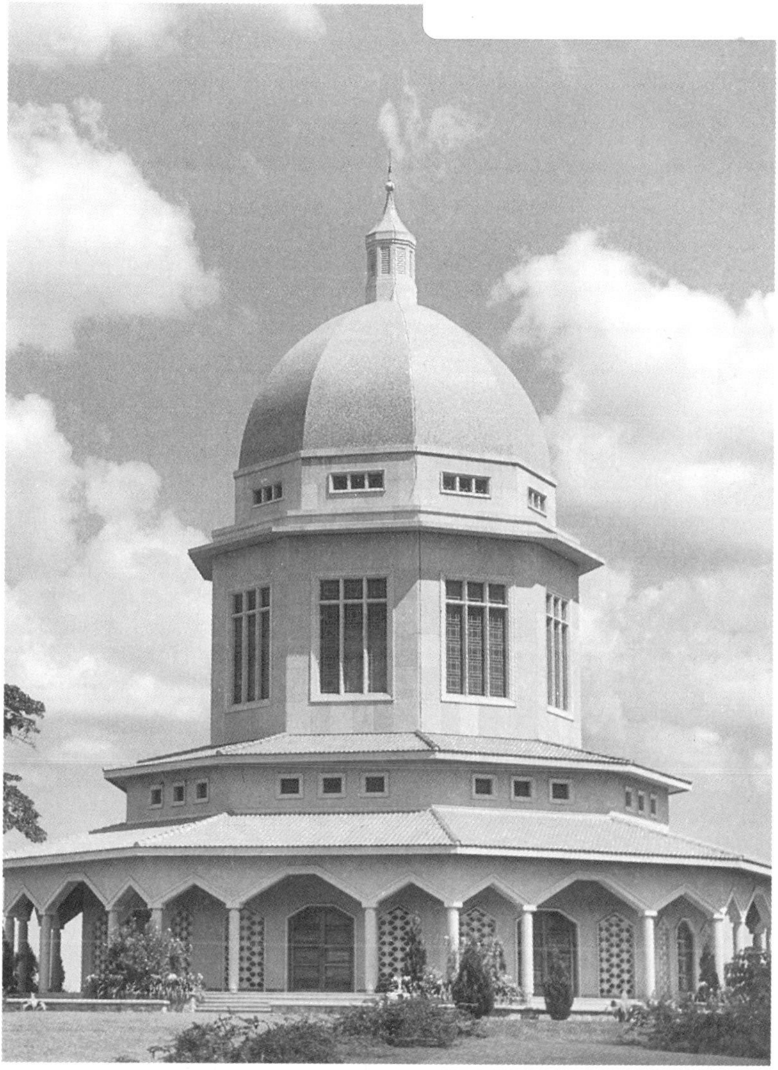

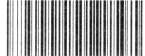

The Bahá'í Temple Kampala

Published by

SKYESET LIMITED, December, 2004

Grey Lodge, London Road, Stroud, Gloucestershire, GL5 2AT
Telephone: (National) 01453 763281; (International) + 44 1453 763281

Author: Philip Hainsworth
Editor/Author: Lois Hainsworth MBE, FCIJ, FRSA

ISBN 09549649-O-X

Cover and content designed by Greenhouse Graphics Ltd

Produced by Greenhouse Graphics Ltd

Printed and bound by Butler and Tanner Ltd

LOOKING BACK IN WONDER

LOOKING BACK IN WONDER

AUTOBIOGRAPHY OF PHILIP HAINSWORTH

FROM 1919 TO 1967

WITH A POSTSCRIPT

BY LOIS HAINSWORTH, MBE

COVERING THE YEARS 1967-2001

Table of Contents

MESSAGE FROM THE UNIVERSAL HOUSE OF JUSTICE

December 17, 2001

We were deeply grieved at the news of the passing of Philip Hainsworth, whose outstanding record of dedicated services in the United Kingdom and in Africa is unforgettable. He distinguished himself through his wholehearted devotion to the beloved Guardian, his staunch perseverance, and his indefatigable efforts to proclaim and teach the Cause. We advise you to hold, on the national and local levels, memorial gatherings in his name. We are also asking the National Spiritual Assembly of Uganda to hold similar memorial gatherings in the Mother Temple of Africa, and elsewhere in the country. Kindly assure his beloved wife and dear children of our deepest sympathy and of our fervent prayers in the Holy Shrines for the progress of his soul in the Abhá Kingdom.

The Universal House of Justice

ACKNOWLEDGEMENTS

Philip wrote this autobiography at the request of many people who had heard him speak of his meetings with Shoghi Effendi, his war experiences and of the exciting developments of the Bahá'í Faith in England and East Africa between 1946 and 1967. He had intended to write a sequel, but appreciated that the years following 1967 were much better documented and his personal involvement in the earlier years was perhaps of greater interest.

This book could never have been published without considerable help and support from our three children, Richard, Zarin, and Michael, who assisted me in various ways and all of whom made suggestions to the text and the selection of photographs.

Many others encouraged and helped me to edit and publish this book: Ian Semple, a friend of Philip's since 1949 and mine of fifty years, who has been a Member of the Universal House of Justice since its formation in 1963, wrote the Foreword and suggested that I write a chapter to summarise the latter part of Philip's life.

Two people gave me exceptional support as well as precious technical advice, without which this book might never have seen the light of day: Alex McGee's help with editing the manuscript, in addition to making supportive suggestions, was invaluable and his encouragement at the outset of the project was inspirational; Hugh Adamson read the proofs, a labour of love from someone who had served with Philip for many years on the British National Assembly, and provided the footnotes as well as other valuable advice and assistance.

There were three areas of his life and service with which I was only peripherally conversant (his work relating to the incorporation of Spiritual Assemblies, his involvement with the Bahá'í Agency for Social & Economic Development (UK), and his service on the National Spiritual Assembly), and at my request three distinguished Bahá'ís have contributed paragraphs to cover these: Kian Golestani, Iraj Poostchi and Hugh Adamson.

My daughter Zarin suggested Greenhouse Graphics, the designer and producer of the book, and Timi van Houten and Ian Crossley gave me great help: the excellence of their work will be apparent.

It was Ken Brookes, a fellow Past President of the Chartered Institute of Journalists, and a member of the British Copyright Council, who suggested that I publish the book and he and his wife, Sandra, offered support throughout. My son Michael and his wife Katherine treated this suggestion with enthusiasm which enabled me to pursue the idea.

The book was written at the request of Bahá'ís, but there are others with whom Philip came into close contact during the years in which he was closely concerned with external affairs work: in government departments, with diplomats, Members of the European and both Houses of the UK Parliaments, the United Nations Association, the World Federalists, the Inter Faith Network, the World Congress of Faiths, the Wyndham Place Trust, the World Conference for Religions for Peace, as well as a great many others.

It seemed to me that a short introductory chapter on the Bahá'í Faith itself was necessary and for this contribution I wish to thank my son Richard, who wrote Appendix 3 on a train between Moscow and Yaroslavl: the best short introduction I have ever read

Others who helped me include Erica Leith; members of the Reviewing Panel of the National Spiritual Assembly of the Bahá'ís of the UK; Shahin Leaver and Iman Fadaei. There were, naturally, others who encouraged and helped me over time and I apologise if I have unintentionally omitted their names.

I wish too to thank the National Spiritual Assembly of the Bahá'ís of the United Kingdom for their creation of a "Philip Hainsworth Library" room in the Sub-Office of the National Spiritual Assembly of the UK (Bridge House (3Fl), 97-101 High St, Tonbridge, Kent TN9 1DP). This is particularly important because, as the reader will soon discover, there is a literal treasure trove of previously unpublished documents in the pages that follow. All of the documents cited in these pages now repose in the "Philip Hainsworth Library" room, which will, at some point, allow access to those undertaking further research.

Lois Hainsworth
Sevenoaks, December 2004

FOREWORD

Philip Hainsworth's life spanned a period of extraordinary development of the Bahá'í community in Britain and throughout the world. Future generations will owe him a debt not only for the tireless exertions with which he served the Cause of God, but for the record he has left of those soul-stirring years. It is a personal record, but all the more precious for that. It reveals, as no impersonal history could, the conditions in which the British Bahá'ís of the mid twentieth century laboured, and the spirit that suffused them. Tracing the course of Philip's own life, it portrays the struggles and achievements of a British Bahá'í during the years of the Second World War, his service in the army, his first experiences in Africa, the labours and triumphs of the Six Year Plan, the burgeoning of the overseas mission of the British Bahá'í community in Africa during the Two Year Plan and the Ten Year Crusade, and draws to a close with Philip's return, in 1966, to initiate over thirty more years of service in his homeland.

It was in 1949, when Philip was serving as Secretary of the National Teaching Committee and living as a pioneer in Oxford, that I met him, received from him my first training in the Teachings of Bahá'u'lláh and found a friendship that I have treasured all my life. He was a man of unflagging drive, of definite views, and bluntness of speech, but with loving patience for the human frailties of others and deep roots of loyalty to the authority of the Divine Revelation. Strong as were his views, he taught me never to fear to disagree with them – because only the Teachings were unfailingly right.

Although this book is an autobiography, it is less about its author than about the historic events in which he took part, and preserves invaluable records of the services of others whom Philip met or with whom he served. It reveals the loving ease of communication that existed between the individual believers of those days and their Guardian, and the vital rôle played by 'Amatu'l-Bahá Rúḥíyyih Khánum. It gives insights into the devotion of the pioneers and administrators of the community, the love that bound them together, and the daily life they had to pursue in addition to their services to the Faith itself.

There are many passages in this book in which Philip reveals a touching self-perceptiveness and underlying humility that is refreshing in any man, and especially in one who has achieved so much. In one of his letters to the Guardian, he writes what might well stand as a testimony to the whole tenor of his life: "I have no ambition beyond being a good Bahá'í, but it is dreadfully hard at times." He well knew, long before it was translated into English, this challenging standard set forth by Bahá'u'lláh in the Kitáb-i-Aqdas: [1]

> This is not a Cause which may be made a plaything for your idle fancies, nor is it a field for the foolish and faint of heart. By God, this is the arena of insight and detachment, of vision and upliftment, where none may spur on their chargers save the valiant horsemen of the Merciful, who have severed all attachment to the world of being. These, truly, are they that render God victorious on earth, and are the dawning places of His sovereign might amidst mankind.

Ian Semple

[1] Bahá'u'lláh (1992). Kitáb-i-Aqdas - The Most Holy Book. Haifa, Bahá'í World Centre., p.84.

PROLOGUE

Again and again, while re-writing the story of more than sixty years of Bahá'í service, I have wondered, "Why me?"

When, in 1939, shortly after the outbreak of World War Two, I was called as a young Bahá'í to appear before a Tribunal in Leeds, Yorkshire, to seek exemption from combatant service, I did not realise that I was just beginning to participate in a series of events which have turned out to be of historic significance. Strangely enough, I never sought them out nor was I often aware of what they meant at the time.

During the past few years, I have given many talks on the precious hours I spent in the presence of Shoghi Effendi and of my personal involvement in these events.

There has been a great demand for these to be made available in print. I have completed detailed memoirs up to the late 1960s but these are far too voluminous for any publisher to take on at the present time. I have therefore extracted sections which I feel may be of especial interest to those, particularly to the youth and new Bahá'ís, who may wonder what it was like to have been involved in the work of the Faith towards the end of its first centenary, through the war years, and in the national and global Plans initiated by the beloved Guardian.

It has always seemed strange to me that people are interested in how I became a Bahá'í. Looking back, it seems that it was just a natural thing to do – no deep study, no real problems: perhaps it was that my father and mother had unknowingly prepared me, for the Guardian once wrote to me, "You were blessed in your parents". They were somewhat apprehensive when I met the Faith, accepted it and told them about it, but some eight years later, they themselves embraced it.

That is how I shall begin the story and will follow with a little of my war experiences, my six weeks in Haifa with the Guardian on my way home after the war, the Six and Two Year Plans, my fifteen years in Uganda and my part in the Global Crusade. I shall also include the full texts of the 15 letters and 16 cables I received from the Guardian.

LOOKING BACK IN WONDER

THE EARLY YEARS 1919 – 38

I was born on 27 July 1919 in Great Horton, Bradford, Yorkshire. My father, George Herbert, was a Yorkshireman and my mother, Lizzie (née Fowler), was from Lincolnshire. Father had been an invalid for as long as I could remember. I left school before my 14th birthday and started work in a worsted spinning mill the day after, as we were in much straightened circumstances. I had hoped to work for a local newspaper, but wages at the mill were better.

I had joined the Scouts about a year before I left school, was very keen on achieving Scout proficiency badges, and became a King's Scout, the holder of the Bushman's Thong and Gold All Round Cords. I was chosen to be one of the twenty Scouts representing Yorkshire at the Coronation of King George VI in 1937, and represented Bradford at the St George's Day Parade at Windsor Castle two weeks later.

Attending the Coronation was my first visit to London and it was there, sleeping on the floor in a huge hall with Scouts from many lands, that I first met people of different races. The bringing together of all these young people from every part of the Empire under the banner of Scouting gave me an even greater thrill than meeting Lord Baden Powell, who visited the hall on that occasion.

Many years later, I visited Malta in the 1970s on behalf of the British National Spiritual Assembly (NSA). When talking with Cyril Crockford, one of the early believers in Malta – a Scot who had lived for most of his life in Malta – he mentioned that he had formed the first Scout Group in Malta and had attended the Coronation. It transpired that he had slept on the stage in Horticultural Hall, some few feet away from where I had slept, in that same Hall, on those same days, in 1937! This was but one of many strange coincidences I have experienced during my more than three score years as a Bahá'í.

ACCEPTING THE FAITH

One day, not many weeks after my 19th birthday, I was on Church Parade with the Scout Troop when it was announced that a certain television announcer, one David Hofman, would be addressing the Young Men's Bible Class on the following Sunday afternoon. His subject would be 'The Bahá'í Faith'. In 1938, we had heard rumours about something called 'television', and that the first station in the world had opened a news service at the Alexandra Palace in London. There were two female announcers and one man – David Hofman. No one had heard of the Bahá'í Faith and no-one was particularly interested. The Young Men's Bible Class had a reputation for being rather hard, critical, and argumentative with its visiting speakers. That particular afternoon the attendance at the Class was a record one, not because of the subject, but to see what kind of a performance would be given by a 'television announcer'. The audience was very attentive and, most unusually, gave a long ovation to Mr Hofman's talk. Not a word of criticism and hardly a question was asked. Ralph Naylor – a Scouting friend – and I, among others, took a pamphlet.

It was a very strange experience for me. I had gone as far as I could in Scouting, and I was too old to wear my Scout shirt with the record number of badges on it. I was doing very well at night school and doing a fully grown man's work during the day, yet here was something of which I had never heard. It was different, no one in our little part of the world had ever met a Bahá'í and here was a man who spoke fluently, using beautiful English and painting such an exciting picture. I felt I must know more – so I found out where there would be a follow-up meeting where I could meet Mr Hofman again: this was to be at the home of Mrs Wilkinson, 20 Southey Place. Many thoughts rushed around my mind during the next two weeks. I wanted so much to be different from all those people I knew; I felt I must try to be better than them, yet I felt I needed to be humbled for the good of my soul. Surely Mr Hofman could do this? I saw in the Bahá'í Faith, with its universal appeal and on a spiritual basis, a way of achieving the vision I had gained from Scouting at the Coronation. I had one important question: if I went into this new Faith, would I be disloyal to Christ, whose Teachings I had so recently sworn to uphold when I had done the 'Squires' Vigil' on being invested as a Rover Scout?

I met a few Bahá'ís in the home of Mrs Wilkinson and they were lovely people, but Mr Hofman had succeeded in giving me real satisfaction. My parents gave the news a mixed reception. Father was always ultra-conservative, and as he grew older and frailer, 'beware of change' was his attitude and mother hoped that this new attraction would not take me away from the Church.

After my second meeting with these Bahá'ís, two weeks after first hearing Mr Hofman, I was in the process of preparing to leave when I was introduced to Herbert Stone, a blind piano tuner and a Bahá'í. He had a most unusual way of squeezing one's hand on being introduced as though he was trying to get to know one through the vibrations from his hand clasp. He leaned towards me and said very quietly, 'Are you one of us?'

Somewhat surprised but quite excited, I replied something to the effect, 'Yes, I suppose I am'. Immediately he called out, 'Joan, make a note of this, Philip is one of us'. Joan Wilkinson, the daughter of our hostess, and the secretary of the Bradford Group, confirmed my name and address: that was how I became a Bahá'í – I never made a formal 'declaration'. There were no such things as declaration cards nor had the Bahá'ís in Britain got around to studying the 'Will and Testament of 'Abdu'l-Bahá' or 'Dispensation of Bahá'u'lláh'. There was a Spiritual Assembly in London, one in Manchester and occasionally one in Bournemouth, as well as Groups in Bradford and Torquay and teaching work had begun in Newcastle. There were about 80 Bahá'ís in total, all in England.

Going home that night on the electric tramcar, I was so excited, saying to myself over and over again, 'I am a Bahá'í'. Again and again I had, on my knees, been beseeching Christ to guide me and protect me from disloyalty. That night I realised, though I could not immediately express it, that in fact the only way I could be loyal to Him was by accepting Bahá'u'lláh. I had read little, but I had absorbed every word of teaching and I had believed.

Looking back to those days, I now realise that there was no real intellectual investigation, no great struggle, no strong issue to be resolved, no big problems to be overcome. I was selfish, full of myself, always trying to be different from others. Yet Bahá'u'lláh, in His wisdom, granted me the bounty of recognising Him. To this day I have never done anything worthy of being granted that bounty. Ralph Naylor also became a Bahá'í shortly afterwards.

In April 1939, Bradford elected its local Spiritual Assembly (LSA) – I was, at 19, too young to be elected a member.

MY FIRST PUBLIC TALK

I had been a Bahá'í for less than a year when I received a card from a Mr AE South of the Peace Pledge Union, inviting me to speak to their meeting on 22 November 1939. It came about like this…

A Miss Joan Brown was studying the Faith. Her mother was from Birmingham and her father from the West Indies. He was a member of the

Bradford Secular Society. I was not then aware that Secular Society members were atheists; they included many of Bradford's intelligentsia, and many were members of the Peace Pledge Union. This movement was for a time banned in Britain because of its association with the 'Left' and the Soviet Union. At that time, I had read only one piece of introductory literature, the 'yellow pamphlet', and a small booklet by Dr Esslemont: 'The Message of Bahá'u'lláh' (a 'green' pamphlet). Joan must have told her father, who told Mr AE South that I was 'a good speaker on Bahá'í', but the fact was that I had never addressed an audience in my life; until I became a Bahá'í I had never discussed religion and on this occasion I, a 20-year-old, had an audience of about 30 rather frightening, middle-aged to elderly men, plus there were four or five Bahá'ís present.

I spoke for 45 minutes without a pause, remembering the points from the pamphlet without any notes. At the end the chairman, Mr South, said that what they had heard was most interesting, that their society could not agree with many of the things I had said but they 'must pay tribute to the speaker's knowledge of his subject'! Little did he know that this was the first proof to me that 'God will assist all those who arise to serve Him'.[2]

THE WAR YEARS 1939 – 46

Ralph, being a little older than me, was conscripted into the Army just before war was declared and before the British National Spiritual Assembly was fully alert to the instructions of the Guardian. During 1939 a great deal of correspondence about the issue of the Faith's position on the war had been exchanged between David Hofman, then secretary of the National Spiritual Assembly, Arthur Norton, chairman of the Bradford Assembly, and Ralph and I. David had also written to the Guardian about the matter.

It will be realised that both Ralph and I, although young, naive and relatively new Bahá'ís, felt the inner conflict of duty to our parents, duty to our country and the need to express our determination to do what was right for the Faith. These letters make very interesting reading but David's letter to me dated 10 May is worthy of note:[3]

> We are not conscientious objectors. We do not resist the government. Killing and fighting are contrary to our principles of human brotherhood and therefore if the government offers exemption from them on grounds of conscience, we take advantage of this offer. If they refuse our application, we do not resist, but bear

[2] Compilation (1988). Lights of Guidance: A Bahá'í Reference File. New Delhi, India, Bahá'í Publishing Trust., Section 1595, p. 579.
[3] Unpublished letter (personal archives).

> arms without any fuss. In addition if they grant our application we will take other forms of service required by government. I believe this is perfectly clear and logical. Again the Bahá'í Faith pursues the golden mean. We are not pacifists neither do we rush to join the army. We will bear arms if ordered to do so, but if the government permit us to serve in some other way we will do that. This is neither resisting, nor causing dissension. Whether the British Government is a bulwark for peace or not is a matter of political opinion. Certain it is that the Peace Plan of Bahá'u'lláh is not being followed by *any* government today. He commanded collective security as a means of establishing the Lesser Peace. Collective security has been abandoned by one nation after another, and it is true that we were in the lead in doing this. The last voice raised in defence of collective security was that of Litvinov and he has been sacked. We have made it very clear that we will only fight to defend our own interests, and peace can never come in that way. As I have written to Ralph: 'No government is in the right today; all are wrong and hopelessly astray. Therefore all we can do is to live in the world order of the Bahá'í Faith, taking no part in political controversy, but remaining loyal to the government under which we live'. I'm afraid this is not a question which can be settled by letter, it requires discussion. But it may be of some comfort to you to think how very much more difficult it must be for the Bahá'ís in Germany, Italy, China and Japan.

War broke out on 3 September 1939, but Ralph was 'called up' before then. He could not, before hostilities began, register as a conscientious objector (CO), as I was subsequently able to do. Consequently he went into an infantry unit and became a signaller, as he thought this would be non-combatant. He was in the 4th Lincolnshire regiment, went to Norway and was driven out by the Germans, and then spent a long time in Iceland. He was brought back for the Normandy assaults, was in the battle for Caen and sustained a bullet in the brain. He recovered well enough to marry, have a family, divorce, remarry, and hold a job until retirement, but he suffered for very many years with severe headaches. He died in May 1992.

EXEMPTION FROM COMBATANT SERVICE

I registered for first-aid work and, in late September 1939, just a year after I became a Bahá'í, I received my 'call-up' papers and immediately sought to register as a 'conscientious objector'. Although as a Bahá'í I did not 'object' to service in the Army, I was obliged to register in order to get 'non-combatant service'. In other words, as the National Service (Armed Forces) Act (1939) made provision for this appeal on grounds of conscience, it was in the spirit of 'obedience to government' that I registered.

In my heart of hearts I had hoped to have 'absolute' exemption and so did my parents, but the words of the Guardian were quite explicit, and were quoted on my application form.

On 18 October, David produced a certificate from the National Spiritual Assembly of the Bahá'ís of the British Isles:[4]

> This is to certify that the bearer of this letter, Mr Philip Hainsworth, of 26 Etna Street, Bradford, is a member of the Bahá'í Faith.
>
> In keeping with the principles of the Bahá'í Faith, he seeks exemption from combatant military service, but is ready to serve his country in any non-combatant manner required, whether at home or at the front, and regardless of whether such service would expose him to danger or not.
>
> *David Hofman, Secretary*

David actually typed the following on my application form that I then had to sign:

> I wish to obtain exemption from combatant military service, as such would be incompatible with my beliefs, which are those of the Bahá'í Faith. (Please see enclosed booklet).
>
> I am most anxious that this should not be, in the slightest degree, prejudicial to my standing as a loyal and devoted citizen.
>
> It is after very serious consideration that I have decided on making this application, for the simple reason that it is due to my belief and my faith which, after all, are as they should be, *the* first consideration.
>
> The following is an extract from the words of the Guardian of the Cause, which were written with a view to their being of use to us as guidance in any such emergency:
>
> > ...appeal to the Government for exemption from active military service in a combatant capacity, stressing the fact that in doing so they are not prompted by any selfish considerations but by the sole and supreme motive of upholding the Teachings of their Faith, which make it a moral obligation for them to desist from any act that would involve them in direct warfare with their

[4] Unpublished (personal archives).

> fellow humans of any other race or nation.[5] Such forms of national work as air raid precaution service, ambulance corps, and other humanitarian work or activity of an non-combatant nature, are the most suitable types of service the friends can render, and which they should gladly volunteer for, since in addition to the fact that they do not involve any violation of the spirit or principle of the Teachings, they constitute a form of social and humanitarian service which the Cause holds sacred and emphatically enjoins.[6]

I have been for some years doing various works of a public nature, such as helping in the training of Boy Scouts; being an active Rover Scout, etc.

I have also, since the outbreak of war, been a part-time stretcher-bearer at the local Ambulance Depot.

These things, taken together with the work of the propagation of our Bahá'í Faith, and the three nights per week which I have been compelled to put in at the College as necessary for my textile education, have taken up the whole of my time for some years.

Philip Hainsworth, 1st November 1939

On registration as a conscientious objector, a Court hearing was arranged and the judge and tribunal had to decide on the sincerity of the applicant and place him in one of four categories: 1. Absolute exemption, 2. Land service, 3. Non-combatant service, 4. Rejected outright.

My hearing was on 24 November 1939. The chairman of the Tribunal was Judge Stewart, with D McCandlish and EC Behrens as members. David Hofman was there as official representative of the National Spiritual Assembly. The judge of the Tribunal to which I was summoned had the reputation of being very hard on conscientious objectors, particularly those who appeared to be trying to get out of military service by pretext. He listened very carefully to what David had to say and asked him some interesting questions, but asked me very little before granting me non-combatant service.

I was placed in Category III. The official findings were that I was 'sincere' and the decision described as 'unanimous'. My parents and I had hoped I would be exempted but when the decision was made, David was jubilant – he said it was exactly as the Guardian had wished.

[5] Effendi, S. (1981). The Unfolding Destiny of the British Bahá'í Community: The Messages from the Guardian of the Bahá'í Faith to the Bahá'ís of the British Isles. London, Bahá'í Publishing Trust., p. 128.
[6] Ibid., p. 123.

After I appeared in the Leeds Court, two local papers carried the heading: 'Persian Faith modifies man's pacifism'.

David wrote about the Tribunal in a report on 'Teaching Activities', and the Guardian published it twice in *The Bahá'í World* vol. VIII, and once again in vol. IX.

I think that it was unique for the Guardian to publish the same item of news three times. Looking back I think that this was because it was the first time in the world that an individual Bahá'í had appeared before a court of law and the Faith had been recognised as the basis for a sympathetic ruling. This decision became a precedent for all Bahá'ís who were subsequently called into the Armed Forces in the British Isles and its overseas territories.

'ABDU'L BAHÁ IS PROTECTING YOU

For many years, Mrs Kenworthy was a resident in York; she moved to Leeds in early 1939 and became a member of the Bradford Group.

On a couple of occasions, Mrs Kenworthy was brought by car to speak to us and these talks are worthy of note. Although old and frail, her mind was razor sharp and she was alert to all world events, speaking with deep insight into what was actually happening. She claimed to have direct contact with the Master and sometimes would say: ''Abdu'l- Bahá is saying to me …'.

One day, after war broke out, I went to visit her, and after providing me with tea, she suddenly looked straight at me and said, ''Abdu'l-Bahá says you are not to worry during the war, He is protecting you!' This was so direct that it sent shivers down my spine. She had first meet the Master in Paris in October 1911 and in December made the journey alone to see Him in Haifa. She passed away in Leeds on 30 August 1942 at the age of 84.

EARLY ARMY TRAINING

At the First Aid Centre, before conscription, I had met Ernest Hartley, and he and his parents were interested in the Faith. He had dabbled in many religious beliefs and was attracted to the Faith.

Interestingly, Ernest had to appear at the same Tribunal on the day following my hearing. I learned afterwards that the cases before his had been very trying and the judge had been very angry with some of those appealing. It was with trepidation that Ernest faced him.

The judge spent some time reading the statement prepared by Ernest which listed the many avenues of search he had pursued and then said, with a smile which completely changed his forbidding appearance: 'You might almost be a Bahá'í!' A flabbergasted Ernest replied, 'I am now studying that, sir!' He was given the same ruling as mine and we were posted to the same unit in the Royal Army Medical Corps (RAMC).

We were called to report together on 18 January 1940 at the Gibraltar Barracks in Leeds, were sent to a unit, the 16th Casualty Clearing Station, in Selby, and put in civilian accommodation together. The unit went 'under canvas' at Ricall (Yorkshire) and then to Helens Bay, Co. Down, N. Ireland. There were about six conscientious objectors in the unit.

In Helens Bay we were billeted in empty houses. Ernest and I, while on the beach, met a 'nanny' of two children, who was a Christian Scientist. Occasionally we went to visit her in the evenings to talk about our religious beliefs but little interest was shown in the Bahá'í Faith. Her name was Beth and she was an Australian. Many years later I went to meet Elizabeth (Lisbeth) Greaves, a fairly new Bahá'í, who lived in the next village to Helens Bay, Crawfordsburn. Lisbeth said how interesting that it was just about that time that she had really become interested in spiritual things. I said jokingly that it must have been the effect of our 'firesides' at Beth's. This became even more astonishing when she said that she and Beth had become very friendly. Lisbeth and Beth had not really discussed religion as far as I remember, but when Lisbeth became a Bahá'í she had written to Beth, who was then living again in Australia. Her letter had crossed with one from Beth saying that she had become a Christian Science 'healer'.

Many of us from Helens Bay would visit Bangor and one elderly lady serving at a canteen agreed to call some friends together at her house to hear about the Faith. It was in the summer of 1940. This was the first real 'fireside' in Bangor, possibly the first in Northern Ireland – even before George Townshend began his firesides in Ahascragh, Eire.

ACTIVE SERVICE NORTH AND EAST AFRICA 1942 – 46

Towards the end of 1942, I sailed for Algeria as a stretcher bearer with a Guard's Brigade in the British First Army, where I had my first experience of active warfare.

In the days before the war, *The Bahá'í World* would carry names and addresses of Bahá'ís around the world, except in Írán, the USA and India, where there too many for individual listings. I had made a note of those in all the countries to which I might be sent during the war. Among these was the address of a Mr Buchucha[7], 115 rue El Marr, Tunis. When the Germans were defeated in Tunisia I was stationed in Bizerta, and as soon as I had an opportunity I took a French-speaking friend into Tunis and we found Buchucha's house. My friend, Horace Warburton, a corporal cook, was a small man but very imperious when he spoke French. He demanded of the frightened little girl who opened the door if this was the house of Buchucha, and asked to see him. The little girl's fear was understandable as we were the first British soldiers they had seen and we had been 'living rough' for several weeks. Mr Buchucha was sitting on a settee as he had some slight leg trouble and answered Horace's question that he was Buchucha with some trepidation. Then I greeted him with 'Alláh'u'Abhá': this was a very moving moment as his expression changed to pure joy. I was able to take them a few things, such as sugar, tea, and chocolate, which they had not seen for some time.

More than thirty years later, I was invited to speak about the Guardian at a summer school in Italy. I had more than one interpreter, but when I told this story as part of an introduction to my later visit to the Guardian, my interpreter, who was very good and translating simultaneously from English into Italian, hesitated for a moment. She later told me that in fact she was 'the little girl who had opened the door'!

We lived for a while in Bizerta and then moved to Sousse for 'a rest' and to prepare for the landing in Sicily. On my 24th birthday, we sailed on a crowded US 'Liberty' troop carrier – everyone was sick! Our unit landed in southern Sicily; we walked up through the centre of the island and took part in actions around Centuripe and Randazzo, on the foothills of Mount Etna. I wrote a poem, 'Epic', verse by verse describing our experiences from November 1942. I also wrote a poem in Centuripe about Etna – it reminded me of Etna Street, where I was born and where my parents still lived. This poem was subsequently published in the *Bradford Telegraph and Argus*, the only time any of my poetry appeared in print.

After the capture of Sicily, our unit took over part of a monastery at Tindari: about 80 percent of the infantry went down with malaria from the river crossings and not taking their Mepacrine. From this vantage point we could see the Messina Straights and were preparing for a landing in Italy.

When we landed at the southern tip of Italy, we went by transport up to Bari and Barletta and made a seaborne landing at Termoli to attack the German Army in the rear. We took over the town hall which the Germans were using as a small hospital. One of the Germans was in bed with malaria and was quite indignant when a stray German bullet came through

[7] Bahá'í Year Book (1939). Bahá'í World (1936-1938) Vol. VII An International Record. New York, Bahá'í Publishing Committee., p. 560.

the window and lodged in his pillow! The situation was relieved by the approach of Canadian tanks, and the Germans had to retreat northwards.

It was in Termoli that a notice appeared asking for volunteers to go to a Selection Board for a new type of commission in the RAMC – 'Stretcher Bearing Officer' – it would be the only Commission, other than Quartermaster in the RAMC, given to non-medical practitioners. I was accepted and sent to Sicily.

THE ARMY SELECTION BOARD

When I appeared at the Selection Board interview I was questioned by a psychiatrist about my parents, my lack of formal education, and so on. I had with me a Bahá'í book and spent much of the interview telling him of the Faith.

A form had to be signed stating that it was understood that it may not be possible to be allocated a commission in the 'arm' of our choice (in my case the RAMC). We were asked to be prepared to make second and third choices. This I refused to sign and had to appear before the Commandant; I explained that I had sought non-combatant service and that I could do my work in the field ambulance more efficiently as an officer than as a lance-corporal, but if I was to be considered for any other arm of service I would prefer to go back to my unit. I was passed through. Some years later I learned that other conscientious objectors who had applied for commissions, such as Ernest Hartley, had had to go back to court and withdraw their CO pleas. It seems that I was the only soldier to obtain a commission without having had to change my position.

Only one other soldier from my unit was accepted by the selection board – a staff sergeant (I was a mere lance corporal) – and we went by ship from Taranto to Catania.

MY FIRST COMBAT EXPERIENCE

In the middle of the night just before we were due to arrive, the ship was rocked by an explosion – either a torpedo or a mine – and everyone had to rush up on deck.

Hearing cries for help from below decks I went to the bow and found that there were several bodies of soldiers who had been killed in their bunks. The deck had been blown open and many were wounded who could not get on deck or were trapped in their bunks. I climbed down, accompanied by a young private and an American naval officer, and we began to get the wounded to a place where others could help. After a while the Staff Sergeant organised a chain of men on the deck above to help to bring out the wounded, and I called for a rope to be tied to the metal sides of some bunks so that the men above could pull on them and allow us to get at the chaps who were trapped and screaming to be brought out, as the water was rising and they would be drowned.

I remember vividly the naval officer trying to tie the rope. Either he was too shocked or incompetent, so I grabbed the rope from him saying 'Let me tie it – I was a Boy Scout!'

When we had rescued as many as possible we climbed up on deck as another boat had come alongside and the troops were being marched onto the good vessel.

I then thought about all my kit lying below so I went to my bunk, which was still dry as the rising water had not yet reached it, got everything into my bag and went on deck, being among the last few to leave the ship. The majority of the troops in the rescue ship appeared to be commandos. We landed safely in Catania and went to sleep in a hall near the docks. Later in the morning we were told that the damaged vessel had been brought into dock; the packs of the soldiers had all been brought on shore and we were told to go and collect our bags. Although I was one of the very few who had brought ashore their own kit, I went to have a look at the ship and saw the damaged bow: it must have hit a mine. The dead bodies were still there and only then did I realise how precarious had been my position when working below decks.

When all the soldiers went to find their own kit they were outraged to find that most of their bags had been slit open and looted. Money, watches and souvenirs had been stolen. They blamed the commandos, but it could have been some of the local populace.

I later discovered that the young Private who had helped was actually on his way home on sick leave. When some officers came to take notes I said that some recognition should be given to that young lad, but that as an RAMC soldier, it was expected of me and of the Staff Sergeant. Much later, after reaching England, I learned that the RAMC Staff Sergeant and another Staff Sergeant had been decorated for 'bravery' in organising the orderly evacuation of the troops. The sick young private and myself who, with the naval officer, had done the dangerous work, were not mentioned!

Shortly after I left, the Unit suffered its first casualties – more than two years after its formation and having passed unscathed through the North Africa and Sicilian campaigns.

I travelled by goods wagon through North Africa and arrived back in the United Kingdom in December 1943. Following my arrival back in

England I was sent to the Officer Cadet Training Unit (OCTU) at Wrotham, Kent and then on leave for Christmas of 1943.

THE HOLY YEAR CONVENTION 1944

In the editorial of the March 1944 issue of the *Bahá'í Journal* (which incidentally was N°. 44) appeared the words:

> That glorious century, with its triumphs and its sacrifices, is ending and on 21 March 1944 another begins, a century which will be in some respects even more glorious, which will bring greater victories for the Cause of God and which will bring ever nearer the goal for which all those noble souls in the First Century sacrificed themselves.

The plans for the Centenary of the Declaration of the Báb and the national Convention, called by the Guardian for Saturday, Sunday and Monday, 20, 21 and 22 May, to enable the Convention to celebrate the Declaration of the Báb at 2 hours 11 minutes after sunset, were then announced. Convention was held at 1 Victoria Street – a basement centre with blackout drapes and shutters, as heavy bombing was expected due to the build up of armed forces in the South of England and the assault on the Continent by the Allies was daily expected. The site is now occupied by the Department of Trade and Industry.

THE FIRST SIX YEAR PLAN IS BORN

At the Convention some 11 resolutions were passed. Excitement rose when, according to those present, a message from the Guardian dated the 3rd of May was presented. It revealed that the Faith was established in 78 countries, with its literature in 41 languages and announced that the Seven Year Plan given to the Bahá'ís of the USA and Canada had been successfully completed. The delegates agreed to adopt a Six Year Plan and to ask the Guardian to set its goals. It was a spontaneous action 'by general consent' and was not even recorded in the Convention Resolutions! Most of the delegates lived to see the triumphant conclusion of that Plan and four of the nineteen were still alive in the Holy Year of 1992. The Guardian's response was:[8] "Advise formation nineteen spiritual assemblies spread over England, Wales, Scotland, N. Ireland and Eire."

[8] Effendi, S. (1981). The Unfolding Destiny of the British Bahá'í Community: The Messages from the Guardian of the Bahá'í Faith to the Bahá'ís of the British Isles. London, Bahá'í Publishing Trust., pp 169.

By that time the five Spiritual Assemblies had dropped to four, which meant that to reach 24 Assemblies by 1950 a six-fold increase was needed. And, as not all the Bahá'ís would be in assembly areas, about a three-fold increase in adult Bahá'ís within six years. The community was only about 80 strong after almost half a century.

NORWICH OPENED TO THE FAITH

My initial officer training was mainly in Kent, but during that Convention, I was undergoing my final days of intensive training as an officer cadet, and was commissioned in the RAMC in Repton, Derby, on 2 June 1944. From Repton I went to an Army Headquarters and was able to go home on 'compassionate leave' for D-Day and then to my first posting in the Norwich 'Nelson' and 'Britannia' Barracks. I had a very carefree time for some months and then had a fever that was diagnosed, in hospital, as malaria. Subsequently I was sent for three weeks embarkation leave (presumably for Burma), but that posting was cancelled and I was eventually sent to North Africa.

From home I went to a Bahá'í summer school at Buxton, 4 – 11 August 1944, and it was at that summer school that I learned of the Six Year Plan and I realised that I had been wasting many opportunities for teaching. Towards the end of my leave, my overseas posting was cancelled and I was to return to Norwich; I determined to use my time to 'open' Norwich to the Faith. On my return, I attended a Quaker meeting on the Sunday morning and read a passage from 'The Hidden Words', which led to an invitation to speak to a men's class. In the evening, I went to a Christian Spiritualist meeting and sat next to Miss Ethel Bird. I told her of the Faith and two weeks later she became Norwich's first Bahá'í. Shortly afterwards I heard that there was a US Air Force sergeant who was a Bahá'í stationed near Norwich – Henry Tellerman. We met and celebrated a Nineteen Day Feast, and from that meeting I wrote my first letter to the Guardian, on 15 November 1944, to which he replied on 27 November[9]:

> *Dear Bahá'í Brother,*
>
> Your welcome letter of November 15, so full of encouraging news, has been received, and the beloved Guardian has instructed me to answer it on his behalf.
>
> He was both surprised and delighted to see how much you have been able to do in Norwich, and that the first 'native' believer has entered the Faith and is actively assisting you.

[9] Unpublished letter (personal archives).

The work in England has, indeed, progressed slowly from the standpoint of enlarging the Faith's membership and establishing new centres and assemblies. On the other hand, however, the British Bahá'ís have consolidated the administration and thus prepared the way for intensified teaching activities. They have also built up a very helpful institution in the Publishing Trust, one calculated to impress the public and aid greatly in their own and other countries' teaching programmes. The Faith there needs more active, devoted young believers like yourself.

Regarding your question concerning your future plans; the Guardian strongly advises you to devote yourself to teaching the Faith in the British Isles. The need is very great for the people, emerging from so much suffering into a still deeply troubled immediate future, to hear of the Cause. Also the recently undertaken Six Year teaching Plan requires a great effort on the part of the English Bahá'ís, and your services are very much needed in this field.

Please convey his loving greetings to Mr Tellerman and Miss Bird. He will pray for them, and particularly for you, that you may render the Cause many services.

With Bahá'í Greetings, R. Rabbání

In the Guardian's handwriting:

Assuring you of my keen appreciation of the spirit that animates you in the service of the Faith, and of my special and fervent prayers for the success of your high endeavour.

Your true and grateful brother, Shoghi

In retrospect, I realised that the declaration of Ethel Bird and the first 'Feast' not only opened Norwich to the Faith but also was the first victory of the Six Year Plan.

There were at that time two old Bahá'ís – Olive Stockley and her mother – in Mundford, Thetford, Norfolk, both disabled and bedridden. They appeared on the first lists of isolated believers but never appeared on the register of believers. I organised a series of meetings and Kathleen Brown (later Lady Hornell) addressed the first one and started a record book about those early days in Norwich.

AFRICA AND HAIFA 1945 – 46

Following a course in Aldershot, I was posted in May 1945 to East Africa, to train an African field ambulance. We boarded ship on 19 May 1945 and sailed on 23 May in a 15,000-ton liner. I used the occasion of the Holy Day to introduce the Faith to many people, mostly Army officers – British, Libyan, Sudanese, Cypriot, Palestinian – and officers of the Palestine Police. We called in Gibraltar and Malta, from which port I posted a letter to Shoghi Effendi, dated 30 May, giving him my future address in Kenya and asking for any Bahá'í addresses in Africa. He replied on 12 June and his letter eventually reached me in Nairobi.[10]

> *Dear Bahá'í Brother,*
>
> Your letters dated November 15th 1944 and May 30th 1945 have been received, and the Guardian has instructed me to answer them on his behalf. He answered your first letter shortly after receiving it; the reply must have not reached you, unfortunately. The clippings you sent, etc., were of interest to him, and he was delighted to see you had been so active in teaching the Cause.
>
> In East Africa we have no addresses of believers, but in the Belgian Congo there is a Bahá'í family, a Persian married to a Belgian woman. Their address is: Mr Vahdat, Agronome Colonie, Kabongo, Province of Elizabethville, in case you have an opportunity to get in touch with them.
>
> The Guardian hopes that at a not distant future date you will again be able to serve the Cause in England. Young and eager workers are much needed to get the work started on a larger scale and reach more of the public.
>
> No doubt you will be able to teach wherever you are, and you may be sure his prayers will be offered on your behalf and for the success of your devoted efforts.
>
> *With warm Bahá'í greetings, R. Rabbání.*

In the Guardian's handwriting:

> Assuring you of my special and fervent prayers for your welfare, your spiritual advancement, the success of your efforts in the service of our beloved Faith, and the realisation of every hope you cherish for its extension and promotion.
>
> *Your true brother, Shoghi.*

These first two letters I had from the beloved Guardian were overwhelming in their content, for although I had not given any significant service for the Faith, he expressed his 'keen appreciation'.

We left the ship in Port Said on 4 June and took a train to Suez, where I tried unsuccessfully to find the Bahá'ís. However, I did locate the

[10] Unpublished letter (personal archives).

Mustapha family in Ismailia after a 12-hour journey and from them I learned how to make contact with the newly formed local Spiritual Assembly of Suez. Its chairman was Iskandar Hanna and the secretary was Girgis Sidarof, both customs officers in Port Tewfik whom I first met in their office in that port. It was during a Feast in Suez that I learned that the report of the Leeds Tribunal had so thrilled the Egyptian Bahá'ís that a play had been written about me, and the court proceedings translated into Arabic. The Suez Bahá'ís also arranged for me to visit the Bahá'ís in Cairo with a brother officer, Lt J Gibbins of the Royal Engineers. As it was necessary to report our arrival in Cairo to the Police, we duly reported and gave our Cairo address as 'Ḥaẓíratu'l-Quds, behind 216 Malika Nazli Street'. We were the first non-Egyptian guests to the centre, and we arrived early while two young Bahá'ís, Tahira Gollestani and Miriam Rúhí, were preparing our rooms.

In 1992, when attending the funeral of Isobel Sabrí, I was reminded of this visit by Gamal Rushdi's wife, who was a small girl at one of the wonderful Feasts I attended. I quote from some notes written of that visit to Cairo:[11]

> That evening, 26 June, 1945, many Friends came to see me and the local Spiritual Assembly had a meeting officially to welcome the two visitors. The kindness of the people, their evident delight at meeting me, the happiness which radiated from them, threatened again and again to overwhelm me completely. The Chairman of the local Spiritual Assembly explained that for many years Egypt, especially Cairo, had been the centre for travellers and tourists, and that Bahá'ís from all over the world had, from time to time, congregated there. Since the war, however, the stream had almost dried up, and it was a rare privilege for them to be able to entertain a brother Bahá'í. He also said that they were especially honoured that the one who was chosen to take such an important step in the history of the Faith (referring to the Leeds Tribunal) should be the one to visit them. This was almost too much for me. I had never dreamt that the appearance before the Tribunal meant so much to them and the rest of the Bahá'í World and I felt very, very humble and conscious of the privilege which had been mine. For once in my life, I could find no words to express myself. After this official welcome two young men, Houssein Gollostani, a student doctor, and Fowsy Zein el Abidin, a teacher of applied art, were delegated to be entirely at our disposal for the whole holiday.

[11] Unpublished notes (personal archives).

This visit to Egypt en route to Kenya was written up in the *Bahá'í Journal* N°. 52, August 1945, pp. 3–4, and no. 53, November 1945, pp. 3–4.

Of the many interesting experiences I had there, that of 29 June was the most inspiring. A certain old Bahá'í, Mohammad Bey Said, was too ill during the visit to the Cairo Ḥaẓíratu'l-Quds, but asked to see me. After calling on him, we went to the house of Taqíy Effendi (Muhammad Taqíy-I-Isfáhání, who passed away 13 December 1946 and was posthumously named a Hand of the Cause of God). At the time I met him he was about 95 years old, though he was quite active, his mind was clear, his voice strong and he kept up a daily correspondence with people around the country. He had had the precious privilege of being in the presence of Bahá'u'lláh when He had been revealing some verses and he described this experience for me. The room in which Taqíy received us was very quiet and restful and there seemed to be a particular vibration in it while we were having coffee, served in small glass cups. When I described this to him through an interpreter, he said that 'Abdu'l Bahá had stayed in that very room and we were using the cups which had been used by the Master!

Eventually I had to return to Suez and on 13 July, we sailed to Mombasa and then moved on to Nairobi by train. It was there that I received a loving letter from the Bahá'ís of Suez, dated 18 July 1945:[12]

> *To our beloved Friend Philip,*
>
> This is written to you by friends whom you have met by a happy chance. Though short that chance was, it was quite sufficient to mix their souls with yours.
>
> They remember you with such love as if it were the love of years. What a quick tie that which unites the hearts - the tie of Faith, knowledge, and understanding. This tie which is never affected by language or country.
>
> You have recorded our names in your pocket book. Do you therefore, remember these happy moments which you spent with us at Suez? You have left in our minds a picture which never fades.
>
> *With all our love and the Greetings of the Bahá'ís of Suez,*
>
> *'Iskandar Hanna.*

My 26 days in Egypt were the most memorable time of my life up to that point.

After some months' training a Field Ambulance in Meru and Isiolo, north of Mount Kenya, during which time I was able to visit the grave of Lord Baden Powell in Thika, the war in Europe finished and then the Far

[12] Unpublished letter (personal archives).

Eastern War ended, so the field ambulance was disbanded. My batman was a boy from Tanganyika – Adam Ali – and my sergeant – Benazir Phiri – was from Nyasaland.

Soon after settling in my new position of training officer in a new East African Field Ambulance, I wrote to David Hofman, who had originally registered for Category II exemption from military service (i.e. work of a non-combatant nature but not in the Armed Forces). He had been released from this at the cessation of the war in Europe and was again working when he could as an actor. He first replied on 6 August 1945, and on receiving my reply, wrote again on 15 September from Dundee, giving me news of his forthcoming marriage with Marion Holley. As these letters convey something of the spirit of those early days of the Six Year Plan, extracts are quoted below.[13]

6 August 1945:

> I was very glad to hear your news. What a wonderful time you have been having! I particularly envy your having met the old boy in Cairo; I had heard of him before. It's a wonderful feeling to travel round the world and know that you will find friends and a warm welcome wherever you go. I'll be interested to hear your views of Kenya....
>
> Come back as soon as you can; we need every available effort for the Six Year Plan. You and Peter ought to be able to get things going in Yorkshire – there's plenty of people up there. I'm proud of the few whom I was able to help into the Faith in Bradford and Leeds, and I hope for great things from you. You will find that Frank Hurst had done an enormous amount of spreading the Message, and I feel certain his work will bear fruit.

15 September 1945:

> I was very glad to get your letter, but first I have some news for you. You probably know it already, as all the girls in the country seem to be writing to you.
>
> I'm getting married very soon. Marion Holley, of whom you may have heard, is coming from San Francisco within three weeks (I hope) and we shall be married right away. I'm planning a Bahá'í wedding at my home. We haven't seen each other for ten years, but what's that to Bahá'ís. We have the same spiritual mother – May Maxwell. I'm wonderfully happy, and feel we shall yet manage that old Six Year Plan, in spite of a typical British start. The Guardian has given his approval and blessing and permission to visit Haifa.

[13] Ibid.

> We have been given a trip for a wedding present. I can only wish you the same happiness one day, Philip. Marriage to a fine Bahá'í girl, who will help you to mould your life and work to the Bahá'í pattern, is the best anyone can ask for here, and I strongly urge you to try and fit yourself for such a day. For the women are ahead of us – make no mistake about that. Especially in the West. The heroes and martyrs and Hands in the West are all women. Martha, May, Keith, Lua etc. Only John Esslemont was worthy to be a Hand.
>
> My own feeling is one of extreme gratitude, to be stabilised at last, with my companion, and to have my work directed to the service of the Cause.... We got up at Speakers' Corner in Hyde Park last Sunday. I broke the ice, Mary Basil Hall followed on, and John Ferraby did the rest. Janet and Angela held the banner, and looked too good to be true. It was a great success and people listening made a close ring around the soap box and asked lots of questions. Some heckling, but on the whole reverent and orderly. Some fine types there. They're going to keep it up.
>
> Well old lad, come home as soon as you can, and get into this SYP (Six Year Plan) with both feet. The Guardian says it's historic and we must not fail. I'm proud of all my spiritual children, but I think you have the capacity, if you go the right way, to do as much as any of them. Some of us are doers, and some thinkers and planners. All are needed, but the right thing is to be the utmost what one can be. You are a doer, so check up on the rules and most effective methods, and then come back and go to it.

For a time I acted as 'quartermaster' for a general hospital in Nairobi and then transferred to the 74th field hygiene section. It was there, about Christmas 1945, that a notice appeared announcing pre-release courses for officers. I saw one on economics at Mount Carmel College, Haifa, and applied at once. I was told that: it was full and, as I was due for early release from the Army, I would not be considered!

Later I was posted to take over the 73rd field hygiene section in Gilgil where there was a small hospital and large Italian Prisoner of War camps. From there I went to Nakuru to have lunch with Marguerite Preston (née Welby), one-time member of the British National Spiritual Assembly who was married to a tea planter Terry Preston – a non-Bahá'í.

THE HAIFA STORY

In Gilgil on 20 March, I met, by chance, Captain Somper, a Jewish officer I had known on the ship. I told him that it was the eve of our New Year's

Day and asked if he would have dinner with me? As I was 'PMC' ('president of the mess council' – in charge of catering) I was able to organise a good meal for him! I learned that he was the Area Education Officer and told him that if he wanted any more good meals he had better get me onto the economics course in Haifa! Exactly 19 days later, I received a cabled notice of acceptance. I left to pack all my effects for shipment to England and finalise details to leave on 17 April 1946. My officer friend never had a second meal with me!

By this time, I was Acting Major but could only wear insignia of Captain. Within ten days I had visited Nairobi, completed the necessary documentation and was in Kisumu on Lake Victoria. On Friday, 19 April, I left by the flying boat 'Campion' and reached Khartoum the following day. I spent the night at the 'Grand Hotel', after failing to locate the local Bahá'ís, and left for Cairo the following morning landing on the Nile at Wadi Halfa and was in Cairo at about 16.00 hours.

Arriving at the barracks to which I been instructed to report, I found them almost deserted and learned to my amazement that it was Easter. I had completely lost count of the days with all the excitement of getting ready to go to Haifa. I then decided to go straight by taxi to the Ḥaẓíratu'l-Quds, hoping at least to meet a few Bahá'ís. I found the place absolutely packed and as I went into the hall I heard a man, at the front of the hall, reading in Arabic. As I entered he was reading out my name! He then saw me, excitedly beckoned me to the front to sit on one of the front seats and who should be next to me but Buchucha from Tunis!

I realised that it was not only Easter but the First Day of Ridván and the secretary of the Cairo local Spiritual Assembly was reading his annual report. As I walked into the room, he had reached the point where the Assembly reported that early in the year the Ḥaẓíratu'l-Quds had been opened to visitors and Philip Hainsworth, an Army officer, had been the first overseas guest.

When the local election took place there was a press photographer present, as it was the first time in Egypt that women had participated in the voting, and this made front page news in several papers. Subsequently the newspapers were given to me to take to the Guardian. The Bahá'ís were highly delighted with this publicity; the Guardian less so as he felt it could have bad repercussions and would arouse too much opposition.

On April 24, I made a day trip by train to Suez accompanied by Hassan Sabrí's father, Abdel Fatah, and met all the friends there again. On returning to the barracks the next day, I found that the rail and postal services were on strike and that we could not go to Haifa. Later it was announced that the courses at Mount Carmel (Middle East Formation

College) would be cancelled and we would be sent to England.

Late at night, however, we learned that the strike had broken and that a train would leave for Haifa at midnight. Only half of the contingent of officers for the college could go, and they would report on the basis of alphabetical order of surnames. I would therefore be on that train, leaving at 18.40 on 25 April. Was this the Hand of Bahá'u'lláh I wondered?

During the afternoon of 25 April, I went to the army stores and bought a leather hold-all. This bag subsequently saw service in many countries, including 15 years in East Africa, and is still being used by our son Richard in Russia, over half a century later!

Also delayed in returning to Haifa was a young man who had just married – Yusuf Jarráh – with his wife Hyatt. They were on the same train and we agreed to meet in Haifa on the morning after our arrival. We could not travel together as I was allocated a first-class seat and they were in a crowded third-class carriage.

The train left on Thursday at midnight and we arrived on Friday afternoon, 26 April. I was so excited to be in Haifa that I went to a cinema that evening!

FOURTEEN HOURS WITH SHOGHI EFFENDI

On Saturday morning I met Yusuf, who was an engineer in 'Akká. His great-grandfather had been a governor of 'Akká prison who had accepted the Faith at the time of Bahá'u'lláh. His wife was also his cousin and the sister of Salah Jarráh. Salah was later a pioneer to Arabia, a 'custodian' of Bahjí and, eventually, of the grave of Shoghi Effendi in London.

It was with some difficulty that I persuaded Yusuf to take me to 'Abdu'l-Bahá's house to let the Guardian know that I was in Haifa and would be there for about five weeks. He said that nobody just 'dropped in' on the Guardian like that, but I insisted that I must let somebody know, perhaps by contacting Mr Maxwell, father of 'Amatu'l-Bahá Rúḥíyyih Kh̲ánum? Reluctantly he took me to what I remember as a downstairs room to the left of the main steps up to the Master's House – it was a small reception room and someone was given a message that we were there. After a while I was told to go to the main steps to be greeted at the door by Rúḥíyyih Kh̲ánum. She made me very welcome and said, 'Shoghi Effendi is very sorry he will not be able to see you today as the mail has just arrived on the train and he has two bags-full to open'. I was stunned – that Shoghi Effendi was 'sorry he could not see me'!

She seemed to know that I would be staying for some weeks and said that there would be plenty of time for me to meet Shoghi Effendi later, but would I care to have lunch with her the next day (Sunday). I was delighted, and plans were made. Rúḥíyyih Khánum said that I should not visit the Shrine of the Báb until the Guardian had arranged a properly conducted tour.

I learned somewhat later that it was the Guardian's habit to tip all his mail onto his desk and then sort it out into piles, one for each continent. The smallest was always that of Africa, but because of his love of Africa he always opened the few letters from that pile first. This had apparently happened on the Saturday morning and he was reading a letter which surprised him considerably. It was from a young Bahá'í who had written to say he was coming to Haifa – not asking permission, just saying he was coming! It was my letter and he was reading it when it was announced that I was in fact downstairs!

On Sunday morning, 28 April, I prepared myself in my best tropical uniform – short-sleeved shirt, shorts, etc., and set off in ample time to catch the bus. After waiting for some considerable time and no bus having arrived, I asked a passing Jewish girl what time the bus came. She answered that because some of the bus drivers were Arab Muslim and had Friday off, some were Jewish and had Saturday off and some were Arab Christians who took Sunday off, there was only a bus service on that route on four days of the week!

Fearing I would be late for lunch, I ran down Mount Carmel to the Western Pilgrim House where Mr Maxwell lived and where I was to have lunch with him and 'Amatu'l-Bahá Rúḥíyyih Khánum. It was quite a long way and the weather was hot, so I arrived very hot and sticky. There was no panic however, no obvious signs of a meal spoiling: Mr Maxwell greeted me and suggested I relax with a glass of fresh orange juice. This I did, and the sweat really began to pour out of me – my shirt was very obviously wet. Suddenly a young Persian servant girl came to the door and simply stated, 'Shoghi Effendi will see you now, please come with me'!

I remember him as a smallish, dapper man in a dark grey suit, a black fez, and brown boots. He shook me warmly by the hand and said how pleased he was to see me. Then, after some general conversation about what I was to do in Haifa, he really made my hair stand on end by saying, 'If you had written to me asking permission to come to Haifa, I do not think I would have given it, but because you wanted so much to come, God has granted you your wish'.

No question of doubt, or of 'maybe', but quite an assertive 'God has granted you your wish'. I found conversation very easy and light, with snatches of humour. All my Bahá'í life I had hoped to meet a Bahá'í who would really make me feel humble, and I had yearned for the day when I would meet the Guardian to experience that humility. But it did not happen. During this and the many subsequent meetings I had with him, I always felt at ease and able to talk frankly with him. It was only years later, when I described my meetings with Shoghi Effendi to groups of Bahá'ís, that I realised it was this 'allowing me to grow' that endeared him to me and why I was so much more able to appreciate his letters in the years that followed when he signed himself '*Your true brother*'.

I must have spent half-an-hour with him on that occasion, telling him of my meeting in Kenya with Marguerite Welby-Preston, of the experiences with the Egyptian Bahá'ís and of the publicity received in Cairo when the women were photographed casting their votes for the first time in a Bahá'í election.

During this meeting, Shoghi Effendi asked if I had seen his new book, *God Passes By.* When I said no he replied, 'I will give you a copy. Please study chapter nine'. When I conveyed to him a message from Marguerite he said she must do as her husband wished and have the children baptised and win him over by love, that her husband's move into Kenya administration should be encouraged and that he hoped she would write to him. I should encourage her to get something about the Faith translated into Swahili – 'something simple'. He stressed the vital importance of the Six Year Plan and expressed the belief that I would teach the Faith in England and other countries. He hoped to see me again soon.

I remember little of the meal with Rúḥíyyih Khánum and Mr Maxwell, but I was shown the library there, where I came across and read with great interest, and on later occasions took notes from the pilgrim notes of May Maxwell. During the lunch, I had learned that there was to be a Holy Day meeting at the Shrine and I said that I would attend. Mr Maxwell said he would ask the Guardian. I responded in amazement, 'But surely if it is a Holy Day for the Bahá'ís, I must go?'

Mr Maxwell explained that it would be conducted in Oriental style, would be entirely in Persian and Arabic – and there would be no English translation. Nevertheless, I could not understand why I could not just 'turn up'!

I was then taken by taxi to the Shrine where Mr Maxwell gave me a delightful and impressive tour of the Oriental Pilgrim House, which had been built by a Bahá'í from South Russia, and then into the Shrine itself. It was a very solid, square building of nine rooms. The middle three were the actual Shrine of the Báb and the three on the side facing the sea were the Shrine of 'Abdu'l-Bahá. The three on the side of the hill, overlooked by a clump of cypress trees, were a closed section used to store precious archives. I could well see why the local populace could have thought, when the Master was building it, that it was a fortress!

Already the gardens were so beautiful that they were the pride of the people of Haifa, though they knew nothing of the Faith. What was so impressive about the gardens was not merely their design, but the way in which the bright green of the grass and hedges and the colour of the roses, flowering shrubs and geraniums were such a contrast to the parched surroundings of the Carmel hillside.

One day, some time later, I was taken into that closed section of the Shrine building by Rúḥíyyih Khánum and shown some of the Archives. I remember her showing me a small box containing some small fragments of wood and dust that had dropped onto the floor. We were both very concerned as she had described how, when the wooden casket containing the remains of the Báb had to be transferred into the marble sarcophagus sent by the Bahá'ís of Rangoon, the box itself was slightly too large so some pieces had to be shaved off to allow it to fit in. The dust and wooden fragments had been carefully collected in this box. I gently brushed these with my fingers onto the cover of my prayer book – it was a very sobering thought.

On the following morning, 29 April, when the economics course met for the first time with the Commandant, he said that some weeks previously he had been told that his lecturers would be posted to Greece to take some pre-release courses there and he had decided to cancel the course. 'For some unknown reason', he said, 'I felt urged to keep the course going, even if it meant that it would run the risk of being deprived of its instructors'. The instructors would first give the outline of the course, with the appropriate reference books, so that if they left the students would carry on with personal study. Within two or three days, they were posted to Greece and I had over four weeks of freedom.

After the morning lecture, we collected our notebooks and course material and were then free in the afternoon to study them while sunbathing on the college veranda. It was then I leafed through *God Passes By*. I quickly realised that it would take some serious study; I was thrilled with the power of its language, but I only briefly glanced at chapter nine. I vaguely wondered why the Guardian had asked me to study the story of Bahá'u'lláh's Declaration, which I had accepted without question in 1938.

At about 15.00 hours, I received a telephone call from 'Amatu'l-Bahá Rúḥíyyih Khánum to say that I should be at the Western Pilgrim House within an hour, when the Guardian would send a taxi to collect Mr Maxwell and me.

As it was still very hot and I did not have time to change into my dress uniform, I arrived in the usual Army officers' dress of khaki shorts and short-sleeved shirt. We walked down the Pilgrim House through rows of male local believers seated, as far as I can recall, on carpets on the floor, to the end of the room where there was a large table piled with oranges and Persian delicacies. Mr Maxwell and I sat on the seats along the left-hand wall facing Shoghi Effendi, who sat in the right-hand corner where the window looked out across the bay to 'Akká. I learned subsequently that this was where the Master had always sat. We had interrupted the meeting, which continued with Persian chanting, with pauses during which an old Persian believer sitting a short distance from the Guardian would ask a question and the Guardian would answer. Apparently my unconscious demeanour and actions had caused a great stir among the gathered believers. I had marched in, sat down, folded my arms and crossed my legs and looked around. This behaviour in front of Shoghi Effendi was to them unforgivable, but of course I only learned of this much later.

After this had continued for quite a while, there was a pause and suddenly the Guardian looked at me and said, 'Have you read chapter nine?' When I said yes, he asked, 'Is there anything you do not grasp?' 'No', said I, and he began to explain certain aspects of the chapter. 'It is purely historical … the ten years since the Síyáh-Chál, the Declaration and the beginning of the Proclamation to the Kings, with Bahá'u'lláh's Tablet to Sultan 'Abdu'l-Azíz written just as the exiles left Constantinople.' He then explained the importance of the Proclamation to the Pope and Queen Victoria and other Western leaders, and of the responsibility which lay upon their shoulders. He quoted what Queen Victoria was reported to have said: 'If this be of God, it will succeed, if not, it can do no harm'. He emphasised that Bahá'u'lláh's Declaration was gradual, not sudden.

There was more chanting, followed by the Feast where oranges and cakes were passed round. The Guardian then led the way to the Shrine of the Báb. At the door of the Pilgrim House, he waited and then indicated, apparently to the chagrin of the local believers, that I should walk with him. On the way he explained how Haifa was the spiritual as well as the administrative centre; that first he had to complete the Shrine of the Báb and then the administrative buildings. He called it the world's geographical centre and said that Bahá'u'lláh had occasionally visited Haifa. He would sit in the circle of cypress trees and had actually pointed out the spot to 'Abdu'l-Bahá where the Shrine should be built.

In the Shrine, first in the room of the Báb and then in that of the Master, the Guardian chanted the Tablets of Visitation, and then we wended our way back to the Pilgrim House. He said he had news of some victories, one of which was the formation of a new Assembly in Rio de Janeiro. He said that he had been able to send a 400-word cable to America in spite of the postal strike, as the government had allowed it to go through on a private line at Barclays Bank and he spoke of its content – the second Seven-Year Plan. He told me of the significance of the United States Convention that year and a great victory: not only did a woman receive the most votes, but moreover she was a Negress (Elsie Austin).He had paused at the top of the path which led from the Shrine down to Haifa harbour and described how the kings and rulers of the world would come up those steps on foot, lay their crowns at the door of the Shrine, pay their respects to the memory of the Báb, and when they had finished their prayers would come out and move across 'to receive their instructions from the Universal House of Justice'. He pointed to a spot up the hillside, which I vividly remembered seventeen years later, when I was present at the first election of the Universal House of Justice as a member of the Central and East African National Spiritual Assembly. I recalled it even more vividly when, at a later International Convention, with other members of the British National Spiritual Assembly, we visited the site selected for the Seat of the House of Justice. It was the exact spot that the Guardian had pointed out to me some 30 years previous!

It was several days later when I learnt how I had shocked all the Persian believers present at that Feast. Firstly, by appearing before the Guardian in shorts and a short-sleeved shirt, secondly by sitting just opposite the Guardian with folded arms and crossed legs and then to be invited to walk with Shoghi Effendi, which was such an honour and I did not appear to appreciate it.

It was only when writing up these notes some 46 years later that I realised why the Guardian had referred to chapter nine – it was on 29 April and we were celebrating the Ninth Day of Ridván. An officer with whom I became well acquainted at this time was a Major Cranmer-Byng, who had come from his unit in another part of Palestine and had his own jeep. He showed particular interest in the gardens surrounding the Shrine of the Báb. He expressed a desire to meet the Guardian as he said that he, Cranmer-Byng, was interested in landscape gardening and he felt that the one who had designed these gardens must be a genius. He was never able to meet the Guardian but he did later take me to Jerusalem and Bethlehem where, in response to Shoghi Effendi's request, I was able to visit the Christian holy places and compare the distressing commercialisation associated with these with the quiet beauty and deeply spiritual atmosphere of the Bahá'í holy places. It was during this time that I visited the village of Samakh where I first met Salah Jarráh. Several years later, this association with Cranmer-Byng was put to good use. When the British National Assembly was considering how we could help George Townshend to earn money with his pen after he left the Church of Ireland and lost all his income, we received a letter from Cranmer-Byng saying that his father had died and he had taken over the job of editing the Wisdom of the East series. He had decided, as a result of his experiences in Palestine, to replace the original issue *The Splendour of God*, published by John Murray, with a new compilation of Bahá'í scripture and asked if we could suggest a person for this work. George was invited and *The Glad Tidings of Bahá'u'lláh* was the result, published in 1949.

During a conversation with Rúḥíyyih Khánum I learnt that she had befriended Ann, the wife of John Seegar, of the Palestine police, who was chief fire officer. Neither were Bahá'ís, but John was the son of Alfred Sugar, a Bahá'í of Manchester, one-time member of the British National Spiritual Assembly, and one who had contributed a great deal, through discussion and correspondence, to my early Bahá'í education. I made contact with John and he took me on my first tour of Haifa in a fire engine which, with its bell clanging, cleared a way through the busy streets of the old town, thronged as they were with large numbers of men in their long garments, astride small donkeys which all appeared to stagger under the weight of their loads.

On 30 April I spent one and a quarter hours with the Guardian, during which time he spoke about the United States' second Seven Year Plan and the goals in Europe, particularly in Spain and Portugal, and that after this Plan there would be a three year 'rest', then the third Seven Year Plan. He stressed how the American Bahá'ís were 'going quicker and quicker', they had to make groups in all the states and provinces, they actually made Assemblies – 'England must do this and it is only by action, it won't do it by itself'. 'Teach and consolidate, study and act, incorporate Assemblies later'.

He wondered why the believers always seemed to be ill in England. He acknowledged the 'war reasons', but said, 'It was the same in the days of 'Abdu'l Bahá'. He said that we must reach the masses who were looking for spirituality, and worry about leaders only so far as to 'gain their benevolence', and leave alone the political leaders. The testing time in England would be when the upper classes came into the Faith. He predicted that there would be much trouble between Capital and Labour and Conservative versus Labour.

On 2 May I took some non-Bahá'ís to the Shrine, met some visiting Bahá'ís from Egypt, and then spent an hour with the Guardian. He spoke a little about 1957 and referred to a 'triumph of the Faith', saying that there could even be the Lesser Peace by then, but he was not certain. It was very important for the Bahá'ís to study and re-study *God Passes By*, especially at summer schools. He explained that the Bahá'í Funds should go first to the teaching plan, secondly to the Publishing Trust and lastly for a new centre. He spoke of the importance of teaching as the 'best profession' and suggested I become a professor of economics at a Bahá'í university!

We discussed again the importance of teaching, particularly of teaching the Faith; that ideally one could devote half of one's time to teaching and the other half to business or one's profession, so that the teaching time would not be a charge to the Fund. This point I discussed again on 27 May.

I told him that my present thoughts were that as I was an officer in the RAMC I felt my future lay in some form of medical career, which meant that I would have to go back to school, obtain sufficient qualifications to enter a university and then register for a medical degree, which could take as long as eight years. The Guardian then spoke of these being times of crisis, which meant that sometimes teaching took precedence over other activities. He felt I should concentrate on teaching the Faith rather than starting a long period of study for medicine. He spoke about developments in the Magalenes and Baluchistan where local Spiritual Assemblies had become incorporated, with an English woman in the former. He also mentioned the Divine intervention during the war which protected the Holy Places, with enemies on three sides and fighting only a few miles from the Shrine of Bahá'u'lláh; bombs had dropped in Haifa on the German colony and on an Arab mosque and cemetery.

The Faith was also being subjected to attacks from within. I had been advised by Rúḥíyyih Khánum and Mr Maxwell of the troubles with Covenant-breakers and the devastating effect it had had upon Shoghi Effendi, even affecting his physical health. Subsequently, in 1947 and through several cables in the year that followed, I had been made aware of some of the problems facing the Guardian in this area, particularly from his own family, and had been moved to offer to be of assistance to him. It was not until August 1992, when I read a presentation copy to Lois and myself of Adíb Taherzadeh's book *The Covenant of Bahá'u'lláh* that I really appreciated the magnitude of these attacks and untold suffering he must have been experiencing all the time I was in the Holy Land.

When I reported on my visit to the Shrines with non-Bahá'ís, he said I should, in teaching any local people, give only the history and the principles of the Faith and not really try to teach or convert. It was a difficult situation and the problems were both 'spiritual and political'.

This meeting was followed by dinner and a long talk with Rúḥíyyih Khánum and Mr Maxwell. It was arranged that on 4 May, I would be taken by Mr Maxwell to visit Bahjí. I called at N°. 10 Persian Street (the Western

Pilgrim House) for Mr Maxwell at 15.30 that day and a taxi was provided to take us to Bahjí.

Of that occasion I noted, 'A wealthy Arab family own adjacent land and they are not very friendly'. A stout wall surrounds part of the gardens. I made a drawing in my notebook that showed the path from the main road along a government farm, then along an unmade road past the Arab house and into a building that I had marked 'rented'. This I visited on later occasions, at the time of the election of the Universal House of Justice and subsequently, when the pilgrims and visitors would rest and take the tea that was generously and continually provided by the Bahá'í custodians.

Overlooking the Mansion was the large, forbidding-looking building owned by the Covenant-breakers. We had to enter the Mansion very discreetly as the Covenant-breakers were said to watch most jealously what happened in the Mansion and the appearance of a British Army officer entering may have caused difficulties. My notes made after reaching home illustrated and described the Shrine and the Mansion and it is interesting to note that while subsequent visits have demonstrated the continual development, extension and beautification of the lands around and within the Haram-i-Aqdas, the interiors have remained exactly as they were on my first visit.

I recorded the story that I was told of the way in which the Covenant Breakers had allowed the property to fall into disuse when 'Abdu'l Bahá was incarcerated and how they had allowed some land to go to a Bedouin family under a Turkish law relating to trees being planted for a certain number of years.

When 'Abdu'l Bahá was in prison, His brother had given Bahá'u'lláh's robe and prayer beads to the Bedouin who, when the Master came out of prison, the Bedouin went to visit Him, wearing the robe and dangling the precious prayer beads under His eyes. The Guardian had managed to buy the Mansion and have it renovated through the assistance of one of the believers who had actually lived there at the time of Bahá'u'lláh. The Guardian had made the hall and rooms (other than the one where Bahá'u'lláh had met with EG Browne and later passed away) into a type of archives/museum, with books, photographs, manuscripts and paintings from all over the world.

On our return from Bahjí, we had dinner with Rúḥíyyih Khánum and John Seegar, and then drove back to college in John's fire engine!

On 5 May, I made a trip by jeep to Nazareth, Tiberius, Samarkh and a Jewish 'Communist' colony (it must have been an early kibbutz). We had dinner with Salah Jarráh, his mother and sister, and later a swim in the Sea of Galilee.

On 7 May, I had an hour's visit to the Shrine followed by one hour with the Guardian, followed again by dinner with Rúḥíyyih Khánum and Mr Maxwell. It was probably at this meeting that the Guardian described how the Persian believers could best obey their government by keeping out of politics. He said we must always obey our government, even if we are called upon to fight, but not get involved in politics, nor even in any political issue, due to the international character of the Faith. Again he stressed the opposition from within the Faith as well as from without. The stronger the Faith became, he said, the greater the opposition. The trouble then being experienced in Persia was that various governments, knowing the integrity and influence of the Bahá'ís, were trying to attract Bahá'í young men to work for them.

He then described how the world was 'zoned', and the responsibility for taking the Faith into Russia would be that of the Germans and the Indians. Egypt would be responsible for the whole of Africa, the USA for Europe and then the rest of the world. When he paused, I said, 'And what are you going to give to the British?' He said, almost without hesitation, but with a smile on his face and a twinkle in his eyes: 'Oh, I think I'll give them Iceland and the Channel Islands', to which I responded in like vein, 'Oh, thank you very much!'

He then went on to speak with great enthusiasm about the Germans. How even one month before the war had actually finished they had re-started their activities, they had had a summer school, started children's classes, formed their National Spiritual Assembly and sent the Guardian a 'newsletter' and their 'annual' report (from April – May 1946). They would take a lead in Europe, which the Master had prophesied; their centre would be in Frankfurt and they would pioneer into Central Europe. On receiving news of Germany's plight, India had sent money to Írán for Germany, which had then sent on $80,000. America had sent cash to Burma for the relief of the Bahá'ís there. The Guardian then made the wonderful statement: 'America needs encouragement; Germany needs nothing; Britain needs to get going!'

I mentioned that I had received a letter from Una Townshend.

He also explained during this meeting that Bahá'u'lláh had had three wives, the first and faithful one, 'Abdu'l-Bahá's mother, was alone and ostracised by the other two. He was allowed four by law, but had three before He made His laws in 'Akká. 'Abdu'l Bahá wrote in a Tablet to an American believer that Isaiah 54 referred to His mother.

On 9 May, I took a fellow officer around the Shrine and gardens. I then went to the Western Pilgrim House, where I browsed among the books and notes in the library, and was joined by Rúḥíyyih Khánum and Mr.

Maxwell, who showed me some new photographs of the gardens and his plans for the development of the Shrine of the Báb – the superstructure of which was to be built as soon as possible. After dinner we went to the House of the Master, where Shoghi Effendi had gone to bed, when Rúḥíyyih Khánum showed a film of the Master in the USA in 1912; colour film of the Shrines in Haifa and Bahjí and three of the 1944 Centenary celebrations at the Wilmette Temple. This lasted until 23.30 and I reached my room in the college at about midnight. I was concerned that Shoghi Effendi had been distressed with news from Amman, where there had been repercussions from the press articles that had appeared in the Egyptian newspapers.

As I was going down Mount Carmel Avenue on 13 May, I passed the gardens and I saw Shoghi Effendi from the road. As it was the proper way for an Army officer to show respect, I saluted him as I went past! I had an hour in the Shrines and had one or two minutes' conversation with the Guardian. During a conversation later with Mr Maxwell, I was advised of the consternation which I had caused at my first public meeting when I sat across from the Guardian with my arms and legs crossed and it was also made clear I should not salute the Guardian!

I called at the Western Pilgrim House on 14 May at 18.30 for a talk with Rúḥíyyih Khánum and Mr Maxwell, when we discussed the question of writing letters to Shoghi Effendi, my father's life and poetry writing, the personality of the Guardian, how Bahá'u'lláh had forbidden hand-kissing, and the Guardian's reaction when some of the devout believers fell on their faces before him and attempted to kiss his hands and even his feet.

This was followed by a long interview with Shoghi Effendi during which time he said the news from Amman was bad; Egypt had to be careful. He spoke about some news he had received from England and how we should encourage teaching at summer schools. His instructions were that we should study Bahá'u'lláh's Writings, which were pure, while the Báb's were not[14], and the Quayyúmu'l-Asmá is very difficult to understand. He told me to talk about *God Passes By*. I believe it was at this meeting, although I did not record it, that Shoghi Effendi said that in the preparation of *God Passes By* he had to go through all the letters of and relating to Bahá'u'lláh and 'Abdu'l Bahá, to search for significant pieces of information. He said that there were many more letters still not collected, some were in the hands of Covenant Breakers and some inherited by families who were not Bahá'ís. He had to examine everything because, for example, Bahá'u'lláh may have been writing a letter to a pilgrim – just a personal letter about his journey home and his family – and an important

[14] Effendi, S. (1979). God Passes By. Wilmette, Ill., Bahá'í Publishing Trust., p. 165

piece of 'revelation' would appear. He had come across one such letter, not yet translated, where Bahá'u'lláh had said that had all those who had accepted Him in Baghdád during His Declaration remained steadfast in the Faith, so great was the power released at that time, that the kings of the world would have in His own lifetime come and laid down their crowns at His Feet! When he said this, I felt my hair stand on end.

Shoghi Effendi then stressed the effects of travel teaching, saying that believers should not be too static. He enlarged upon the afflictions levelled upon Bahá'u'lláh and 'Abdu'l Bahá, from without and within the Faith, from friend and foe and from clergy, State and kindred. He suggested that I should study and teach in England until the end of the Six Year Plan and then in Europe and, perhaps, in Africa. He again referred to Egypt and said that the Cause there suffered from attacks from without and from a lack of wisdom within – they were overzealous and should not propagate the Faith aggressively. Other things to which he referred were party politics, saying that we may vote for an individual on a personal basis or an associate, but should not ally oneself with any party; philanthropic ventures which depend upon finance; the status of women; that the figures 9 and 19 are associated with unity but have no other particular significance.

He also pointed out that the Báb's Dispensation lasted nine years, that Bahá'u'lláh's Ministry was for 39 years, and that of the Master for 29 years – a total of 77 years.

On 16 May, I had another long interview with Shoghi Effendi and was able to convey news that I had received from England about the use the community had obtained of a caravan and that 14 people had offered to work for the Faith. He was delighted, and when I spoke about having a travelling exhibition in the caravan said, with a twinkle in his eye, 'The English are good at exhibitions'. He stressed that perseverance is needed and added, 'Convey to the English that it is even more important to pioneer to Africa than the Six Year Plan'.

He spoke about evil, saying that it is a vacuum – an absence of good – but it is the consequences of evil which appear to make evil appear to be positive. The forces of nature require education.

Speaking of the Prophet Muḥammad, the Guardian explained that He was a rich merchant who had many amanuenses to record the Qur'án during His 23 years ministry. The Guardian said that Bahá'u'lláh stated that the Qur'án is authentic, and of the many thousands of recorded Ḥadíths (traditions), those quoted by Bahá'u'lláh are authentic.

Shoghi Effendi further said that the Bayán of the Báb had been corrupted, but that the works of Bahá'u'lláh are practically free from corruption. He explained that the sufferings inflicted upon Bahá'u'lláh came from the state, religious authorities and His own hypocritical followers, and that although there had not been too much in Baghdád, the sufferings had increased in Adrianople due to the involvement of Ṣubḥ-i-Azal, and the worst of them had been in 'Akká.

Of metaphysics, he said that real visions are very rare, and that souls will retain their identity and interact in the next world.

I spent 18 May in 'Akká with Yussuf Jarráh. First we visited a friend in the police station and then went to 'Akká Prison. It took me about one and a half hours to get to see Major Grant, the prison superintendent, which only happened after I had used my rank as an Army officer to get by his subordinates. He allowed me to see the Cell of Bahá'u'lláh and to take photographs. There were, at the time of my visit, no prisoners in the cells immediately adjacent to that which Bahá'u'lláh had occupied.

One person who took me around in 'Akká was a Christian Arab and he tried to tell me of the 'wickedness' of Shoghi Effendi and told slanderous stories about the treatment of the Holy Family. They were so patently untrue that I just told the man he was completely misled, but so effective had been the lies of the Covenant-breakers that he thought I was naive and had been hoodwinked, which illustrated the constant pressures under which the Guardian had continually to work. I learned many years later that the Guardian had been very concerned about what had been said to me, as he did not wish my faith to be tested. After this I spoke with the superintendent for about half an hour and then went with Yussuf to the Garden of Ridván – about one and a half miles from 'Akká, and then on to Bahjí. I took an abundance of black and white photographs. I had another long talk with Shoghi Effendi on 23 May, when he spoke of Megiddo and Jerusalem and made comparison with the Holy Places. He explained to me that the Shrines were free from ground rent, taxes and rates, both government and municipal, and that no other religion had the same privileges. All our land was open to the public, no buildings were rented out, all produce was given to the poor. When the Catholics had tried to get the same privileges, they were told that they could have them if they gave the same undertakings.

Shoghi Effendi told me that there was nothing in the Writings about the Tomb of Bahá'u'lláh. At that time, the American National Spiritual Assembly had land at the Shrines through a 'Palestine Branch' and this privilege would be later extended to all National Spiritual Assemblies and even to some local Spiritual Assemblies. Because it is the spiritual centre of the world, Shoghi Effendi said that nothing must disturb it. He told me that the Trans-Jordan situation was very bad. The Amír was becoming king and desired the Caliphate, hence Amman was a centre for fanatical Islam so it was very difficult for the Bahá'ís there – there were no newsletters, nor correspondence, and no teaching going on.

My last interview with Shoghi Effendi was on 27 May. He began by saying that he had news of some Covenant-breakers living in England and that I should warn the National Spiritual Assembly that unless they were 'contained' and the friends shunned them completely, all the work of the Six Year Plan would come to nothing.

After this, he asked why the British did not do as the Americans did and set up budgets for pioneers and travel teachers. I replied by saying that the British would not do this. They would not take money from the Fund as they were very fearful of setting up what might be considered a type of paid clergy. He then explained in detail what Bahá'u'lláh had said about deputisation, that if a Bahá'í could not pioneer or teach, they should 'appoint someone in their stead' and that was what the Fund was for, to make possible the spread of the Faith. He then said: 'I will write to the British National Spiritual Assembly about this'.

COMMEMORATION ASCENSION OF BAHÁ'U'LLÁH

Shoghi Effendi said that he understood I wished to go to Bahjí the following evening to attend the commemoration of the Ascension of Bahá'u'lláh (03:00 hours 29 May). He said that I should go to the Western Pilgrim House and wait with Mr Maxwell for a taxi that he (Shoghi Effendi) would send for us. This would take us to the Mansion in Bahjí, where he had arranged for us to sleep for a few hours as we were not accustomed to the 'Oriental' way of chanting and praying throughout the evening, preceding the actual 'three hours after midnight, when Bahá'u'lláh passed away'.

Prior to our visit, Mr Maxwell reminded me about dress and I said that I would wear long sleeves and trousers in any case, against the mosquitoes. We were taken by taxi and were shown into separate rooms in the Mansion. I seem to remember that mine was across the hall from that where Bahá'u'lláh had passed away. Years later, when I visited the Mansion as a pilgrim and went into that room, I was told that it was the one Shoghi Effendi used when he stayed there, and I was delighted to see by his bedhead two photographs I had taken in 1952 of the first Spiritual Assembly of Kampala, Uganda, and one of myself with the other first pioneers to Uganda. I also saw, in the old visitors' book in the adjacent room, my signature and what I had written on that visit.

At about 2.15 on 29 May, we were awakened and went to join the Persian and Arab friends sitting among the olive trees outside the Shrine of Bahá'u'lláh. There was one line of chairs facing the assembled believers and at the end of the row furthest away from the Shrine but facing it, sat Shoghi Effendi. Mr Maxwell and I were led to seats along the row, quite a number of chairs from the Guardian but with no one else between us.

Chanting continued very much along the pattern of the Feast in the Pilgrim House on the 9th Day of Ridván, with pauses during which the Guardian would speak in Persian, presumably explaining some of the passages chanted. I was spellbound. I sat lost in contemplation, that I, the only visitor, the only one from the British Isles likely to have had that privilege, was sitting here on this special occasion in this very special place and in the presence of Shoghi Effendi. Suddenly there was a silence, I looked up towards Shoghi Effendi, and he said, 'You are getting more like a Persian every day!' I realised that with my legs tucked underneath the chair, my head bowed and my hands in my lap, I was indeed in a pose much like some of my Persian friends and so much in contrast to my posture at the Ridván Feast. This again, even on this solemn occasion, was an example of the delightful humour that, alas, not very frequently in those days, flashed to the surface.

I recalled that in one of the many meetings with Rúḥíyyih Khánum she had remarked how happy she had been with my meetings with the Guardian, when we had had a laugh together.

Very shortly after this, the Guardian led the way to the Mansion and indicated that Mr Maxwell and myself should be among the three or four believers who would accompany Shoghi Effendi into the very room where Bahá'u'lláh had passed away. It was there where, with the chanting of a Persian believer and with Shoghi Effendi kneeling at the side of the bed, that we experienced that awesome moment of three hours after midnight on 29 May 1946. In the years that followed, my memories of that occasion flooded back to me whenever I was called upon to speak to a gathering on the night of the Ascension. This was never more poignant than the day in May 1992, 46 years exactly after that experience in 1946 when, with my wife Lois, I was among the nineteen Bahá'ís representing the United Kingdom among the 3,000 or more gathered in the Ḥaram-i-Aqdas on the centenary of His Passing.

On that day in 1946, Shoghi Effendi was so overcome with emotion that he had to be assisted to his feet. He led the way to the Shrine where he laid his head on the Threshold and then stepped back for Mr Maxwell and I and the other believers who followed to pay our respects to the Beloved. After this, he chanted the Tablet of Visitation and sat for some time in silence. He then rose, again laid his forehead on the threshold, and stepped back for Mr Maxwell and myself. I was not aware that he had not left the Shrine and was not only astonished but overwhelmed when, after I was about to back away, he came forward, collected two handfuls of rose petals from the threshold and placed them in my hands! He then backed away and I never saw him again.

By this time it was dawn, and we travelled back to Haifa in the waiting taxi. It was my last day in Haifa and so, when all was packed, I went down to the Master's House to call and say 'Goodbye'. Rúḥíyyih Khánum answered the door and said, 'The Guardian is very busy writing the letter to the British National Spiritual Assembly, but he said 'goodbye' to you this morning in the Shrine. He did, however, ask me to give you this envelope.' It contained no note but £15 in English pound notes. The significance was clear – He was demonstrating the meaning of the letter he was then writing to the British National Assembly!

It was only in 1992, when Lois and I were having a private lunch with Rúḥíyyih Khánum and Violette Nakhjavání in London at the Royal Academy of Arts, that I reminded her of this event and she learnt that the envelope had contained £15 – the Guardian had never told her!

I had been in Haifa for almost five weeks and had had twelve meetings with him – a total of about fourteen hours. I could not have kept a full record of all that was said during those priceless hours and from the scrappy notes which still exist from those days, I am not sure which were of things actually said to me and which were from the many happy meetings with Rúḥíyyih Khánum and Mr Maxwell, or the notes I had taken of things I came across in the library at the Western Pilgrim House. These included the following:[15]

- To teach Muslims with courage: Obtain a knowledge of the Qur'án – Rodwell's translation the best for use but Sale's more authoritative.
- Know the Faith: State the truth even if science does not at the moment agree. It does not matter if we do not presently have all the proofs – ours is Revelation, science will later prove it.
- Palestine question: The war of 1914 drove away the Turks. The Balfour Agreement allowed the entry of Jews; persecution by Hitler compelled their migration to Palestine. Palestine will become great by Jewish capital and British administration. Haifa is the greatest centre and therefore will suffer greatest tests.
- Status of women: All the greatest teachers in the Faith have been women and all Americans – he listed about ten. These included Mr and

[15] Unpublished notes (personal archives).

Mrs Hyde Dunn, exemplary settlers; Martha Root, an itinerant teacher; May Maxwell, for her service in Canada and Paris; Marian Jack, for her times in Bulgaria; Mrs Thornburgh Cropper, and others.

- Administration: local Spiritual Assemblies should be strengthened and obeyed, and gain experience to act as courts in the future.
- When pilgrimage is allowed: the pilgrims will come for nine days. (I was there for a month and am therefore blessed!)
- Teaching efforts, schools, temples, etc.: These are to be paid for only by our Fund – our gift to humanity.
- Stress justice: Though justice must be tempered by mercy.
- Leaders are weak: Strength is in the masses, but it is not often realised that the masses lead the few. Ends do not justify the means. Never revert to a method which is against the Cause to promote it – never lie. The Cause is based on truth. Once religions oppose the Cause, this releases power which will bring about their own destruction.
- Obedience to government: Obey the government, but do not recant your faith. If it's an administrative matter – obey; if it is a spiritual one, do not. If it only retards growth, obey; if it dishonours the Faith, do not obey. If government says do not teach, obey, but one should never obey if it means violating a spiritual principle. We need not obey if the government is merely discouraging, but only if it is legally forbidding – we must be sure of text of the law. We may be weakened, but not humiliated.
- Leaders of Islam and Christianity: They are fighting to prevent Bahá'í being recognised as an independent religion.
- Great destiny of America: Persia is Cradle of the Faith, but America is the birthplace of the administrative order.
- Inspiration of life of Ṭáhiríh: Her life inspired the son-in-law of Albert Einstein to write a play and he wanted to become a Bahá'í; he had been advised to publish it first and then register as a Bahá'í.
- Unfaithful wives of Bahá'u'lláh: They both became Azalis, as did all His sons except 'Abdu'l Bahá and the Purest Branch (Mírzá Mihdí). Azal's betrayal was the first time in history that an appointed 'successor' was the opponent to the next revelation. In all other Faiths it was a 'rebel' who had caused schism. Professor EG Browne was influenced by Azal.
- All 'isms': They are often very good as an experiment, but man-made organisations break up as they expand. Their expansion is the cause of their split. In the Faith, expansion simplifies the administration.
- 'Bahá'í News' USA: It is not competently presented; it needed more vigour, and more international news to be included.
- Egypt: Needs competent workers to tackle its responsibilities.

- United Nations: It will have setbacks. Shoghi Effendi did not personally believe that there would be war with Russia.
- In the future: It will be research for the Germans, contemplation for the Persians, and execution (activity) for the Americans.

RETURN TO ENGLAND

When the National Teaching Committee learnt of my forthcoming release from the Army and of my visit to Haifa, Marion Hofman wrote to me, as its secretary, and was eager to get me back to settle in a goal town'.

The letter was dated 8 May 1946 and I received it in Haifa:[16]

> The Teaching Committee has heard with great joy the news that you would spend a month in Haifa, before returning to England, and already we are anticipating your home-coming and an account of your wonderful experiences.
>
> As you know, the Guardian has confirmed the choice of nine goal towns of the Six Year Plan, and has advised us to form Assemblies in them as rapidly as possible. At the Convention the delegates adopted a resolution to complete this initial phase of the Plan as rapidly as possible, but in not more than two years, and to attain the first five assemblies by next Convention.
>
> Such an achievement will require truly superhuman effort and sacrifice, and means particularly that all those who are able must arise to pioneer. The committee realises what a valuable service you could render, should you find it possible to settle in one of the goal towns upon your demobilisation. Knowing that you may already be making plans for employment and residence, we bring this urgent matter to your attention, and hope most earnestly that you will be able to lend your full weight to the pioneering of one of these key communities....
>
> May I add a personal word to say how pleased David and I were to receive your letter yesterday. We were really thrilled with all your news. The summer school committee was already planning to invite you to speak, but I will send the good news of your coming to the chairman, Geraldine Cooper, and will also ask Dorothy Ferraby to book a room. Please give our loving greetings to Rúḥíyyih Khánum whom we hope to write soon. Our thoughts are daily in Haifa with the Guardian, and you are indeed blessed to meet him. We have

[16] Unpublished letter (personal archives).

> already shared your letter with Alma (David is playing in Cheltenham this week), and will pass it on to others.

It was signed by Marion Hofman and there was a post script in David's handwriting:

> It really was a joy to have your letter, and to hear of all your good news. The Cause of God has certainly led you into wonderful experiences, and I want you to know that I am very proud of having had something to do with bringing you to the Faith. You have made really good progress – which is the important thing for all of us. The youth group here is getting very active – radio-active almost and I know you will be a great help to them. They have a suggestion at present to descend on goal towns en masse and hold rallies. Hugh McKinley is buying a motorbike so as to be able to get to all the goal towns.... Marriage is a good thing. I cannot wish you more than a true union with a nice Bahá'í girl – under the blessing of the Cause.... You are very privileged to meet the Guardian and enter the Shrine. We hope to do both before too long. In the meantime please convey our loving respects to him and think of us again in the Holy place. And give our loving regards to Rúḥíyyih Khánum. It will be good to see you home again, but don't think you're coming for a rest!!

After leaving Haifa on 30 May I travelled back by train to Sidi Bish near Alexandria, where there was a special camp for transport back to England. I met Bahá'ís in Alexandria, learned of a young couple in Sidi Bish and went to stay a night with them. I was very moved by their hospitality, particularly when I found that they had put me in the only bed in the house and they slept on the floor – even though the wife was in very advanced pregnancy with their first child.

Some thirty years later, when I was National Spiritual Assembly secretary, an air hostess from Sudan acted as courier with letters from the Sudan National Spiritual Assembly to the Universal House of Justice, which I had to post to them. After several visits over a number of months I learned that her mother, the secretary of the National Spiritual Assembly of Sudan, was the Sidi Bish lady, and the courier was the unborn child during my 1946 visit.

I travelled to England via Alexandria and Marseilles, then by train to Calais, across to Dover and, after demobilisation from the Army, I went home.

It is interesting to note that had I not become an officer, I would not have gone to East Africa, would not have got to see the Guardian, and would not have been equipped later to go as pioneer to Uganda and get a job in the Uganda Medical Service.

THE FIRST SIX YEAR PLAN THE YEARS 1946 – 1950

When I returned, my mother told me she had been attending Bahá'í meetings while I was away: when I asked her why she had not become a Bahá'í she replied, 'Because nobody asked me!' This was soon remedied. I discovered that the National Spiritual Assembly had been discussing a letter from the Guardian addressed to the newly formed National Youth Committee. This committee had had its first meeting in mid-May and had written to the Guardian on 16 May and he sent the following paragraph in reply, dated 4 June 1946: 'The Guardian has enjoyed very much meeting with Captain Philip Hainsworth, who had the unique privilege of being in Haifa for over a month, and he feels sure that upon his return to England he will lend great impetus to both the Youth and the teaching work.' I was appointed to the National Teaching Committee (NTC) and made chairman of the National Youth Committee (NYC). Hassan Sabrí from Cairo, who had come to study motor mechanics at Loughborough at the end of 1945, was on this National Youth Committee, as were Alma Gregory and Hugh McKinley.

Marion and David Hofman had pioneered to Northampton, having married on 21 October 1945. She had wide teaching experience, had worked with Leroy Ioas on the American National Teaching Committee which had won the first Seven Year Plan and was now on the British National Spiritual Assembly and Secretary of the National Teaching Committee.

Marion wrote to me on 21 June 1946:[17]

> I have been trying to contact Marion Norton, our chairman, about arranging a time for consultation with you at our meeting this weekend. Apparently she is out of town, for I get no answer by phone. So this morning I telegraphed you, and I hope it has been received. The suggestion is to come to Manchester for lunch with the Committee. We shall go at about 1 p.m. Then after lunch we are consulting on pioneers, and this would be a most logical time to meet with you to hear first-hand about the Guardian's suggestions for the Plan, and also to talk about your own pioneering plans. I hope, too, that we can talk a little about co-ordinating the youth

[17] Unpublished letter (personal archives).

> work with teaching, for this is tremendously important – and more so, since I have seen the Guardian's letter to your committee.

She wrote again on 10 July 1946:[18]

> Many thanks for your postal with the good news of your recent meetings.
>
> This will confirm your consultation with the Committee at the last meeting. It was agreed that the three months of your leave will be spent in Bradford, giving much-needed help in Leeds and Bradford in preparation for the separation of these communities and the formation of the Leeds Assembly. Success in this task will be a very notable contribution to the Six Year Plan. Because of the importance of this work, and also because we do not want to take you away from your parents just now, the Committee has not planned to send you to other goal towns for the present.
>
> The Committee and the National Assembly are both overjoyed that you will be able to settle in Nottingham in October. A cable has been sent to the Guardian giving him the good news of five pioneers. We have also heard from Mrs Brown of their great happiness in hearing of your coming. We are hoping to consult with the Nottingham friends at Summer School and detailed plans for more intensive teaching can be worked out then. Any other details connected with your move can be discussed at future meetings of the Committee. The Committee is confident that you will contribute just the qualities needed in the Nottingham Group at present, and we all deeply appreciate your decision to go.

Very shortly after arriving home there was a National Spiritual Assembly meeting at which I was invited to report on my meeting with the Guardian. At that meeting of the National Assembly there was a feeling that the Six Year Plan should include 'teaching the masses'. This was contrary to the Guardian's words to me so I cabled him and he replied to me on 28 June 1946:

> 'Teaching masses never prime objective concentration goal towns primary consideration.
>
> *Love, prayers, Shoghi*'.

It was to this meeting of the National Spiritual Assembly that I explained the background to the Guardian's letter of 29 May and his very strong emphasis on protection against the Covenant-breakers; appropriate action was taken.

It was that letter of 29 May 1946, with its instruction about pioneering,

[18] Unpublished letter (personal archives).

travel teaching and deputisation; its guidance to 'organise the work on a new basis', the need for 'a planned and consistent form of teaching' and to follow the pattern of the American and Indian Bahá'ís by financially assisting pioneers and travel teachers, not for a moment confuse this type of support with the creation of a paid clergy', that set a new direction to the Six Year Plan and was the basis for its ultimate victory.[19]

After settling in at home I realised I must pioneer quickly but as my father was virtually bedridden and my mother was exhausted, I could see no way that I could leave home, although I was prepared to go at once if the National Teaching Committee wished. I also wrote to the Guardian and he replied on 27 July 1946.[20]

> *Dear Bahá'í Brother,*
>
> Your letter of June 17th was received, and the beloved Guardian was delighted to receive your good news; both of the state of the Cause in England and the acceptance of the Faith by three new people in Egypt.
>
> He hopes that the way will open for you to both enter the pioneer field and also provide for your dear parents. He was very sorry to hear of your father's condition, and assures you he will supplicate for him in the holy shrines, that Bahá'u'lláh may assist him and bless him, and that God's will for him may be done.
>
> What the Guardian meant by appealing more directly to the masses is that the British Bahá'ís must try to acquaint the public with the teachings through public meetings and disseminating literature; this still does not mean they are in a position to launch activities on a scale comparable with what is being done in America: as he told you, their primary consideration at the present time must be to bring people into the Faith, in order to speedily achieve the goals of the Six Year Plan. This has precedence over everything else.
>
> He hopes the Summer School will be a great success, and wishes you well in your devoted efforts to stimulate the friends to take immediate action! You may be sure he will pray for you and your family.
>
> *With loving greetings, Rúḥíyyih Rabbání.*

In the Guardian's handwriting:

> *May the Beloved guide every step you take in the path of service,*

[19] Effendi, S. (1981). The Unfolding Destiny of the British Bahá'í Community: The Messages from the Guardian of the Bahá'í Faith to the Bahá'ís of the British Isles. London, Bahá'í Publishing Trust., pp 185-7.
[20] Unpublished letter (personal archives).

> *bless every effort you exert for the promotion of the Plan, and fulfil every desire you cherish for the advancement of the Faith in your country. Your true brother, Shoghi.*

My feeling was that I could go, but the National Teaching Committee (NTC) asked if they could consult on the letter and also consult my mother, as the committee (Marian Norton, chairman; Marion Hofman, secretary/treasurer; Connie Langdon Davies and myself) was meeting in a private hotel in Bradford.

The committee's interpretation of the letter was that I could only pioneer if adequate preparation had been made to look after my father and give mother some relief. Once these conditions were filled, I could pioneer to Nottingham.

A word should be said here about the Guardian and his letters. In Britain we were aware of the Guardian in a very general way but not at all conscious of his station, of his person, of his accessibility. To write to him was almost unthinkable. It was Marion Hofman initially, and then David who realised that the only way the British Isles could win its Six Year Plan would be when the believers began to 'turn', as the Master's Will had said, to the Guardian. He must become a real living reality to the friends and, it seemed, four people in particular would be able to inspire that love and awareness: Marion – a brilliant and moving speaker; Hassan Sabrí, young and full of the love and reverence for the Guardian instilled in him by his father; David Hofman; and myself, who had been so recently with him. At gatherings, on teaching tours, in seminars, whenever possible, we developed this theme.

The National Youth Committee began to write to him and published his letters in their *Bahá'í Youth Bulletin.* Believers, particularly those who arose to pioneer, began to write for guidance, the National Spiritual Assembly turned more readily to him and the National Teaching Committee wrote to him. A study of *Unfolding Destiny* gives some indication of the increase in correspondence from 1946 onwards, but the excerpts from individual letters, though quite substantial, do not reflect fully the large number of letters received, as only those sections which had guidance of a permanent value were selected for that publication.

As soon as a letter was received by the National Spiritual Assembly, a committee or an individual, copies were immediately typed or hand-copied and shared between the growing band of devotees.

Naturally all letters of general significance to the National Spiritual Assembly were duplicated for members and then published in the *Bahá'í Journal.* It is impossible to describe the excitement with which any message, letter, or cable, to any body or any individual was received, read, studied, read aloud and consulted upon repeatedly. Articles were written and messages from committees were sent out using quotes from his messages and explaining the considered implications of these letters and cables.

Gradually the whole community learned 'to turn' and miracles were witnessed. One such 'miracle' was towards the beginning of this period, when the National Teaching Committee had consulted on my letter from the Guardian of 27 July 1946 and reached the decision previously noted.

A MIRACLE

My mother consulted the National Teaching Committee (without my being present) and went home. Within a few hours our next-door neighbour, Mrs Joy, came in and said she had suddenly felt that she ought to come in more often and help my mother! That same evening my father's sister, who did not often call, came to express similar sentiments to Mrs Joy's, and by the time I got home from the committee meeting mother felt the Guardian's requirements had been met and I could go off to Nottingham! The operative words picked out by the committee were: 'and also provide for your dear parents'! The next part of the paragraph was not that my father would recover but that 'God's will be done'.

It was about this time that I received a personal letter from Rúḥíyyih Khánum dated 19 September 1946:[21]

> *Dear Philip,*
>
> I was so very pleased to hear from you as I have been sort of waiting for a letter from you. Don't take to heart what I wrote to Marion about the 'polishing' – we all need it in one way or another in this world and I feel you can do so much for the Cause we love so dearly that you should go on and on fitting yourself to better serve it and exemplify it in every way. We all should – as my mother used to say that the teachings are a never-ending education: she said it was a school she had been studying in for 35 years!
>
> All your news I shared with the Guardian – the whole letter in fact, and he was very pleased, particularly about the summer school attendance and the youth work.
>
> As the Persians say 'Your place was empty'. We missed you very much after you left – but you were lucky to come! So many have perforce been refused the last few years!

[21] Unpublished letter (personal archives).

The Guardian and I have been able to get a little rest and consequently feel much better. He was very tired when you were in Haifa – and so was I. I really made very poor company for even the pleasure – the *real* pleasure – of having a pilgrim was overshadowed by my feeling so run down. I feel ever so much better now.

I was very sorry to hear your father is so ill. I know this is hard for you to see – but we have to accept these trials in life and hope they make us better, along with their suffering.

I do wish you great success, dear Philip, in your work for the beloved Cause. Do let me hear how you get on and your news in general.

Of course I think it is far too early to put yourself in the hands of a drum-major of a wife, but mind the example you show others – young people today are longing for examples as you know yourself.

With affectionate greetings, Your Bahá'í Sister, Rúḥíyyih.

The committee decided that I should spend July, August, and September in the Leeds/Bradford area and if the conditions were met, I could go to Nottingham. I also attended my first summer school after the war, at Cromford Court, Matlock Bath, which began on 27 July, my 27th birthday. It was attended by 110 people – a record number.

In early October 1946, I went to Nottingham where I arrived unannounced. It was gratifying to receive, shortly after my arrival in Nottingham, a letter from the National Spiritual Assembly dated 18 November 1946:[22]

The Assembly has asked me to write you to express our appreciation of the efforts you have made in pioneering for the Six Year Plan. It has not been easy for any of those who have gone pioneering, and we realise that in your case too, a great effort has been needed. It is through sacrifices such as these that the Plan gains the spiritual strength which will eventually enable the Bahá'í community to achieve the goals set us by the Guardian.

John Ferraby, Secretary

Very shortly after my pioneering, not only did my mother have considerable help but my father expressed to Arthur Norton that he too believed, when Arthur, at his bedside, read a prayer of the Báb. Arthur treated this as a deathbed declaration as father passed away shortly afterwards and was given a Bahá'í funeral in Schoolmoor Cemetery. The

[22] Unpublished letter (personal archives).

Guardian cabled on 24 October 1946: 'Profound loving sympathy praying fervently soul dear father.'[23]

During this time in Nottingham Kathleen Brown was a pioneer; Lizzie Lacey, of Ilkeston, Derbyshire, was a member of the Group; Hassan Sabrí was at Loughborough Technical College; and Richard (Dick) Backwell pioneered there and we shared a flat for a while.

'Clarie' Lacey became a Bahá'í; Mrs Keary, a dedicated Bible student, accepted the Faith and later pioneered to Belfast; and Mr Maxfield was elected chairman of the Group. In January 1947 John Henshaw declared, which raised the number of Bahá'ís to nine.

By this time, on the instructions of the Guardian in a cable of 7 June 1946, the National Teaching Committee was concentrating on the re-establishment of the Torquay and Bournemouth Assemblies and the 'five most promising goal towns'.[24] These were Northampton, Leeds, Nottingham, Birmingham, and Liverpool, which between them required 25 pioneers or new believers. When these were achieved, the Guardian said we could have an increase in delegates to 'twice 19' and on the completion of the Plan 'three times 19'.[25] No sooner had we been able to report some teaching activities when the Guardian immediately gave us a new glimpse of our path ahead. The National Spiritual Assembly cable of 30 June 1946[26] and his reply of 6 July are illuminating:[27]

> Assembly renders loyal gratitude beloved Guardian's generous gift, guidance. Birmingham, Northampton, Nottingham, Leeds, Liverpool chosen attainment assembly status this year. Five new pioneers Gregory, Hainsworth, Wilkins, Joe, Elsie Lee. Eighteen travelling teachers circulating June, July. Youth work organised. Summer School registration broken all records. Sending plan organisation teaching. Humbly begging prayers.

The Guardian replied:[28]

> Delighted bright prospects. Achievement this year's goal will constitute turning point fortunes plan, landmark British Bahá'í history. Sustained concentration essential. Convey pioneers,

[23] Unpublished cable (personal archives).
[24] Effendi, S. (1981). The Unfolding Destiny of the British Bahá'í Community: The Messages from the Guardian of the Bahá'í Faith to the Bahá'ís of the British Isles. London, Bahá'í Publishing Trust., p.188.
[25] Ibid.
[26] Unpublished letter (personal archives).
[27] Effendi, S. (1981). The Unfolding Destiny of the British Bahá'í Community: The Messages from the Guardian of the Bahá'í Faith to the Bahá'ís of the British Isles. London, Bahá'í Publishing Trust., p. 189.
[28] Ibid., p. 189.

> travelling teachers assurance loving appreciation, abiding gratitude noble response. Urge exert simultaneously efforts establish this pivotal year nucleus future Assembly both Scotland, Ireland. Praying continually increasing evidences nation wide expansion, progressive consolidation dearly beloved English Bahá'í community.
>
> *Shoghi'*

It is of interest to note that the community was beginning to grow. At Ridván 1945 there were 118 voting believers, of which 40 were in London; by Ridván 1946 the total had grown to 145 throughout the British Isles (of which 14 were still on the voting list in 1992).

Being appointed to the National Teaching Committee meant regular meetings and a great deal of travel teaching. My appointment as chairman of the National Youth Committee was equally exciting and demanding. From the beginning, the Guardian encouraged us with our *Bahá'í Youth Bulletin* and this was produced by myself, as editor, with Alma Gregory the committee secretary, who would type everything out and take it to the printer in Northampton. We were very fortunate in that for almost all of the early issues we had a letter from the beloved Guardian to go on our first page.

I can still recall the excitement of putting together the first issue and writing my first editorial – the first time I had really written anything for publication. As it was the first, perhaps it should appear in this autobiography:

> THE GREAT ADVENTURE[29]
>
> The wars are over, but a greater adventure is awaiting. A vast army, with legions in many lands, is organising its resources and sending out its reconnaissance patrols, which are already engaged in the preliminary skirmishes. The army is the Army of Youth, preparing for the fight for Happiness, Peace and Goodwill. 'The future is in our hands', they shout. 'The world is at our feet'. Eager, impatient, Youth are searching for the Way.
>
> It has ever been thus, for that turbulent entry into Maturity, with all its unknown possibilities and responsibility, is *the* greatest Adventure of all. 'Did Youth but know', cried the Sage – but the youth will never know his individual destiny. Yet today, he may glimpse a brilliant future: a future which has been likened to the 'coming of age of the entire human race'. The attainment will not be easy, and resistance will be stern.

[29] Personal archives.

> The 'patrols' have contacted the enemy. Generals Doubt, Uncertainty, Misbelief, and other well-known warriors, are leading the Opposition.
>
> Bahá'í Youth all over the world constitute these 'patrols'. Of those in America, the Guardian of the Faith wrote: *'Though lacking in experience and faced with insufficient resources, yet the adventurous spirit which they possess, and the vigour, the alertness and optimism they have … shown, qualify them to play an active part in arousing the interest and securing the allegiance of their fellow youth ....'.*[30] From India, Persia, Egypt, Germany and other countries too, the Call has been answered, and victories won.
>
> British Bahá'í Youth, conscious of the need for more active workers for the first 'systematic crusade' in the second Bahá'í century, have undertaken to produce this magazine for *their* 'patrols'; may they find it a useful handbook for their glorious work.

We had talked with Bernard Leach – potter and artist – about our proposed magazine, and he sent us a design for the front cover – we loved it.

On 26 December 1946, the beloved Guardian wrote of the first copy:[31]

> This is an important new undertaking, and must be established as a firm innovation on the part of the British Bahá'í Community. He hopes it will gradually become the means of interesting and attracting many new souls to the Faith.
>
> In fact the Youth work everywhere in the Bahá'í World is dear to his heart, and he attaches great importance to it. The young people, who will inevitably grow up to shoulder all the work of the Cause, are really its hope, and should be one of the most active factors in its propagation. Through their courageous adherence to the high moral and ethical standards set out by Bahá'u'lláh, and through gaining a mastery of his many, diversified, and profound teachings, they can shape, to a great extent, the development and aid in the rapid expansion of their beloved Faith in the various countries in which they labour. They should be made to realise their responsibility is heavy and their privilege very precious.

And in the Guardian's handwriting:

> *May the Beloved bless abundantly the work which your Committee*

[30] Effendi, S. (1984). The Advent of Divine Justice. Wilmette, Ill., Bahá'í Publishing Trust., p. 69.

[31] Effendi, S. (1981). The Unfolding Destiny of the British Bahá'í Community: The Messages from the Guardian of the Bahá'í Faith to the Bahá'ís of the British Isles. London, Bahá'í Publishing Trust., p. 192.

has so nobly initiated, remove all obstacles from your path, aid you to realise every hope you cherish, and carry out every plan you conceive, for the furtherance of the interests of our beloved Faith and of its God-given institutions.

Your true brother, Shoghi

For the first article we were indebted to Louis Ross Enfield, who drew our attention to the poem which was, and still is, often quoted to give an entirely opposite meaning to what it actually portrays:[32]

O East is East, and West is West
And never the twain shall meet

But the next lines are often forgotten:

Till earth and sky meet presently
At God's great judgement seat;
But there is neither East nor West,
Border, nor breed, nor birth,
When two strong men stand face to face
Tho' they come from the ends of the earth.

So successful were our first two issues that they rapidly sold out and eventually reached youth in 36 countries.

Marion Hofman had been corresponding with a young Bahá'í in California, United States, who had become a Bahá'í after being directed by her tutor to study the Faith for her work towards obtaining a degree in international relations. After a great deal of research into British law, we were able to get for her a British passport. This was by invoking a very old law that enabled her to claim British rights because her father had been born in Egypt. She was Isabel Locke (later to become Isobel Sabrí), a pioneer to Africa in the Two Year Plan, and later a Counsellor in Africa and a member of the International Teaching Centre.

She first arrived in Birmingham where she was the guest of David and Marion Hofman, and then visited the Nottingham friends. Hassan Sabrí and I went to meet her at the station but the fog was so dense we had to abandon my car on the way to the station. The train was hours late and we almost despaired of being able to find her, though we eventually did.

Some days later I took her to my home in Bradford to spend some days with my mother. It was still cold and wet but we were able to dry out at home. Mother still lived in the house where I was born, which had no hot water or bathroom, and the only toilet was outside the house, down some stone steps to an underground 'loo'. Mother described this geography to Isobel, but after what seemed to be an unnecessarily long absence, I asked

[32] Rudyard Kipling, "The Ballad of East and West".

my mother to see how she was. A look of horror came over her face – 'Oh, I'd forgotten', she said 'I painted the seat this morning and it's probably not dried'! A rescue operation was duly completed but I'm sure Isobel would long remember her first visit to a working class house in Bradford.

Shortly afterwards she pioneered to Edinburgh to form the first 'nucleus' in that 'pivotal centre' and was on the first Assembly of that city in 1948.

At the end of August, I participated in a new 'teaching seminar', developed by David and Marion Hofman in Northampton, which led to the declaration, among others, of Betty Reed and enabled Northampton to be able to cable the beloved Guardian in October that it had enrolled its ninth believer and thus become the first goal Assembly to be formed in the Six Year Plan.

The Guardian responded to this news briefly but making three important points, which were to be the key points for all future new assembly formations: [33]

> Rejoice historic accomplishment consolidation imperative. Praying fervently success increase membership. *Love Shoghi.*

This work in Northampton allowed David and Marion Hofman to pioneer to Birmingham on 3 October 1946. Efforts were being made to raise pioneers and intensify teaching in the five top priority goal towns and the two 'pivotal centres' of Dublin and Edinburgh.

After attending the summer school, Dr Mohyi Said from Egypt, who was studying in Edinburgh for his FRCS, was able to organise the first fireside there on 25 September. I was the speaker and six contacts were present.

It was *Bahá'í Journal* N°. 58 of November 1946, headed 'Organising on a New Basis', that really began to stimulate the country with news of victories. It started a long series of reports from the National Teaching Committee and carried two photographs of that historic summer school which cabled the Guardian and to which he replied: 'Overjoyed. Praying ever-increasing success, Deepest appreciation high endeavours'. Shoghi'.[34]
That issue also reported my pioneer move to Nottingham and the declaration of my mother and father. By November 1946 the National Teaching Committee was able to report to the National Spiritual Assembly that only eight believers were required in the first five goal towns, that

[33] Cable (personal archives).
[34] Effendi, S. (1981). The Unfolding Destiny of the British Bahá'í Community: The Messages from the Guardian of the Bahá'í Faith to the Bahá'ís of the British Isles. London, Bahá'í Publishing Trust., p. 189.

numbers had risen from 20 in January to 38, and that there had been twelve adult and three youth new believers, with eleven pioneers since the start of the intensified teaching. When it is realised that these had come from a community still totalling only 183 adults and 3 youth, this was a quantum leap, yet two and a half years of the Six Year Plan had gone by and only 28 per cent of the total task had been accomplished.

The National Teaching Committee also recommended that the forthcoming teaching conference, to be held in Manchester 4 – 5 January 1947, be dedicated to the 25th anniversary of the Guardianship. The National Spiritual Assembly approved and asked permission of the Guardian, to which he replied on 21 November:[35]

> Approve. loving appreciation. Praying success. *Shoghi.*

David and Marion then asked Rúḥíyyih Khánum if she would write something for us on these 25 years, and her most inspiring words were reproduced in a 23-page booklet *Twenty-five Years of the Guardianship.*

About this time Lizzie Lacey of Ilkeston, Derbyshire – a member of the Nottingham Group – received a letter from an old pen friend from Germany. She had had correspondence with her before the war but had lost touch. Now that the German Bahá'í community was experiencing a resurgence, this lady had written to say that her son was a prisoner of war (POW) in England. He was in a POW Camp halfway between Nottingham and Ilkeston. We decided that I should don my Army uniform as a recently released Captain of the RAMC, visit the POW Camp and say that I wished to meet with Private Gerhardt Bender. This was successful and I was given a room. The lad was marched in, in proper military style, and was very frightened at being called to meet a visiting officer. I dismissed the sergeant who brought him in and as the door closed greeted him with 'Alláh'u'Abhá'. He just wept with joy – we had a long chat and before I left, I arranged to call for him and escort him to a 19-Day Feast.

1947

The teaching conference was held in Manchester on 4 – 5 January 1947. Seventy-five Bahá'ís attended, with 65 at the peak sessions. It was an outstanding occasion, as the cable sent to the Guardian implies:[36]

> Dedication to twenty-fifth anniversary Guardianship, our rock of strength, source of guidance, raised Teaching Conference fresh

[35] Ibid., p. 192.
[36] Cable (personal archives).

> heights vision, endeavour. Conference gratefully, joyously, humbly offers beloved Guardian loyal steadfast devotion. Pledges service as never before.

He responded on 12 January:[37]

> Profoundly moved message. Greatly appreciate noble sentiments. Praying depths grateful heart continued success magnificent collective efforts.
>
> *Deepest love. Shoghi*

It was after this conference that I wrote a long letter to the Guardian to which he replied on 18 February 1947. Through his secretary he said:[38]

> He wishes he more often got such glad news in one letter! It seems that at last the Cause in England is really getting into its stride, and that the British Community of believers are beginning to show forth the fruits of the many blessings showered on them – for England was one of the first countries of the West to hear the Divine Message, and was blessed by two visits from the Centre of the Covenant! Surely the older Bahá'ís must be astonished to see new centres springing up in a matter of months after years of an almost static condition! It shows that wherever and whenever the friends arise to serve, the mysterious power latent in this Divine Cause rushes in to bless and reinforce their labours far beyond their fondest hopes....
>
> He is very happy to hear you are established as a pioneer, with a business of your own, and you may be sure he will pray for your material as well as spiritual success in this goal town.
>
> As to the bulletin: he suggests you try and make it as universal in appeal as possible, with news included of outstanding work being done by the Bahá'ís in other lands, in the form of well-written articles.
>
> Your dear father's death, though for him a blessed release, must have been very hard for your Mother and for you as well, to bear. You may be sure the Guardian will pray for his great happiness and progress in the next world.
>
> PS He thanks you for sending the clipping and programme! He has heard nothing from Mrs Preston in Kenya. Can you find out if the pamphlet is being translated into Swahili and how she is getting on?

[37] Effendi, S. (1981). The Unfolding Destiny of the British Bahá'í Community: The Messages from the Guardian of the Bahá'í Faith to the Bahá'ís of the British Isles. London, Bahá'í Publishing Trust., p. 193.
[38] Ibid., p. 445.

He feels her presence there is an important opportunity to serve the Faith. Please assure her of this and encourage her constantly in your letters.

The footnote in his own handwriting was staggering:

Dear and Valued Co-worker,

I was deeply touched by your letter, and I truly admire your services and the spirit which animates you. You are often in my thoughts and prayers, and I will continue to pray, from the depths of my heart, for your success, your happiness and continual spiritual advancement. Persevere in your noble endeavours.

Your true and grateful brother, Shoghi

It was interesting to note that at the time Shoghi Effendi was writing his 16 February letter to me, I was writing to him on behalf of the Group of Nottingham. In this letter, signed by all nine members of the Group, I was able to confirm the acceptance of the Faith by its ninth member, originally announced by cable. We were four pioneers and five local believers. Four of the community had already written directly to the Guardian, but on different occasions. We were able, in this letter, to express in a somewhat inadequate way the consciousness that was beginning to pervade the whole community, largely generated by the dedication to the 25th Anniversary of the Guardianship at the teaching conference six weeks before. We wrote:[39]

We are now beginning to realise, still dimly, perhaps, our absolute dependency upon the life-giving power of Bahá'u'lláh now flowing through the Guardian. We are aware, too, that it is only our small capacity that is limiting his creativity, and we beg, in all humility, that at the Holy Threshold you will ask that we might grow ever more conscious of this, and that we may become better instruments for you to work with.

To this letter he graciously responded on 8 April:[40]

Dear Bahá'í Friends,

Your letter, dated 16 February, was received and read by our beloved Guardian with great joy, and he has instructed me to answer it on his behalf.

The news of your group having reached Assembly status was a source of deep satisfaction to him, and demonstrates what the friends can do, once they put their shoulder to the wheel!

[39] Unpublished letter (personal archives).
[40] Effendi, S. (1981). The Unfolding Destiny of the British Bahá'í Community: The Messages from the Guardian of the Bahá'í Faith to the Bahá'ís of the British Isles. London, Bahá'í Publishing Trust., p. 409.

You have every reason to feel proud of your achievement, and he hopes you will, through your correspondence and contacts with your fellow believers, encourage them to follow your example and forge ahead, in spite of every obstacle, with determination, confident that once we do our part, God is never failing in His.

He hopes your numbers will steadily increase and that many young people will be attracted to the Faith, as the part they have to play is very great and, also, their need of the Faith is very great.

You may be sure his loving prayers will be offered for you, and for the success of your labours, in the Holy Shrines.

In the Guardian's handwriting:

May the Beloved bless your efforts in the service of our beloved Faith, and enable you to deepen your knowledge of the essentials of His World Order, to increase your numbers, to extend the scope of your activities, and to fulfil every desire you cherish for its promotion and consolidation.

Your true and grateful brother, Shoghi

During this time, the National Teaching Committee and National Youth Committee were carrying on their meetings, writing encouraging letters to the believers and attempting stimulating articles for the *Bahá'í Journal* and the *Bahá'í Youth Bulletin.* The members of these communities were all going out travel teaching, so life was very full.

Una, daughter of George Townshend, had been released from the Services and settled in Dublin in September 1946, thereby 'opening' this 'pivotal centre'; Joan Giddings from Bradford had joined Rose Jones, resident believer in Cardiff, completing the 'nucleus' in that centre; Isobel Locke had joined Dr Said in Edinburgh and so a real beginning had been made in what the Guardian had described as 'virgin territories'.

Ursula Newman became the first travel teacher to visit Dublin in December and I went for four days in March. During January, I had also participated in a 'Bahá'í Week' in Leeds. On several occasions during this time, I had the privilege of sharing the platform with visiting pioneer teacher Honor Kempton. Honor was on her way to take up a pioneer post in Luxembourg where she added lustre to the already outstanding achievement of opening up to the Faith the territory of Alaska. I also did a ten-day teaching project in Bournemouth.

It was during this teaching and this committee work that I moved into the 'third phase' of my own understanding of the life, the rôle and the person of our Guardian.

Firstly, as a young Bahá'í, I knew nothing about the Guardian or the

Guardianship – I had just known that I must, some day, meet him. Then came the actual privilege of being in Haifa, having 12 interviews with him. It was a kind of unreal period of my life – almost six weeks of being in Haifa when I never knew when I may meet him again or what might happen. The third period was developed by my close association with Marion and David Hofman, Hassan Sabrí and by such outstanding visitors as Honor Kempton, Lucienne Miguette and Edna True, but even more by my relating the stories of my Haifa visit, by studying every word he had written that I could lay my hands upon. Marion Hofman, in a brilliant article in the *Bahá'í Journal* N°. 60, seemed to sum up what I was feeling:

> For the working of the Covenant of Bahá'u'lláh through the person of the Guardian is a miracle of guidance in these shepherdless and chaotic days. Around us humanity struggles from blow to blow. Within the Cause, and *only* within the Cause, are sure leadership, undeviating judgement, far-reaching vision. Through the Guardian pulsates this marvel and bounty: the unique and continuous manifestations of Divine Guidance from its appointed Dayspring. The rôle of the Guardian is to lead. The rôle of the friends is to turn with humility and devotion, and to respond and follow with gladness and ever-increasing power.
>
> We stand now at a cross-roads in our personal and community life. By our own free act we chose to be the first Bahá'í community to embark on a collective enterprise in the second century. The confirmation of the Guardian rests on that choice. We have richly profited by his guidance. We are forewarned in this crucial year by his knowledge that we cannot and dare not fail, that the task we have so freely chosen is pivotal to the whole future of the Faith in Britain, to the very future of the nation itself.
>
> Indeed, we begin to see an even larger perspective. For is not our Six Year Plan but one flank in a wider campaign, a mighty endeavour for the 'spiritual regeneration' of Europe? It is a struggle already engaging the believers of both hemispheres. For us in Britain, advancing on a major sector under the soundly-based leadership of one of the two National Spiritual Assemblies of Europe, it is a thrilling and glorious hour.
>
> As our forces consolidate and move forward in unison, do we not all secretly rejoice? Do we not welcome with eagerness the favour of God? Do we not cherish in our hearts as never before 'the power of the Covenant' which like 'the heat of the sun … quickeneth and promoteth the development of all created things on earth?'

As we moved towards our national Convention, the National Spiritual

Assembly and National Teaching Committee were working all out to achieve the five goal towns, re-form Bournemouth and achieve the 'virgin territory nuclei'. Northampton, Nottingham and Birmingham had the required number of believers and plans were made for the settlement of pioneers in Edinburgh, Dublin and Bournemouth. We were extremely aware of the words of Shoghi Effendi written 26 February 1947:[41]

> *Dear and valued co-workers,*
>
> The present crucial year, now drawing to a close, may well be regarded as one of the most memorable in the annals of British Bahá'í history.

He gave us for the first time a glimpse of our collective destiny:

> Upon the success of the Plan they are now so diligently and devotedly prosecuting, must depend the scope and effectiveness of their two-fold task of proclaiming the verities of their Faith to their fellow countrymen at home, and of implanting its banner abroad amidst the peoples and races of a far-flung Empire.

It is difficult, more than half a century later, fully to appreciate the effect of these words on the handful of Bahá'ís then dedicated to the goals of the Plan. About 150 adult Bahá'ís in some 30 centres, with Assemblies assured in only seven towns, faced the task of more than tripling the number of assemblies, doubling the number of believers, developing the 'virgin territories' of Scotland, Ireland and Wales – all within three years – plus the Guardian telling us that we had a rôle to play throughout the British Empire!

It was not until years later that we began to realise that as he saw the capacity of the believers increasing, Shoghi Effendi was able to share with those believers a part of the great vision he had for the development of the Faith worldwide. To the recipients, however, it was stimulating, even exciting, and we were always moved to redouble our efforts. We were comforted with the thought that if the Guardian could see that potential in the community, it must be there – the goals are possible, the believers will arise and new believers will be found. Even after those early letters of the Plan we began to live for the day when another letter came, if to the National Spiritual Assembly, to get our hands on a copy, to read it aloud together, in our groups or committees, whenever a few Bahá'ís were together. Sentences would be underlined and picked out for talks, for conference themes and for inclusion in our letters and other correspondence.

[41] Ibid., p. 195.

An example of this was my editorial for the May 1947 edition of the *Bahá'í Youth Bulletin*:

> THIS REMARKABLE EXPLOIT
>
> In the 'days of stress, of turmoil, and danger' of 1940, we were thrilled with these words of our beloved Guardian, 'I cherish the brightest hopes for you … be assured, persevere and be happy'.
>
> Little did we realise then how prophetic were his words, for one month later brought: 'the rising generation will erect a noble structure that will excite the admiration of their fellow countrymen.' and slowly, in accordance with our gradually awakening consciousness, he unfolded the picture in successive letters.
>
> To Convention, 1941, he stressed the 'priceless opportunities (of the) present hour' to be followed later in that year by praise for the 'truly heroic example' as we passed through the 'valley of spiritual death,' thus 'laying a magnificent foundation for the spiritual edifice their hands are destined to raise in their native land.'
>
> Then came that challenging, inspiring letter of 18 July, 1941, containing, 'They are increasingly demonstrating their right to be called champions of the Cause of God and manifesting their ability to follow in the footsteps of the early heroes of their religion.'
>
> Thus words of encouragement flowed to this country by cable and letter, until that memorable occasion – the Guardian's cable to Convention 1944 – 'Advise formation nineteen spiritual Assemblies spread over 'England, Wales, Scotland, N. Ireland and Eire'.
>
> The Plan was launched, the time for action had arrived, the strength of the 'foundation' was to be tested, our worthiness to be proved. The very tone of the Guardian's messages changed. We were approaching maturity as a community, and such words as 'The English believers stand identified with this Plan.... The immediate destinies of the entire community depend upon it … the greatest collective enterprise … urge supreme united collective effort' all indicated the magnitude of the task, and its importance.
>
> At last came the 'crucial, pivotal year', 1946/47, the 'turning point', the crisis – not only in our Plan but in the very history of the British peoples. We may not, for many years, see that year in its true perspective, nor realise how linked our particular rôle was with that crisis which so severely tested the whole of the country in that trying winter. Yet we do know this: the Goal was achieved and the victory won. As reward we were assured that 'success … has raised immensely' the community's 'prestige' and 'this remarkable

exploit' has indicated that 'total victory will ultimately be achieved at the appointed time.'

The picture was then unfolded a little more – 'the two-fold task of proclaiming the verities of their Faith to their fellow countrymen at home, ... and implanting its banner abroad amidst the peoples and races of a far-flung Empire,' is to be a fitting sequel. The future is bright, the 'unspeakably thrilling task ... awe inspiring obligation ... s priceless opportunity' is ours, but nothing less than total, all out effort, can bring the desired success.

Let us then, dear Friends, remember, as we re-dedicate ourselves to this year's work, those pregnant words of the Guardian: 'exertions Youth vital,' and demonstrate that this 'rising generation' can, and will, be worthy of our trust.

On 15 to 16 March 1947 the first regional youth conference was held in Nottingham. At this time almost any Bahá'í under the age of thirty was classed as 'Bahá'í youth' and at least 50 per cent of the pioneers and teachers were in this category.

At the beginning of March, I was able to take some firesides in Dublin, and before the Fast was able to enjoy the abundance of food which was available, in contrast to the relatively meagre rations of the still war-affected England.

There was a tremendous build-up for our Convention that year – it turned out to be significant in many ways:

- The year described by the Guardian as the 'crucial year' had ended in triumph, with many goals achieved.
- For the first time it was held in a new area – Birmingham – preceded by a public meeting with two non-Bahá'ís and five Bahá'í speakers.
- It was the first time the annual reports had been mimeographed and sent to delegates in advance.
- A letter dated 7 April from the Guardian to the NYC had arrived on the night before Convention and could be shared with the friends.
- On a personal note, I was elected to the National Spiritual Assembly and then appointed Assistant Secretary. (We had fourteen two-day meetings scheduled for the year).

On 15 May 1947, I received a picture postcard from Rúḥíyyih Khánum:[42]

Dear Philip,

Here is your 'wee note' written just the minute I finished reading

[42] Unpublished (personal archives).

your letter. You are really very often remembered with much affection I assure you. I will write a real letter some day! Daddy is away in Cyprus for a much needed real rest – first in seven years – the dear. Shoghi Effendi and I are both more rested and are in better health than last year but just about as busy or busier!

Try writing for the 'Herald of the South' and 'World Order' Magazines as they need it. To be a professional seems to me to be a stiff job but you might try it if you want to.

More some other time. I was thrilled to see such a young NSA and you on it too.

With much Bahá'í love to you, Rúḥíyyih.

Shortly before the Convention, the Guardian had began to press for the resignation of Rev. George Townshend from the Church of Ireland and he responded magnificently, so the Guardian was able to cable on 18 June 1947:[43]

Overjoyed Townshend's memorable decision noble action commendable determination settle Dublin. *Shoghi.*

The National Spiritual Assembly advised George that I would go to Dublin and give every assistance. In August, the National Spiritual Assembly appointed Dorothy Ferraby and myself as 'Trustees' and sent me over to Dublin to buy a house in Dundrum for the Townshend family, which they had found and liked.

In early July I had received a lovely letter from Rúḥíyyih Khánum dated 24 June 1947, which was in response to a chatty letter I had sent to her on 30 April:[44]

My dear Philip,

I am always so happy to hear from you and I often remember your visit here.

You seem to be fulfilling the Persian proverb 'The pea in every soup'. In other words, the person who is in everything. I see your name on the NSA, etc., etc., etc., and I must say I am very glad because I know you have had a dynamising effect on the work in England since you went back.

I am sorry that your father passed away so soon after your getting home, but it was nice that you could see him again. So often our dear ones die without our having that last comfort.

[43] Effendi, S. (1981). The Unfolding Destiny of the British Bahá'í Community: The Messages from the Guardian of the Bahá'í Faith to the Bahá'ís of the British Isles. London, Bahá'í Publishing Trust., p. 202.
[44] Unpublished letter (personal archives).

Marion and David seem to me, judging by their letters, to take the attitude that no one before ever had a baby, least of all a baby like theirs! However I suppose we can pardon them a certain amount of swelled head upon such an occasion. Judging from Marion's last letter to me she is toying with the idea of abandoning the baby on a Bahá'í doorstep in order to answer the cry of the teaching work. But this I am afraid she cannot do, because after all the baby would then have a perfect right to ask why it was had in the first place.

I am sure it will please you to know that I am feeling very well this year and manage to keep going just about day and night. The Guardian is also very well and in view of all the work we have to do, this is certainly providential. Dad was away in Cyprus for six weeks' vacation; the first in seven years and is much better for it. The old man 'Q' Mars, as you so cutely put it, is also well and as devoted as ever. So are all the other servants.

No doubt you know that an American Bahá'í is now helping us with the work here. The first question everyone asks her is 'When did you come and when are you leaving?' They cannot quite figure out how she got here at such a time and I must say she is so pleased about it, she can't quite figure it out either!

Daddy's presence here is quite a problem to the Authorities. They can't seem to figure out why he didn't get evacuated! But it looks as if that was going to be alright too. From your own experiences, you can surmise that although this is no time to have company, we are, none of us, in the danger one might be led to believe we are in through reading the newspapers! Every now and then a bomb goes off, but all anyone does is to open one eye and say drowsily: 'I wonder what they blew up that time', and turn over on the other side. Of course conditions may get worse – who knows? All we can do is hope for the best and in the meantime it is still no place for pilgrims, so you see how lucky you were to 'slip through' the way you did.

The way the work is going in England is really beginning to make us sit up and take notice and it seems to me that at last the British Bahá'ís are beginning to figure on the Bahá'í map in a big way.

Well Philip, I assure you it would give us all the greatest pleasure to stuff you once more with a good Persian dinner and it's a pity I cannot send you one by parcel post.

With love to you and all the Friends, Rúḥíyyih

PS: Shoghi Effendi is very anxious to get the Swahili Bahá'í booklet – how is it coming? Do keep on pressing the matter!

In October 1947 we had a powerful cable from the Guardian calling on us to 'ensure triumphant termination present phase plan; to maintain at all costs status newly formed Assemblies' and to focus attention on the 'establishment of firm foundations historic Assemblies of Scotland, Wales, Eire ere termination current year'.

Looking back over my teaching activities during this period and subsequently, I realised that I had, in addition to taking that first fireside in Edinburgh, also spoken at the first public events in Dublin, Cardiff and, later, Belfast and Swansea.

1948

Nineteen forty-eight began with a wonderful Teaching Conference in Birmingham, 17/19 January, where, according to the subsequent report in the *Bahá'í Journal* – 'The audience of eighty-five was unanimous in its appreciation of this radiant visitor, who so endeared herself to them, that only with great reluctance could they be persuaded, an hour after the meeting had terminated, to catch their last buses.' 'This visitor' was Dorothy Baker, whose inspiring contributions, at the pre-conference public meeting; during the National Assembly session and in a period devoted to pioneering, brought a new awareness of the significance of the Faith to all who attended of the significance of the Faith. I was privileged to have some time with her on several occasions and on one such occasion we stood hand-in-hand facing Buckingham Palace, saying a prayer and wondering if we could get in and tell King George about the Faith. We met again years later when she visited Kampala as a Hand of the Cause.

Since I had returned to England in 1946 and had been appointed Chairman of the National Youth Committee, I had been active in the Youth work, chairing its sessions at summer schools, editing the 'Bahá'í Youth Bulletin', working on the National Teaching Committee, travel teaching, taking public meetings and firesides, participating in seminar-type meetings as well as attending all the National Spiritual Assembly meetings. I was at the same time secretary of the Group (and then local Spiritual Assembly) of Nottingham. One youth activity was a Regional Youth Conference in Manchester on 29 – 30 November, 1947, which was significant, not only in arousing youth dedication for the Plan and stimulating pioneer offers. It also witnessed the acceptance of the Faith by a man well beyond middle age who almost immediately pioneered to Belfast and later to Sheffield and became, in the Ten Year Crusade, the Knight of Bahá'u'lláh for Orkney – Charles Dunning.

During the following months, on behalf of the National Teaching

Committee, I met with and helped to plan the services and settlement of several believers from overseas and newly enrolled Bahá'ís. These included Jean Court, Bruce McCombe (Whiteman) and from Persia, Noura Faridian, Violet Samandarí, Talieh Agah, Bahieh Jalili, Tahereh Vatanparast, Pouran Mahboubi, Iraj Poostchi, Ata-ollah Khoshbine, Adib and Zarin Taherzadeh, Shomais Ala'i and others.

On 23 February,[45] I wrote to Shoghi Effendi saying that although he had told me I should not hesitate to write to him, it had been more than a year since I had last written. There were three reasons for this:

1) I knew it was good news that he needed most and that all ours had been conveyed to him by the National Spiritual Assembly and National Teaching Committee and I did not have any of my own to add, so I did not wish to take up his valuable time;
2) I needed time to plan to write to him as otherwise I would write on and on for pages (as it was my letter ran to about 16 pages of handwriting);
3) I had been waiting to be able to write of some positive achievement worthy of the bounty that had been granted by my visit to Haifa, but instead I was most dissatisfied with myself and really needed his guidance.

I referred to what I termed the 'tiredness' of the community; radiance and joy seemed to be ours on only rare occasions, and I gave as an example of this radiance the effect of the visit of Dorothy Baker. The light-hearted joy and radiance in everyday life seemed a thing of the past and was only recaptured at summer schools, the teaching conference and the regional Unity Feast, held in Manchester on 15 February. It was almost as though the gloom and despair of the peoples outside the Faith were being projected into our lives. I mentioned some withdrawals and inactivity and said that I felt it was like leaves dropping off a tree in the wind or sea leaving a foam on the shore; that the community becomes stronger, healthier and purged of those too weak to bear the 'growing pains'. After writing at length along these lines, I then asked him the question: 'How much do you really want to know?' I wrote: 'I believe that if a cable were sent – e.g. "In grave difficulty, please advise", you could give a complete and detailed answer as the very act of turning is sufficient. Is anything more than a mere statement, such as this, really necessary?'

I rambled on at some length in this vein and mentioned my discussions on this matter with Dick Backwell. I then came to my immediate problem relating to my business and the way it was failing from a bad period in that particular trade, the shop being in a poor locality, and my spending more time on serving the Faith than in concentrating on trying to make money. I

[45] Unpublished letter (personal archives).

described my own analysis of my weaknesses and inability to be worthy of the bounties so far showered upon me and begged his prayers. I suggested several paths which I might follow and sought his guidance. I then switched to writing about getting a pamphlet translated into an African language and closed by reaffirming my offer made previously to go anywhere in the world and do anything he wanted me to do.[46]

His answer, written almost by return on 4 March 1948, was astonishing:[47]

> *Dear Bahá'í Brother,*
>
> Your letter to our beloved Guardian, dated February 23rd, has been received, and he has instructed me to answer you on his behalf.
>
> Regarding the various matters you asked his advice and opinion about.
>
> It is not surprising, in view of the gloom overhanging the entire world, and in conjunction with their run-down, exhausted state due to war conditions and present circumstances of life in England, that the British Bahá'ís should sometimes reflect the state of their countrymen! It is a pity; and they should certainly try, as believers, to be cheerful and radiant; but he feels the greatest sympathy for them, and considers that when their present achievements are assessed in future, people will give them a double measure of praise for having done so much when they were least fit to do it. The spirit of determination, and their perseverance, are truly outstanding.
>
> Just because some people have lost their vision of the Cause, or never had a proper grasp of its implications before entering it, and leave the fold, should not cause undue discouragement. There are bound to be such cases, and although every moral support should be given them if they still wish to withdraw, they fall off – as you said – like withered leaves from the Tree of the Faith, and do it no real harm.
>
> He likes to be provided with facts by the friends, when they ask his advice, for although his decisions are guided by God, he is not, like the Prophet, Omniscient at will, in spite of the fact that he often senses a situation or condition without having any detailed knowledge of it.
>
> As to your own plans, he feels that you should not leave Nottingham at present, where you are not only needed by the local Community, but where you have a store. He suggests you make a

[46] Ibid.
[47] Ibid.

serious effort, through devoting more time to your business, to getting it on its feet, and at least in a condition to dispose of, if you don't think it worth continuing.

He is very anxious to have the pamphlets in African languages gotten out – both the one Mrs Preston was to see to, and the one you mention you can get done, at least the translation, by an African. He suggests you write Mrs. Preston, and urge her to get the Swahili one done quickly (he himself has heard nothing from her at all), and you make suitable selections for a small pamphlet to be sent to your African acquaintance and translated into Chinyanza. He is delighted at the prospect of having this done, as our publications are now translated and printed in 50 languages, two are being translated into 12 additional languages. One of these 50 is Tegrinia, an African tongue.

He urges you to never feel discouraged, or that you have in any way failed in your services; on the contrary you have done a tremendous lot of work for the Cause since your return to England, and he is very happy over your accomplishments, and assures you he will pray in the Shrines for the solution of your problems and the fulfilment of your heart's desire.

With Bahá'í love,

R. Rabbání.

In the Guardian's handwriting:

Dear and valued co-worker,

I wish to assure you in person of my everlasting gratitude for the historic and magnificent work you have achieved in recent years – a work of which I feel truly proud. You should be happy, grateful and confident, and persevere in your great task, which the Beloved, I feel sure, will continue to bless and guide. The spirit you have imparted to the friends after your return from the Holy Land has been responsible for the success you achieved. May the Beloved sustain you in your high endeavours.

Your true and grateful brother, Shoghi

His 'everlasting gratitude' for the work I had achieved – 'a work of which I feel truly proud' – gave me renewed vigour but made me realise how much more I had to do to become really worthy of his words.

On 29 March, the National Spiritual Assembly cabled the Guardian that only 12 believers were needed to complete the initial phase of the Plan, and among the pioneers to have arisen was my mother.[48] The National Teaching Committee decided to send her to Nottingham where she immediately found a job night-nursing an elderly man which gave her a small income, with food and accommodation – she was then 69 years old.

On 15 April, the National Spiritual Assembly cabled the Guardian, 'Teaching Committee report all goals assured'.[49] From its first meeting after Convention we cabled[50] the Guardian that the National Spiritual Assembly membership was unchanged except that Alma Gregory had replaced Ursula Newman and that Marion Hofman had been appointed chairman of the National Teaching Committee and myself as its secretary. I moved into a rented three-bedroom house in West Bridgeford, Nottingham with my mother and hired my first secretary – Muriel Hayter – who later became a Bahá'í and secretary of the Nottingham Assembly when we left.

The Guardian's cable of 25 April 1948 contained some most moving phrases that stirred the National Teaching Committee to even greater efforts:[51]

> Acclaim triumphant conclusion initial stage epoch making Plan … Concourse on High applauds brilliant feat unitedly achieved British followers Faith Bahá'u'lláh. Sister communities East West marvel victory won such magnitude so short period by community so sorely afflicted so small numerically so circumscribed in resources yet so alive so sound so resolute…

On 29 April, the Guardian sent one of his most powerful letters to date to the British Bahá'ís. In this letter he spoke for the first time of the 'glorious destiny ordained for the British Bahá'í community by divine providence', and went on to spell out the needs of the final phase of the Plan.[52]

By June, the National Teaching Committee was able to report that with the winning of all the goals of the initial phase, there had been 122 new believers enrolled since 1944 – more than doubling the national community in four years, and almost 40 per cent of these in the past year.

In early September mother and I attended the summer school in Ashover, Derbyshire, along with 140 other participants, including Charles Mason Remey – then celebrating his 50th year as a Bahá'í. For us it was

[48] Unpublished cable (personal archives).
[49] Ibid.
[50] Ibid.
[51] Effendi, S. (1981). The Unfolding Destiny of the British Bahá'í Community: The Messages from the Guardian of the Bahá'í Faith to the Bahá'ís of the British Isles. London, Bahá'í Publishing Trust., p. 211.
[52] Ibid., p. 214.

spoiled by mother being taken ill and we had to return home where a specialist reported a terminal illness.

I cabled the Guardian:[53]

> Mother seriously ill Summer School specialist pronounced incurable condition less than year live. Beseech prayers strength enable her spend remainder life service.
>
> *Loving devotion*

To which he replied on 18 September:[54]

> Deeply grieved news dear mother. Assure you fervent prayers deepest love abiding appreciation your magnificent services.
>
> *Shoghi*

He wrote again to me on 17 October:[55]

> *Dear Bahá'í Brother,*
>
> I am acknowledging on behalf of our dear Guardian your letter of some time ago, because he is anxious to assure you of how deeply concerned he was to hear your Mother's health is in danger.
>
> It seems very hard indeed that after losing your dear father you should be faced with this new sorrow – he hopes the doctors are wrong, and that she will be spared to serve with you for many more years. He will certainly pray for her recovery, and he wishes you to assure her that as *your* mother she is dear to him and often remembered.
>
> Your own indefatigable services are, as you know, deeply valued by him; and he urges you not to lose heart but to persevere, with your radiant spirit and your usual courage and determination.
>
> The Cause in England seems, in spite of financial handicaps, to be going forward in Seven League boots. He is truly proud of the British believers, and this is more than he could say in the past, when the work for years seemed to be stagnating! Those days are now past forever, he feels sure.
>
> You know his loving prayers and thoughts are always with you.
>
> *With Bahá'í love,*
>
> *R. Rabbání.*
>
> PS. Please assure your secretary also of his prayers. Likewise Mrs Alma Gregory.

[53] Unpublished cable (personal archives).
[54] Unpublished cable (personal archives).
[55] Unpublished letter (personal archives).

In the Guardian's handwriting:

Dear and valued Co-worker,

Your constant and noble efforts, exerted with such determination and devotion, evoke my highest admiration, and will, no doubt, be richly blessed by the Almighty, Whose Cause you love and serve so well. You are often in my thoughts and prayers, and I will continue to beseech on your behalf the sustaining grace of Bahá'u'lláh.

Your true and grateful brother, Shoghi.

This letter reached me just after the National Spiritual Assembly meeting of 22 – 24 October which issued its 'newsletter N°. 6,' in which it announced the arrival in the UK of Dr Lotfu'lláh Hakím (whose settlement in Sheffield as a pioneer I had to arrange), the passing of Mrs Wilkinson of Bradford (in whose home I had studied and accepted the Faith), and the arrival for teaching tours of Mrs Routh and Mrs Hutchinson-Smith (from Australia) and Marion Little (from the United States), whose schedules I had the privilege of organising and several of whose meetings I chaired.

As 1948 drew to a close, another part of my life took a strange turn. Shortly after being elected on to the National Spiritual Assembly, a close relative of one of our members sought consultation. This young man was in trouble and in a letter presented to the National Assembly confessed to an enormous number of cases of theft. He was very repentant and wanted to become a Bahá'í. The National Assembly decided to call in the police and I had to sit with him in a side room until the police came to take him away, in case he attempted to 'make a run for it'. He was told that if he accepted his punishment with the right spirit and studied the Faith while in prison, he could be accepted as a Bahá'í on his release. For his confession and promise to live a better life and with the support given to him in court, he was given a light sentence and was released in May 1948. He came to Nottingham to work and live in accommodation I found for him, and was accepted as a Bahá'í. He was paid an adequate salary from a factory owner that was subsidised (unknown to him) by his father.

During his time in prison, he wrote to the Guardian and part of Shoghi Effendi's illuminating reply through his secretary appears in *Unfolding Destiny*[56]. Reference was again made to him in the first paragraph of the letter of 23 June,[57] written to his relative. He did not like the work and was

[56] Effendi, S. (1981). The Unfolding Destiny of the British Bahá'í Community: The Messages from the Guardian of the Bahá'í Faith to the Bahá'ís of the British Isles. London, Bahá'í Publishing Trust., p. 449.
[57] Ibid., p. 451.

not physically strong and wrote again to the Guardian who replied on the 23rd of December 1948, again through his secretary, saying:[58]

> He is very glad to see you are now living the life of an active Bahá'í and keeping in close touch with dear Philip Hainsworth, who is a fine friend to have, with his devotion to the Cause and his optimism.
>
> The Guardian urges you not to be discouraged by any setbacks you may have. Life is a process of trials and testings, and these are – contrary to what we are prone to thinking – good for us, and give us stamina, and teach us to rely on God. Knowing He will help us, we can help ourselves more. …

In 1949, I was able to dispose of my business and as secretary of the National Teaching Committee was given a little financial help. I carried around, as a sales representative, several different categories of goods, including items of carpentry made by the Nottingham factory which had employed our new Bahá'í. The factory prospered, moved into larger premises, the owner bought a bigger house and car, finally overstretched himself, got badly into debt, lost everything and I had to visit him in prison some six months later!

In the meantime, Marion and David Hofman had moved into Oxford. Connie Langdon-Davies, another member of the National Teaching Committee, had moved in so, in order to centralise the committee and enable it to meet as frequently as the work demanded, I rented a flat at 179 Woodstock Road and moved in with my mother.

My mother was reported as a pioneer to Oxford but as I was still 'officially' a member of the Nottingham Assembly, my National Teaching Committee secretary and I were elected as delegates to the Convention for Nottingham!

Convention that year, 1949, was held in Manchester, with Ḥasan Balyúzí as chairman and myself as vice-chairman. Unfortunately, Ḥasan was too ill to carry on and I had my first experience as Convention chairman.

My first attempts to put pen to paper for the Faith had been published in the *Bahá'í Youth Bulletin*' in which I wrote the editorials as well as several articles: 'The Great Adventure' (September '46), 'The Golden Opportunity' (December '46), 'Their Privilege very Precious' (March '47), 'The Bahá'í Administrative Order' (Part I, March '47; Part II, May '47, Part III, September '47), 'This Remarkable Exploit (May '47), and 'The Sooner they Prepare' (September '47).

[58] Ibid., p. 452.

I was released from the National Youth Committee in 1948, when I became secretary of the National Teaching Committee and then I was commissioned to write articles and reports for the *Bahá'í Journal* – many followed during the next three years – 'The Supreme Challenge' (*Bahá'í Journal* N°. 70), 'Have you bought a book this week?' (*Bahá'í Journal* N°. 72), and my first annual report for the National Teaching Committee, which ran to 7,000 words. In October the National Teaching Committee started a series of 'news bulletins', the first one of which announced the results of the first public meeting in the new goal area of Sheffield on 16 September, called at short notice in association with the summer school. Twenty-four newcomers and 36 Bahá'ís attended, with David Hofman as speaker and myself in the chair.

The next issue of the bulletin, reprinted in the *Bahá'í Journal*, announced the first full scale public meeting to be held in Oxford, in the Town Hall, on 20 October. Marion Hofman spoke on 'World Unity through World Religion'; David Hofman was in the Chair and 42 non-Bahá'ís were present. My mother was sitting on the back row and in front of her was a young man who seemed very interested in what was being said. At the end, as he was about to go, she spoke to him and asked him if he would like to know more. When he said, 'Yes', she said, 'You must come round to our flat, my son has an information meeting there every week on Wednesdays' (or Thursdays, or some other such day – I cannot remember which). It was one of those firesides to which people would be invited but so far no one had yet turned up. He came as invited, and to the next and the next – no one else came, but he became a Bahá'í. He was at Pembroke College. His name was Ian Semple, and he was later to be a National Spiritual Assembly member, Auxiliary Board member, member of the International Bahá'í Council (1961 – 3) and member of the Universal House of Justice (from 1963).

For my 80th birthday, Ian sent me the following message, received I received at a party given for me by our daughter, Zarin, in Basingstoke, Hampshire on 25 July 1999 with all my family (except Richard) and about 40 friends:[59]

> *My Dear Philip,*
>
> I can hardly credit that it is almost 50 years since you took me under your wing at that meeting in Oxford Town Hall and invited me to the firesides at your and your dear mother's flat, where you taught me the Faith and kept me supplied with books I could scarcely put down. You have my eternal gratitude for those early days and for

[59] Unpublished letter (personal archives).

> your friendship ever since. Now, I hear, your 80th birthday is approaching and you will have the blessing of celebrating it in the midst of your wonderful family with Richard to join you not long thereafter.
>
> May Bahá'u'lláh bless you and yours and grant you many more years of service and joy in His Path.
>
> *With deepest love and every good wish,*
>
> *Ian (10/07/99)*

That same issue of the 1949 bulletin reprinted in the *Bahá'í Journal* announced that mother was seriously ill in Radcliffe Infirmary and asked the community for its prayers. Behind this lies an interesting story. The 'incurable' condition diagnosed after summer school 1948 was reticulosis, or cancer of the white blood cells – causing her spleen to grow to an enormous size. The specialist at the Oxford hospital said it must be removed and as she was so uncomfortable she was willing to have it done.

Some few months previously I had written to the Guardian saying that I had collected some quotations together to make a pamphlet for translation into African languages, giving the first one the title 'Do you know in what day you are living?', from the Master's first public address in London. I was planning for it to be translated into Swahili by Adamali and into Chinyanza by ex-Sergeant Phiri. I had enclosed the English draft. I wrote again on 16 October requesting his advice on the two matters previously mentioned in August – the pamphlet and my own future after the Six Year Plan.

The reason for this second letter was, firstly, that the Chinyanza translator, having nearly finished his work, was asking for some money. Secondly, mother and I must soon make a decision about the house we still had in Bradford and whether she should sell her furniture, as she was then 70 and might not live for very much longer. However, she needed somewhere to go if I was called away to some other country after the Plan was won. If she were well enough to travel, then she would want to go with me. While she was prepared to 'burn her boats' I was reluctant to encourage her to do this if there were a prospect of our parting in the not too distant future. In my letters of 4 January and 22 August 1949 I had reported on mother's general improvement and the Guardian replied on the 30th of October 1949. Before I received the letter, I had to cable:

> Mother undergoing most serious operation beg prayers. Pamphlet sent you August now translated Kiswahili, Chinyanza awaiting your advice. *Loving devotion*

To which he replied on 3 November:[60]

> Assure dear mother ardent loving prayers. Answer letter mailed. Urge translation printing pamphlet. *Shoghi'*

His letter of 30 October 1949 was received the day after the cable. Paragraph 4 was of particular significance:[61]

> *Dear Bahá'í Brother,*
>
> Your letters of January 4 and August 22, were received, and the beloved Guardian has been anticipating answering them for some time, but the pressure of his work has held up a lot of letters of late. He regrets the delay – the material you enclosed in them was also received and he thanks you for sending it.
>
> Mrs Preston wrote the Guardian three letters about herself and her work – or contemplated work. She seems to be now ready to take hold and do some teaching, and the Guardian advised her about this, and also that she need not send any pamphlet to him for correction, but should consider the British National Spiritual Assembly the natural source of advice and help in these matters. He urged her, however, to keep in close contact with him.
>
> The thing he is anxious to see is *a* pamphlet in Swahili (and as many other African languages as possible!). He was, therefore, very pleased over your action and leaves it to you to push the matter further. You should perhaps send a copy of your material to Mrs Preston for consultation. It seems her husband is helpful and speaks Swahili himself, so he could judge of any translation you get back.
>
> It pleased the Guardian very much to hear your dear mother is so much better. You were blessed in your parents and he will pray she may be spared to you for many years to come. Give her his love.
>
> As regards your own future plans: in view of the precarious state of the Plan in Britain he does not think you can at present decide what you will do when it is over. He advises you to wait until it is over and the needs of the immediate future take shape. The best general plan for you to make would be to contemplate getting work for the next year or so in the British Isles, to go on with your services for the Cause there, and keep in mind the desirability of going at a later date to some place in Africa to establish the Cause.
>
> All that you have done and are doing he most deeply appreciates. You have been of invaluable assistance to the work there since you

[60] Unpublished cable (personal archives).
[61] Unpublished letter (personal archives).

went back, and he envisages for you many future distinguished services.

With warmest Bahá'í love and greetings, R. Rabbání.

In the Guardian's handwriting:

Dear and valued co-worker,

Your strenuous, valiant and persistent efforts, exerted with such zeal and devotion, to ensure the success of the Plan are, indeed, worthy of the highest praise. I increasingly admire your accomplishment and feel deeply thankful for the exemplary spirit you demonstrate. My fervent and loving prayers surround you in all your activities, and I feel confident that the Beloved is well pleased with the standard of your achievements. Persevere in your high and meritorious endeavours and be happy and confident always.

Your true and grateful brother, Shoghi.

In the meantime, the operation was to take place on 6 November beginning at 10 A.M. Late the night before, the sister in charge had telephoned to say that at the last moment the surgeon had been called away and would not be able to operate the following morning. I said: 'Look, sister, tomorrow morning people all over the British Isles will be praying for the successful removal of my mother's spleen, if the surgeon does not do it she'll probably give birth to it!' Early the following morning the sister rang to say that the reason for the surgeon's visit elsewhere had been cancelled and he would operate as planned. He did, and it was highly successful – not only that, but it was the largest spleen ever removed and she had made hospital history! When she recovered from the anaesthetic, she decided to get out of bed and walked to the toilet. The surgeon was so amazed with her progress that after a few days he asked her permission to go with him to the lecture hall where he was presenting her case to fellow surgeons and students. She agreed, and he insisted on her going by wheelchair to the lecture. After he had described the case and shown the x-rays on the screen he said, 'Would you be able to stand up to demonstrate that you can move?' She said 'Can you waltz?', got up, and waltzed around with the surgeon to the ovation of the audience.

I cabled the Guardian on 8 November: [62]

> Letter, cable received, deep gratitude. Mother making remarkable recovery. Airmailing Swahili translation to Preston. Consulting NSA next meeting. Obtaining preliminary estimates printing.
>
> *Devotedly, Philip.*

[62] Unpublished cable (personal archives).

The National Spiritual Assembly agreed to transfer my membership from Nottingham to Oxford, raising the number there to 10, and at the 19 Day Feast on 22 November 1949 the election was held with all members present, except mother who sent her postal vote from hospital. An Assembly was elected, with Dick Backwell representing the National Spiritual Assembly: David Hofman, chairman; Marion Hofman, vice-chairman; Philip Hainsworth, secretary; Constance Langdon-Davies, treasurer; Cyril and Margaret Jenkerson (later pioneers to Cyprus); Jean Campbell (new believer – later a pioneer to Malta); Louise Charlot (Alma Gregory's mother); and Lizzie Hainsworth (my mother).

The same issue of the *Bahá'í Journal* (N°. 76) which reported this also carried the story of the history of the Faith in Norwich from my first visit in 1944 which had, earlier in the year, formed its Assembly and received its first letter from the Guardian. The issue also carried the teaching bulletin which confirmed that the date of the teaching conference had been changed to 3 – 4 January to make possible the attendance of Amelia Collins, who would speak on the Saturday evening, as the Guardian was 'praying utmost benefit' from the visit. The session would be called 'Victory Within Sight'.

I was very privileged to spend some time with that wonderful soul, 'Milly' Collins, whom the Guardian loved so much, and whom he appointed vice-president of the International Bahá'í Council in early 1951, and a Hand of the Cause in December of that same year. We shared our feelings about the Guardian and she came to our home for a meal. Before she left London, she wrote me a note:[63]

> *Philip dear,*
>
> Have just finished reading your precious messages from our beloved Guardian. Thanks from the depths of my heart for giving me this bounty – What a glimpse of Paradise we had last evening. I shall always cherish the memories. To your blessed mother my affectionate greetings and gratitude for her big part in making the evening a heavenly feast. My niece joins in appreciation for the generous gift of chocolate.
>
> May Bahá'u'lláh's choicest blessings descend upon you both, you two precious pioneers.
>
> *Milly*

On the 12 December,[64] I wrote 700-word letter to the Guardian expressing gratitude for his cable and letter of 30 October and confirming the remarkable recovery of mother after her operation. I explained that I

[63] Unpublished letter (personal archives).
[64] Unpublished letter (personal archives).

had shared my plans and quotations for the African language pamphlets with the National Spiritual Assembly but 'they could not offer any assistance during these few remaining months of the Plan'. I further outlined the actions taken, with getting the Swahili and Chinyanza pamphlets (about 6,000 words each) ready for the printer; that copies of the Swahili had gone to Mrs Preston in Kenya; that Richard St Barbe Baker had warmly approved the translation but I doubted if his Swahili was good enough to translate a foreword. I also described the difficulties of getting a good translation of the pamphlet in Hausa. Richard Backwell's father, for many years a district commissioner in Nigeria, was attempting a Hausa translation, but he felt it was not a good one. I had sought the help of the International Africa Institute and the School of Oriental and African Studies, but they had referred me to ministers (ex-missionaries), who refused to help because of the religious beliefs expressed in the pamphlet.

I said I was still trying to find a translator. I asked the Guardian's advice on whether I should try to raise the money for the printing from other sources or take it up again with the National Spiritual Assembly. I estimated that I would need £50 or £60 to have 1,000 copies printed in each of the two languages.

This letter was typed and in a covering note, I apologised for typing it, told him of declarations in Newcastle and Glasgow, and included a message of love and gratitude signed by my mother.

The answer was dramatic: On 27 December the National Assembly received a cable:[65]

> Deliver £60 Hainsworth from National Fund for publication Swahili Chinyanza languages. *Shoghi.*

On 12 March,[66] I had been able to advise the Guardian that the Swahili page proofs would be ready within a week, including a preface by Mrs Preston and a foreword by Richard St Barbe Baker, that the Chinyanza translation was being given to the printer and Mr Backwell had completed the Hausa translation. I suggested that we printed one in English, making a set of four to be used by pioneers and travel teachers. I made some other suggestions about their use and their future development. I also gave him the latest news on the pioneer front.

His gracious cable was sent immediately, on 19 March 1950 and a fuller reply was sent soon afterwards: [67]

[65] Effendi, S. (1981). The Unfolding Destiny of the British Bahá'í Community: The Messages from the Guardian of the Bahá'í Faith to the Bahá'ís of the British Isles. London, Bahá'í Publishing Trust., p. 237.
[66] Unpublished letter (personal archives).
[67] Unpublished cable (personal archives).

Arrangement set of four premature print Hausa Chinyanza also cable amount required.

Deepest appreciation, Shoghi.

I was obliged to cable again on 23 March: [68]

Difficulties typesetting slightly increased cost Swahili pamphlet but confident can produce 2,000 each all three pamphlets total £120. NSA already authorised £70. Will not need balance until after Plan overwhelming amount work closing weeks prevents pushing next two.

Deepest love, Philip.

His subsequent letter of 28 March 1950 also served to indicate the terrible strain under which he was working and the suffering at the hands of the enemies of the Faith:[69]

Dear Bahá'í Brother,

Your letters, dated October 16 and December 7 and 12, 1949, and March 12 1950, have been received, as well as St Barbe Baker's letter to you.

The beloved Guardian, having been in touch with you by cable, and being more over-worked this year than ever, delayed answering. You know, from what you saw here, how inefficient – to understate the matter – his servants are. The work at the shrines has vastly increased and of necessity, for as the first part of the building will soon be finished, the grounds around it have been entirely remodelled to fit it better and show it off. All this he has been forced to superintend and plan personally. The attacks and status of the enemies you know about. So that in all he is very tired.

He was, however, cheered and pleased to hear about the new African language pamphlets. This is really a most valuable service you have rendered. As he cabled you, he does not feel an English pamphlet is essential now, and only adds to expenses. He thinks you should consult the NSA (after Plan's end!) about points 1, 2, 3, regarding the type and printing extra material. Generally speaking, he feels some cards with the basic principles would be an advantage. He leaves all details about the appearance of these pamphlets to your judgement and any advice the NSA gives.

He was very happy to see St Barbe Baker and Mrs Preston had co-operated with you, and he would like you to particularly thank Mr

[68] Ibid.

[69] Unpublished letter (personal archives).

Backwell Senior for his contribution in making the Hausa translation.

Although these three translations may *not* be perfect, they are an important beginning and give us a lever in hand, so to speak.

He admires your mother very much, and is delighted her operation was a success, and that she is back at your side. Regarding her home: he does not see why see feels compelled to part with it at this stage. Can she not derive an income from renting it temporarily until you both see clearly what your future plans are? Your loyalty and devotion are deeply appreciated, you may be sure.

With Bahá'í love, R. Rabbání.

In the Guardian's handwriting:

May the Almighty bless, sustain, and guide you in your constant, and deeply appreciated labours, remove every obstacle in your path, and enable you to win still greater victories for His Faith and its nascent institutions.

Your true and grateful brother, Shoghi

THE AMAZING FINAL DAYS OF THE PLAN 1950

The National Teaching Committee was meeting at least weekly and was almost frantically following up every offer of pioneering or teaching. The Teaching Conference was immensely inspired by the visit of Milly Collins and by the Guardian's cable, which was telephoned from London in the middle of the Conference and galvanised everyone present. It contained such phrases as: 'feel moved address this eleventh hour my last fervent appeal ... seize opportunity arouse entire body followers Faith Bahá'u'lláh British Isles save fortunes plan now hanging balance … one last supreme sacrificial sustained effort designed ensure total victory now within reach.'

The Báb's farewell address was recited, as well as the Tablet of Visitation, but what really moved everyone present to new heights of dedication was the recitation of the Tablet of Ahmad by the distinguished guest, Mrs Amelia Collins. Before the conference finally closed the National Teaching Committee was already implementing decisions of the conference and consulting on pioneering offers.

The conference cabled the secretaries of all Assemblies and Groups: 'profoundly shaken and inspired by Guardian's cable just received. Urges you call every believer to a special meeting immediately.'[70]

With a copy of the cable, the National Teaching Committee enclosed a letter addressed to every believer which was posted that same evening. At the conference, I had to present graphically the needs of the Plan using a six-foot map, first showing the growth of the Faith throughout Britain. In the first 40 years of the Faith there had been only three local Spiritual Assemblies formed, then Bradford and Torquay in 1939 and then, in 1944, a total of 130 believers accepted the Plan of 19 new Assemblies. At the time of that conference, with only 15 and a half weeks before the end of the Plan, 47 new believers or pioneers were needed in 18 goal towns or weak Assemblies. Of the 98 people attending that crucial conference, 40 had become Bahá'ís during the Plan and 34 had pioneered. Many offers of pioneering and teaching even came from those who were already in pioneer posts – including one from my mother who offered to go with Connie Langdon-Davies to Belfast!

In April 1949,[71] the Guardian had given permission to form Assemblies as they reached their number during the last year of the Plan, which was why Oxford could form its local Spiritual Assembly in November. By February 1950, Newcastle and Stockport had also formed.

The National Teaching Committee, centred in Oxford, was meeting frequently. As the Plan drew to a close, the meetings became almost daily. Every believer was known to them and all were called upon to teach as never before, to travel teach or to pioneer. Heroic steps were taken, some pioneers moving to new goals once their own area would allow; one old lady in her mid-70s settled in no fewer than seven goal towns.

As if drawn by a magnet, believers from other countries came to settle from Canada, Australia, Holland, Denmark and youth from Írán particularly helped to fan the flame.

The teaching conference, 1949 – 50, representative of the whole community, was overwhelmed with the news from the National Teaching Committee that with only 15 weeks of the Plan still to run, 32 believers were needed in the eight Goal Towns plus 15 believers in 10 of those already won. While it was almost too much to expect that these would be gained by confirmations of new believers, the National Teaching Committee was planning to fill gaps by pioneers.

[70] Unpublished cable (personal archives).

[71] Effendi, S. (1981). The Unfolding Destiny of the British Bahá'í Community: The Messages from the Guardian of the Bahá'í Faith to the Bahá'ís of the British Isles. London, Bahá'í Publishing Trust., p. 228.

Shortly before this time, we had heard that the chairman of the Canadian National Spiritual Assembly, John Robarts, had been visiting relatives in Bristol and the National Teaching Committee had been very impressed with his teaching methods. We decided to seek approval of the Guardian to ask the Canadian National Assembly to release him for a couple of weeks to help us win the goals of our teaching plan. The Guardian, the Canadian National Assembly and John all agreed and I had to fix up a detailed schedule for him to visit the places where we felt he could best serve the teaching work.

In his brief visit, he did tremendous work: he would ring me up in the early hours of the morning whenever he received declarations which helped to achieve goals; all this added to the excitement of those days.

On 28 March, the National Spiritual Assembly cabled the Guardian:[72]

> John Robarts here for fortnight's tour sent by Canadian NSA help complete our Plan. Three declarations Glasgow one Brighton … 26 gaps remain.…

He responded immediately, writing on 30 March:[73]

> Deeply appreciate participation John Robarts appeal further sacrifice, greater heroism, firmer resolve, nobler consecration ensure total success plan now hanging balance....

And then came his most astonishing offer:[74]

> For my part utmost can do is stretch period plan to July ninth date commemoration martyrdom last remaining chance offered hardly pressed yet gloriously striving community should be instantly seized ere it is irretrievably lost.

This so shook the National Teaching Committee that they would have none of it. 'We will get the plan by the due date of 20 April', they told the National Spiritual Assembly, and they began to put into operation all their contingency plans.

The 72nd pioneer of the Plan, Sam Scott, who when he read the message was in his 84th year in a nursing home in North Yorkshire, moved to live with a Bahá'í in Norwich saying, 'Victory will assuredly attend our efforts if we are faithful'.

On 31 March, the National Spiritual Assembly was able to cable:[75]

[72] Unpublished cable (personal archives).
[73] Effendi, S. (1981). The Unfolding Destiny of the British Bahá'í Community: The Messages from the Guardian of the Bahá'í Faith to the Bahá'ís of the British Isles. London, Bahá'í Publishing Trust., p. 240.
[74] Ibid.
[75] Unpublished cable (personal archives).

> Confirmations, pioneers reduced gaps to 14 straining utmost complete Plan by Ridván.

On 10 April, they were able to send another cable:[76]

> Joyfully transmit Teaching Committee report arrangements made complete Plan by Ridván earnestly entreat prayers Bahá'u'lláh seal victory.

The Guardian replied on 12 April:[77]

> Rejoice evidences approaching victory praying with increasing fervour.

The National Spiritual Assembly met on 15 – 16 April and afterwards cabled:[78]

> Total victory assured loving gratitude bounties beloved Guardian assistance whole Bahá'í world,

And, on 19 April:[79]

> Joyous Ridván greetings from National Assembly and 24 local assemblies British Isles.

On 21 April, he replied:[80]

> Share joy reciprocate noble sentiments. Heartily congratulate national elected representatives triumphant community, indefatigable national teaching committee, all subsidiary agencies particularly self-sacrificing pioneers who so outstandingly contributed signal victory reverberating Bahá'í world.

Our greatest reward was, however, his cable to the Convention when with a voice filled with emotion, the National Spiritual Assembly chairman Ḥasan Balyúzí read to the rejoicing friends:[81]

> Heart flooded joy striking evidence bountiful grace Bahá'u'lláh enabling valorous dearly loved Bahá'í Community British Isles triumphantly conclude first historic Plan half century British Bahá'í history.
>
> Herald, Author Faith, Centre Covenant, Concourse on High acclaim superb collective achievement immortalising opening decade

[76] Effendi, S. (1981). The Unfolding Destiny of the British Bahá'í Community: The Messages from the Guardian of the Bahá'í Faith to the Bahá'ís of the British Isles. London, Bahá'í Publishing Trust., 240.
[77] Ibid.
[78] Ibid.
[79] Ibid.
[80] Effendi, S. (1981). The Unfolding Destiny of the British Bahá'í Community: The Messages from the Guardian of the Bahá'í Faith to the Bahá'ís of the British Isles. London, Bahá'í Publishing Trust., p. 241.
[81] Ibid., p. 245.

> second Bahá'í century unprecedented history Faith British Isles, unrivalled annals any Bahá'í community European continent.
>
> Unparalleled percentage members community responding pioneer call throughout Bahá'í world since termination apostolic age Bahá'í Dispensation.
>
> Historic pledge British Bahá'í Community nobly redeemed. Tribute memory Martyr Prophet Faith worthily paid.
>
> Spiritual potentialities prosecute subsequent stage unfolding mission fully acquired.
>
> Triumphant community now standing threshold catching first glimpse still dimly outlined future enterprises overseas....

Messages flowed in from many parts of the world and I was particularly happy to receive several personal letters. The following are excerpts from three of these of particular interest.

From Milly Collins, Wilmette, Illinois, United States, 3 May:[82]

> *Dear Philip and all the loved ones!*
>
> Was I thrilled, was I grateful to Bahá'u'lláh, and to our beloved Guardian when I was met with *the* news on my return from Haiti – where the one and only Assembly was lapsing into group status, the only Assembly in Haiti (it was saved).
>
> First I thought I'd call you by phone – but it cost too much! and so I wired – I sent it c/o NSA as I thought you would all be gathered at your Convention, but a line from Ferraby indicates it will be turned over to NSA when re-elected. I did so want all those blessed ones to get my greeting.
>
> Our dear brother, Bernard Leach was in Wilmette only one day – I sent him all the reports I had from you as he was not up to date, but of course that was some time ago before the 'miracle' news came. Perhaps John Robarts told you when their NSA was in session he called me up asking what I would suggest about one of them going to assist – my reply was 'call up or cable them at once.' Dear John certainly rendered you all a sacred service.
>
> How constantly my prayers and thoughts have followed you all – now I am relaxed on this matter!
>
> To you all my abiding deepest love, and am I proud of you
>
> *Affectionately,*
>
> *Milly.*

[82] Unpublished letter (personal archives).

From Honor Kempton, Bahá'í European Teaching Committee, Geneva, Switzerland, 8 May:[83]

> *Dear Philip,*
>
> Well done! My most sincere congratulations for such a glorious victory. I cannot tell you how moved I was to read your report and the cablegram of our beloved Guardian. I do not think I have ever read such a beautiful message from the Guardian. To me the sweetest passage is 'Tribute memory Martyr Prophet Faith worthily paid'. That is so beautiful that I felt I must tell it to the whole Bahá'í World.
>
> You have the 'spiritual potentialities to prosecute subsequent stage unfolding mission' that also is a great tribute from the Guardian to the Bahá'ís of Great Britain. With that tribute goes a great responsibility but I know that it is one that you will take and you will emerge triumphant in the year 1953 with all your tasks achieved.
>
> Your year of respite will be one of the busiest you have ever experienced – consolidating the victories already won and planning for still greater victories. How wise our Guardian is – how much wiser it is to have this new plan to keep you going and to not allow a 'slump' which so often happens after a great all-out effort. So, in April – or rather at the first Centennial of the year Nine marking the mystic birth of Bahá'u'lláh's prophetic mission in the Síyáh-Chál at Tehran – you will finish your plan and we in America will finish our second seven year plan and there will be a tremendous celebration. I hope it can be altogether. How thrilling it will be....
> Your report was a splendid piece of work.

From John Robarts, Toronto, Canada, 15 May:[84]

> *Dear Philip,*
>
> You have been very kind and extremely generous in your praise of my efforts on behalf of your Six Year Plan. I appreciate them all perhaps more than I should, but most of all appreciate the friendship and the love which you, and others, have showered upon me.
>
> It was a most priceless privilege to have been permitted by Bahá'u'lláh to take that tour. I shall hope to be worthy and to never cease to thank Him for it.
>
> That wonderful British spirit did something for me, and for Canada, and for the whole Bahá'í world. Bahá'u'lláh must have planned it

[83] Ibid.
[84] Unpublished letter (personal archives).

> that way, that so many of us would be brought to your shores to witness such an amazing spectacle. You British Bahá'ís were magnificent in your pioneer service, in your dedication, in your courage and faith in the face of such odds. I admired that spirit so much when I first recognised it last August, and I am so grateful now that I was prompted to do a little something about it.
>
> On the personal level, Philip, you did a tremendous piece of work. Everywhere I found a deep sense of devotion to and gratitude for you and your efficiency. One great satisfaction to me is the sure knowledge that through all eternity I am going to have a close and intimate pal by the name of Philip Hainsworth....

The British National Spiritual Assembly took the unprecedented step of printing in the *Bahá'í Journal* an open letter of appreciation and gratitude to the National Teaching Committee.

That tremendous cable to the Convention gave us the details of our Two-Year Plan: 'After one year respite' which was to consolidate the 19 Assemblies 'painstakingly established', form 'nuclei three dependencies British crown ... translation, publication, dissemination Bahá'í literature ... three African languages, addition to three already undertaken course first plan.' Thirty-four resolutions were made at the Convention and no. 20 read:[85]

> A vote of thanks was passed to Philip Hainsworth who through his initiative has achieved the first publication of a Bahá'í pamphlet in three African languages, thus bringing distinction to the British Bahá'í Community and paving the way for our greater responsibilities regarding African literature.

A letter from the Guardian to the National Teaching Committee dated 28 March was received at the time I was engaged in drawing up the final report of the National Teaching Committee to the National Spiritual Assembly. This report ran to almost 10,000 words and was my longest piece of writing to that date. It was bound together with the annual reports of the National Assembly, the Publishing Trust and the National Child Education, National Youth, Overseas (University) Students, Assembly Development and Summer School Committees. This was the first time that the delegates had a set of annual reports for their study prior to Convention. The main purpose of the report was to combine the presentation of statistics with the spirit of excitement that flowed in from all quarters with the winning of our first Teaching Plan. Of these statistics, along with the names of all believers involved, the following are worthy of note.

[85] Unpublished (personal archives).

In that one year:[86]

- 46 pioneers carried out 49 projects.
- 40 adults and 3 youth accepted the Faith.
- A teachers' conference in Liverpool set the pattern for similar conferences in Belfast, Newcastle, Glasgow, Blackpool, Brighton, Cardiff and Manchester.
- A six-week course was developed, with the title 'The Changeless Faith of God'.
- A mail-out of postcards displaying Bahá'í principles and inviting investigation was used with good effect in the cities of Sheffield, Cardiff, Blackpool, Blackburn, Edinburgh, Liverpool and Belfast.
- There had been 16 full-weekend meetings of the National Teaching Committee (with over 350 hours of consultation) and, for the last few months of the Plan, the Committee was meeting every second night. Sixty-one consultations with local Spiritual Assemblies, Groups and individuals (some 33 held outside Oxford) had taken place; 36,000 words of reports to the National Spiritual Assembly and more than 40,000 words of minutes had been typed.
- In his 12-day visit, John Robarts 'witnessed' 18 declarations.
- During the whole of the Plan, 85 pioneers carried out 126 projects.
- Of those 85, 55 were native-born and 13 came from overseas specially to help win the Plan.

THE AFRICA PLAN

After Convention 1950, the National Spiritual Assembly changed the committee structure and formed two major national committees – 'Consolidation' and 'Africa' – appointing me secretary of the former and a member of the latter.

The Africa Committee began work on the Two-Year Plan. The Consolidation Committee took over the rôle of the National Teaching Committee as well as that of the Assembly Development Committee and appointed six Regional Committees, so I continued to have a heavy Bahá'í workload. It became necessary, however, for mother to move back to Bradford, where my brother Jack had managed to find a little flat for her not far from where he lived. I continued to live in Oxford.

On 19 July, I wrote to Marguerite Preston in Kenya, sympathising with her at the shock she must have felt when it became clear that the three

[86] Unpublished notes (personal archives).

territories to receive the attention of the British Two-Year Plan did not include Kenya. This was because Kenya had already been 'opened' by her, but she was assured that wherever pioneers settled, they would be in the nearby territories of Uganda and Tanganyika and would be able to assist her in her work. I quoted to her from a postscript to a letter from the Guardian which had been published in the *Bahá'í Journal*, explaining why Kenya was not a goal of the Two Year Plan.

The Guardian had written a long letter to the National Spiritual Assembly on 15 June[87] and a postscript on 28 June,[88] explaining the goals of the Africa campaign. News from the Holy Land also indicated the suffering he was experiencing at the hands of his own family and the Covenant-breakers. These were all discussed at the Summer School held in Cottingham, near Hull, Yorkshire, which was attended by 170 people representing 11 nationalities, and the participants agreed to send a cable to the Guardian pledging loyalty and assuring him of fervent prayers for protection. I felt personally moved to send him a cable:[89]

> Waves love from this school surely helping during present difficulties sufferings dearly loved Guardian. Desire humbly re-affirm personal devotion loyalty eagerness serve any part world. Chinyanza pamphlet almost ready. Longing hear news triumph Covenant.
>
> *Deep love, Philip*

To which he responded on 21 August 1950: [90]

> Deeply appreciate sentiments. Exert utmost effort assist highly meritorious African project.
>
> *Loving fervent prayers, Shoghi*

One highlight of this school for me was that I decided to run a midnight 'fireside' for young people. At 31 I was still considered a youth! A young nurse from London had just become a Bahá'í and she brought a friend to the school who knew very little about the Faith. The nurse was Ira Snace (I think she was Latvian) and her friend was Brigitte Hasselblatt from Estonia. Brigitte accepted the Faith at my first fireside. She was a radiant Bahá'í and pioneered to Bournemouth; later she became the Knight of Bahá'u'lláh for Shetland, went to America, settled in Finland and finally pioneered to Estonia in 1990. The next time I met her after that Summer

[87] Effendi, S. (1981). The Unfolding Destiny of the British Bahá'í Community: The Messages from the Guardian of the Bahá'í Faith to the Bahá'ís of the British Isles. London, Bahá'í Publishing Trust., pp. 247ff.
[88] Ibid., p. 252
[89] Unpublished cable (personal archives).
[90] Ibid.

School in 1950 was in December 1990, at the first conference of the Bahá'ís of the Soviet Union held in Moscow! Later, in 1996, Lois and I stayed in her flat in Tallinn, Estonia.

On 22 August I wrote to the Secretary of the National Spiritual Assembly asking him to put on the Agenda some thoughts I had about doing more for Africa during the 'year of respite' to strengthen the African Committee and to appoint someone to the Consolidation Committee who would be 'in training' to take over from me in a few months' time. I opened the letter:[91]

> A further study of the Guardian's messages sent since Convention has strengthened a feeling that whilst the Guardian may not *ask* us to do more than we are doing before the Two Year Plan starts, he may very well warmly welcome any offer we may make to commence operations in Africa in the very near future.... The present world situation, with its possible effects on trade and transport; the joy which the Guardian feels when some progressive step is made, and the indications which I gather from his letter of the 15th June that the launching of the Africa campaign will bring about that extra potency which is required to meet the needs at home, prompt me to ask the NSA to give very serious thought to the whole African project early in the meeting. We should certainly try to understand the implications of the messages sent to the Persians and to Hassan Sabrí, and work out some policy before consulting with Hassan, and I would also appreciate some personal advice on how I might implement a cable I have received from the Guardian....

I then listed three ways in which I was trying to serve the Plan and asked, 'If the NSA would consider this is "exerting utmost effort assist highly meritorious Africa project?" If not, what more can I do?'

On the day following I received another cable dated 22 August 1950:[92]

> Assure you fervent prayers mother. Abiding appreciation exemplary services. *Shoghi.*

I wrote a letter of about 1,400 words to the Guardian in September, that dealt with the following:[93]

- Re-affirming the contents of my cable.
- My consultation with the National Spiritual Assembly on his last cable.
- That I was working hard to wipe out my debts and straighten out my

[91] Unpublished letter (personal archives).
[92] Unpublished cable (personal archives).
[93] Unpublished letter (personal archives).

financial affairs to enable me to get to Africa as soon as possible. I realised the challenge of the work in Africa and begged his prayers that I become worthy to pioneer there, as I had had the feeling ever since my army service in Africa that I should return.

- I expressed my yearning to visit Haifa again, even for a few days on my way to Africa, then visit the friends in Egypt and Mrs Preston in Nairobi.
- I spoke about my mother, who was living in Bradford and miserable at being out of the mainstream of activity and of her longing to serve the Cause more. She wanted to go with me to Africa and hoped to end her days there. (I did not mention that at the Convention she had, unknown to me, been the first one to respond to his cable and offer to pioneer to Africa. The committee had consulted at its first meeting on her offer and decided to tell her that it would be best for me to go there first and as soon as I had settled, to send for her to join me).
- I raised the question of the conduct of a pioneer to Africa. Should a pioneer let it be known at once that he is a Bahá'í or should he first seek to establish himself in the eyes of the community in general? Pioneers to Africa will need to have work before they go as it will not be possible to go as a visitor and then seek employment.
- I asked whether, once a pioneer gets to his goal country, he should seek immediately to go to the tribal native or quietly follow up whichever avenue opens up.
- I was happy to enclose the printed Chinyanza pamphlet and tell him that the Hausa mss. had gone to the printers.

His letter of 20 October 1950 answered all my points:[94]

> *Dear Bahá'í Brother,*
>
> Your two letters, one undated, and one dated April 19, have been received by our beloved Guardian, as well as the pamphlet – which he was delighted to see.
>
> He would be delighted to see you go as a pioneer to Africa and to later have your mother join you. She seems the true heroic pattern!
>
> He feels that in as far as possible the African pioneers should seek to get a job which will take them to one of the countries chosen and ensure employment for them there. It does not seem wise or necessary for a Bahá'í to stress the fact he or she is going there to teach. A people's religion is their own business, and they can talk about it privately as much as they like without neglecting their employer's work.
>
> Also, he feels no rules can be laid down about how to teach.

[94] Unpublished letter (personal archives).

Usually one teaches those receptive souls one finds. The same should apply to the beginning of the work in Africa. Any direct teaching work with the more primitive tribes would have to be done after finding out the best and most tactful way of doing it. The first step is to get to Africa, and, in view of the cost involved, and the state of the Fund, the pioneers should make every effort to get sent out there or at least get employment after arriving, thus relieving the Bahá'í Fund as much as possible. If this fails, then of course all the expense will have to be paid by the Fund.

The Guardian is very pleased over the publications in African languages, and greatly appreciates what you have accomplished in this field, as well as your many other services.

He will certainly pray you may settle your affairs satisfactorily at home, and then find a way to go to Africa.

At present no pilgrims are permitted, as you know, but he feels sure some day you will again be a welcome guest in Haifa.

With Bahá'í love, R. Rabbání.'

In the Guardian's handwriting:

May the Almighty bless your strenuous, constant and high endeavours, and enable you to enrich continually the splendid record of your valuable services to His Faith and its nascent institutions.

Your true and grateful brother, Shoghi.

As mentioned earlier, I had been instrumental in helping in the settlement of Lotfu'lláh Hakím when he first came to England at the request of Shoghi Effendi. On 14 November the Guardian cabled to the National Spiritual Assembly:[95]

Kindly arrange departure Lotfullah Hakim, Haifa, for necessary service.

I wrote to Lotfu'lláh and he replied on 30 November, from which letter the following excerpts are taken:[96]

My very dear Bahá'í Brother,

Your very sweet and valued letter of 26 November is at hand for which I thank you very deeply. I cannot find any word to express my heartfelt thanks to all the friends here in British Isles. They all without any exception have showered me with their love all the

[95] Effendi, S. (1981). The Unfolding Destiny of the British Bahá'í Community: The Messages from the Guardian of the Bahá'í Faith to the Bahá'ís of the British Isles. London, Bahá'í Publishing Trust., p. 255.
[96] Unpublished letter (personal archives).

time that I have been here. They (you and NSA specially) all have been so good and so kind and so loving. How can I forget them. It is impossible. You be sure that I will always remember them whenever I visit the Holy Shrines. Please pray that I may become worthy to do His wish. I do not know what the 'necessary services' are. I will certainly keep in touch with the friends in British Isles and I long from the bottom of my heart to hear and if possible to see the progress of the Cause of God here.

I will certainly let NSA know of the health of the beloved Guardian, Rúḥíyyih Khánum and etc. And any news of interest I may have whether photos or etc. And if I can be of any service to you, dear one or any of the friends at any time while I am there please do not hesitate to let me know. I will do my best very happily. I always look forward to hear good news of you and the friends and of the progress of the Cause here....

How I wish I could see you before leaving England. At any rate you have my best wishes for your work in Africa. You be sure that Bahá'u'lláh, the Master and the Guardian will always be with you and will guide you to do His will....

I hope your mother is keeping well. My warmest Bahá'í love to her, please....And with warmest Bahá'í love to all the friends there and of course not forgetting your own dear self.

Yours in His Service, Lotfullah.

Soon after his arrival in Haifa, he wrote on 30 December:[97]

Alláh'u'Abhá, My very dear Bahá'í Brother Philip,

I have not forgotten and shall never forget your affection and brotherly love especially of that evening ... that you took the trouble to come up to London to say goodbye to me. I was very much affected by it. I know you represented the NSA and the love of all our friends in British Isles. How can I ever forget this wonderful love. I am grateful to Bahá'u'lláh, the Master and our beloved Guardian otherwise who am I unworthy person with so much love having poured upon me. You be sure that you all will always be remembered at the Holy Shrines whenever I visit and will pray for you all.

The beloved Guardian, I am glad to say is very hopeful of the Africa project. And he has great confidence with British Bahá'ís. He read parts of the Africa Committee report to us at table the other day and spoke so highly of you all. I hope to write about this and

[97] Unpublished cable (personal archives).

other news later on to John so that he may share them with the friends. I have promised to write him from time to time news of here for the friends there.

However please excuse this short note I am looking forward to hearing the report or news of the Manchester Teaching Conference.

I expect you will have heard that our dear friends Mrs Collins and Mr Remey are here as well. They arrived two days before me. They both send their love to you and all the dear friends in British Isles.

With warmest Bahá'í love to you and all the dear friends.

Yours in His Service, Lotfullah.

My letter to the National Spiritual Assembly of 22 August had been taken seriously and several actions were taken. Hugh McKinley was moved from the National Youth Committee and appointed secretary to the National Teaching Committee from November, and I was actively consulting with the Africa Committee (of which I was a member) to see how I could quickly get to a pioneer post in one of the three selected territories (Uganda, Tanganyika and the Gold Coast). Hugh had been somewhat overwhelmed with his new rôle and had written to the Guardian asking for his prayers. In his reply of 30 November, the Guardian wrote:[98]

Philip Hainsworth will be missed very much, but his services in Africa will redound to the glory of the British Community.

Nigeria was not one of the selected territories, as Bahá'ís were reported to be there, neither was Kenya due to the presence of Marguerite Preston (Welby). It was agreed that I must find employment, but due to my lack of academic qualifications, I could not apply successfully for any advertised post. The only possibility was for post as a Scout Commissioner for Uganda. While I had had a great deal of experience as a Scout, I had neither experience nor training as a Scout Officer. I applied but did not even receive an acknowledgement.

Meanwhile I was still secretary of the local Spiritual Assembly of Oxford, actively travel teaching and helping with the preparations for the new Africa pamphlet translations. It is of interest to note that in his letter of 28 June 1950 to the National Spiritual Assembly, the Guardian had enlarged upon the value of literature in new languages:[99]

Entirely aside from any additional literature it might be possible to get out in Hausa and Swahili he feels your objective must be to print

[98] Unpublished cable (personal archives).

[99] Effendi, S. (1981). The Unfolding Destiny of the British Bahá'í Community: The Messages from the Guardian of the Bahá'í Faith to the Bahá'ís of the British Isles. London, Bahá'í Publishing Trust., p. 253.

> at least a pamphlet in three languages other than those Philip Hainsworth has tackled. It must be borne in mind that printing in new languages kills two birds with one stone – not only does it enable the Faith to reach new elements, but it also enriches our literature and is excellent as a means of calling the attention of the public to the universality of our Cause and the extent of our world-wide activities!

As noted earlier, my mother had returned to Bradford to live in a small old-peoples' flat near my brother, Jack. She was reasonably happy to be near Jack and her four grandchildren, but I did not realise until after she died how much she missed her life at the centre of Bahá'í activities. Each time I visited her, we talked about the possibilities of our going to Africa, but my brother, not sympathetic in any way at all to our way of life, could only criticise me for wanting to take mother away.

Eventually I was able to hand over the files of the National Teaching Committee and the secretarial duties for the Consolidation Committee to Hugh McKinley and pioneered with Bob Cheek to Blackburn. A new Bahá'í became secretary of the local Spiritual Assembly of Oxford with quite a prestigious address – Ian Semple, Pembroke College, Oxford!

A MOST EVENTFUL YEAR 1951

The new calendar year began with a flourish. On 29 December 1950 I took mother to the first Africa Committee Conference, held as the first such gathering in the new London Bahá'í Centre at 103 Earls Court Road, London W.8. (having moved there from 158a Old Brompton Road, London SW5). At this conference we met Mr Músá and Mrs Samiyyih Banání and their daughter Violette Nakhjavání who were in England preparing to pioneer. Violette's husband, Mr 'Alí Nakhjavání, then the youngest member of the Persian National Spiritual Assembly, was still in Írán finalising his and Mr Banání's business affairs.

We received the news that our first pioneer in the Africa Campaign, Miss Claire Gung, would be sailing on the 'Warwick Castle' on 4 January to Tanga (Tanganyika) and plans were made for a party to see her off at Liverpool Street Station. We also learned that Ali's brother, Jalál Nakhjavání, had passed through Kampala, Uganda, on his way to pioneer in Dar-es-Salaam. He had arrived in East Africa from Írán on the 18th of December.

On the way home from London to Bradford, we spent a relaxed day at the Cardell farm with Ted and his father and mother and then, on the following weekend, 6 – 7 January, I chaired the annual teaching conference in Manchester, which had been given the theme 'This Propitious Hour'. Reportedly, the highlight of this important conference was the Sunday afternoon session entitled 'The Sacredness of its Mission', with speakers Professor Zeine Nuradin Zeine ('The Bahá'í Way of Life'), David Hofman ('Faith in Action') and Ḥasan Balyúzí ('Infant Institutions'). A record number – over 75 participants of 11 nationalities, representing 20 out of our 24 local communities, helped to make it a most memorable conference.

On 17 January the National Spiritual Assembly received a cable from the beloved Guardian advising that he 'highly approved pioneering Africa' of Músá Banání with the Nakhjavánís; the telegram went on to say that he was 'praying for his success and entire family'.[100]

BRITISH BAHÁ'Í COMMUNITY THE 'CHIEF AGENCY'

On 25 February, the Guardian wrote a long letter to the National Spiritual Assembly which, in its opening sentence, indicated the pressure under which he was then working, as it acknowledged no fewer than 29 letters from the National Assembly covering the period 19 June 1950 to 20 February 1951. He noted, through his secretary, that:[101]

> …cable communications between himself and your Assembly attend to the essential work in between letters'. He appreciated the Chinyanza pamphlets we had sent and then outlined a principle which was later to affect my service in Africa:
>
>> He feels that, although it is preferable that the three pioneers to each virgin country should be in one town or at least as near to each other as possible, it should not be considered the essential point at this juncture. The most important thing of all is to get the pioneers out there and established if possible in some self-supporting work. Once this has been done, the work within the country itself can be gradually organised and plans made to consolidate it in a more practical manner.

In his own handwriting however, he made the most staggering statements, the significance of which did not become apparent until many years later. These should be studied from pages 260 – 3, *Unfolding Destiny*. I quote a few:

> The magnificent spirit of devotion and the initiative and resourcefulness demonstrated in recent months by a triumphant

[100] Ibid., p. 257.
[101] Ibid, p. 258.

> community…merit the highest praise. By their organising ability,... by the tenacity, sagacity and fidelity which they have displayed in the course of its opening phase; by their utter consecration…they have set an example worthy of emulation by the members of Bahá'í communities in both the East and the West.... On it, … will devolve the chief responsibility of guiding the destinies, of supplying the motive power, and of contributing to the resources of a crusade which, for the first time in Bahá'í history, involves the collaboration, and affects the fortunes, of no less than four National Assemblies, in both Hemispheres and within four continents of the globe….To be singled out as the chief agency in the prosecution of a task of such dimensions, such significance, and the harbinger of events so glorious, is indeed at once an inestimable blessing and a staggering responsibility with which the British Bahá'í community…has been honoured at so critical and challenging an hour in the fortunes of mankind....

How could anyone then be content to remain at home?

It is interesting to note that in the National Spiritual Assembly's Supplementary Report to Convention 1951 it was stated that on the 'First Day of Ridván there were 274 voting believers, of which 55 were of Persian origin'.[102] This meant that the community had increased its numbers threefold in one decade, the Persian element being 20 per cent.

PREPARING FOR AFRICA

By this time, it was increasingly obvious that I was not going to find employment in either Uganda or Tanganyika and it was to these two territories that I felt particularly drawn, due to my wartime experience and the smattering of Swahili I had learned. We also learned that Jalál Nakhjavání had set up in business in Dar-es-Salaam as a ship's chandler and was well on the way to getting a permit to remain in Tanganyika. An interesting piece of historical information had come to light. His father had visited Britain in 1915 on the instructions of 'Abdu'l-Bahá. He had also been very involved in the construction of the Bahá'í House of Worship in Ashkhabad and had passed away in Baku shortly before Jalál's brother 'Alí was born. Jalál had offered to do what he could to help in the settlement of any pioneer. The following plan was therefore evolved: Jalál would offer me employment as a salesman/manager; the salary would be paid but given

[102] Unpublished (personal archives).

to me in advance in England as a pioneer budget and I would seek to represent some UK companies in East Africa.

With the desire to help in my pioneer move, Mrs Marian Norton offered to deputise me for three months. Her husband Arthur would provide me with samples and details of the cloths he manufactured so that I would be his official sales representative in East Africa. Without Marian's very generous offer it is doubtful whether I would have got to Africa and the whole pattern of my life would have been different.

By this time consultations had been taking place with Mr Banání and his family and it was felt by the Africa Committee that they would encounter some difficulties in travelling in East Africa due to their Persian passports. These, for the ladies, had to be issued in their maiden names as the Persian authorities did not recognise Bahá'í marriage, so in the eyes of the passport authorities in Persia, they were not married. This meant that in any hotel in East Africa Mr Banání would be sharing a room with a lady who did not have 'Banání' in her passport and Miss Banání and her small daughter would be in a room with a 'Mr Nakhjavání'. It was therefore decided that instead of going by ship to Dar-es-Salaam as planned, I would travel with the Banání party by air, and would use my 'captain's title' to make the hotel bookings in whichever part of East Africa we were to visit. As Mr Banání and Mr Nakhjavání had been asked to visit some of the Persian friends in Geneva, en route, the airfare London/ Geneva/ Rome/ Cairo/ Dar-es-Salaam would be more expensive than the boat fare, so Mr Banání would meet the difference in cost.

At the same time a few other Bahá'ís, Mr and Mrs Muḥammad Rúḥu'lláh Yazdaní and the two Farhoumand brothers (both doctors) and their families were ready to go to Kampala, Uganda. Eventually, though, these friends went to Dar-es-Salaam.

In the meantime, mother was very supportive, but a little unhappy that she could not come with me, although she realised the wisdom of my finding a place to settle and then coming to join me.

From his new position as secretary of the Consolidation Committee, Hugh McKinley wrote on 12 June:[103]

> *Dear Philip,*
>
> We have learned that you have now obtained your visa and permit for Africa, and that you will leave by air on 18 June. Warmest congratulations!
>
> The committee – and its secretary – feels rather at a loss for words in saying farewell to you: we know very well what a tremendous

[103] Unpublished letter (personal archives).

> debt the whole British community owes to your ceaseless efforts in every sphere of Bahá'í activities, and hope that you can, in turn, measure by this means, our loving admiration of all that you are and deep appreciation of all that you do.
>
> We shall all sadly miss the heavy clash of ideas, as well as the temporary withdrawal of your strong and individual views from the work here at home; we hope to see these all doubled when you return here, as you will in the course of time, after laying foundations in far more arduous and unfavourable conditions in Africa.
>
> Be sure that our loving thoughts and prayers for your success in His Cause will accompany you wherever you go; please pray for us too – that our 'base' may exceed itself in giving support to your 'front-line'.
>
> *With most loving greetings, In His Fellowship, Hugh.*

Before I flew to Africa, in order to anticipate potential employers' requests, I prepared a résumé and obtained some up-to-date references from Arthur Norton, Lady Hornell, the National Spiritual Assembly and Thomas Hansford. Thomas was soon to take up employment in Dar-es-Salaam and became part of the first Dar-es-Salaam Bahá'í Group.

THE JOURNEY TO AFRICA

I had a quiet, fairly uneventful farewell and, after my last National Spiritual Assembly meeting on 15 – 17 June 1951, joined the Banánís and Nakhjavánís when 'Alí arrived in England. We flew to Geneva on 18 June, just too early to receive the significant cable from the Guardian dated the 22nd of June 1951 that included:[104]

> Brief span two years destined witness first fruits historic continent-wide crusade will ere long terminate. Valorous British Bahá'í Community, central pivot machinery now set in motion, chief agency prosecution mighty divinely propelled enterprise must, aware urgency task, act speedily resolutely despatch without delay volunteers, settle pioneers, disseminate literature, initiate teaching activities, establish fruitful contacts, ensure steady enrolment fresh recruits among tribes races far-flung virgin territories. Transmitting additional contribution one thousand pounds ensure vigorous

[104] Effendi, S. (1981). The Unfolding Destiny of the British Bahá'í Community: The Messages from the Guardian of the Bahá'í Faith to the Bahá'ís of the British Isles. London, Bahá'í Publishing Trust., p. 265.

> prosecution colossal sacred task enabling well-tried followers Faith Bahá'u'lláh British Isles write worthily first page historic memorable undertaking constituting opening phase their glorious spiritual mission overseas.

Little did we realise as we set off on that Monday morning what would happen during the following eventful 10 months, though when that cable caught up with us we were beginning to feel something of the significance now being attached to our journey by the beloved Guardian.

He cabled a second message on that same date: [105]

> Assure departed pioneers fervent loving prayers surrounding them.

Fourteen of the London friends came to the Kensington Air Station to see us on our way and many photographs were taken. We were later to learn that on that very day, Mrs Jalál Nakhjavání and her brother, Farhang Naimi, and the two Nakhjavání children had arrived in Dar-es-Salaam to join Jalál.

In Geneva some of the many Persian youth who had settled in Europe, particularly in Switzerland, freed from the restraints of life in their native country, had been causing problems for the Swiss community and so a meeting was called for the one-night stopover to enable Mr Banání and 'Alí to talk very strongly to them and to stress their Bahá'í responsibilities. A report of our visit was sent to the Guardian and I wrote to him on 28 June – the letter was posted, I think, in Dar-es-Salaam as it was too risky to write to Haifa from Cairo, our next port of call.

After the one-day stopover in Geneva, we flew to Rome for a couple of days where we had some delightful meetings with Ugo and Angelina Giachery – pioneers from America.

MY REPORT TO THE NATIONAL ASSEMBLY

In the very first report I made to the National Spiritual Assembly from the Heliopolis Palace, using BOAC letterhead paper, and dated 26 June 1951, I referred to the 'spiritual humility and generosity of Mr and Mrs Giachery and his enthusiasm for the work he is doing for the Guardian': the purchase, checking and shipping of the stone and marble for the Shrine of the Báb. As I was leaving, Ugo presented me with a small 35mm camera – it was the first camera I had ever possessed.

From Rome, we went to Cairo, where the Egyptian National Spiritual Assembly had been advised of our visit. It had been suggested that we meet

[105] Ibid., p. 266.

with the friends in Egypt and that I should meet with the National Assembly to consult with them on the Africa project. When we left Cairo to go to Dar-es-Salaam via Khartoum, Entebbe and Nairobi, the plane had engine trouble and turned back. Because of the delay, we had four days in all to meet with the friends and have our various consultations.

My letter of 26 June contained information which gives an insight into the situation in Egypt at that time, I shall quote substantial sections from that report:[106]

> Due to engine trouble, we had to return to Cairo for two days, so am taking the opportunity of sending you my first report. As it refers to important matters, will you please have a copy made for all members?
>
> EGYPT

1. Please, in future, do *not* mention – Haifa, Israel, money from Egypt, in letters to Egypt. Instead use indirect references, such as 'world centre', 'our most holy enterprise', etc. Every letter, incoming and outgoing, has to pass the Censor. Great consternation was caused by your letter with regard to the Shrine money from Egypt going through the Bank of England, and by Mason Remey's letter and annual reports of the International Council, which carried the PO Box 155, Haifa, address on the envelope.
2. We are wondering if the non-arrival of letters from you, such as minutes, etc., have been thus delayed, or if you have sent them on to Dar-es-Salaam. We are naturally very eager to receive any new advice from the Guardian.
3. Many attacks on the Faith are now being made in the press here, and the situation is such that the friends dare not write to you to tell you these things. Consequently I am posting this on arrival in Nairobi.
4. Sending money to any country from Egypt is illegal, and even for business special permits are necessary.
5. As the friends cannot send a letter asking you or anyone else, to ask the Guardian if, and how, they should send money to the Shrine Fund, I am writing to him on their behalf, from Dar-es-Salaam. I will ask him to advise me or you as to the best way. If he advises you, will you please use the following 'code':

> 'Our international office advises proceed business we discussed with Arthur Norton Esq.'
>
> or

[106] Unpublished letter (personal archives).

'Suggested business with Beirut warmly approved by our international office, if such is possible'.

or

'Our international office does not advise further business transactions for the present'.

The first one is to be used if the Guardian would like the money to be sent through business channels to our Shrine Fund and passed as part of our contribution through the Bank of England, with Arthur advising the Guardian as to how much came from Egypt, but asking the Guardian to send a receipt to Arthur for the total only. Please write the answer, and not cable.

6. Consultation: We are certain that Bahá'u'lláh guided our steps to Egypt, and He spoke through us. Oh, but it was needed, and we believe miracles have been achieved. Apart from what has been done to further individual, local, national and international consciousness, we, the puny channels, have been confirmed and strengthened. Our schedule has included approximately:

a. NSA: four hours; 19 Day Feast: two hours; NYC: one and a half; Youth meeting: one hour. Individual members of the NSA, LSA and youth, etc.: many hours.

b. With a few exceptions the Africa project was not a real thing to them, either with regard to their own part or to the international aspect. The spirit of pioneering was almost non-existent: the co-operation of National Assemblies just a vague idea which was to be pursued by Britain, and so on.

c. Today, we feel sure, it is different. My own personal impressions are as follows, and I am sending them so that you can compare them with what actually develops later – it will help you to get a closer understanding of the Egyptian NSA.

d. International co-operation is being discussed at national, local and individual levels;

e. Plans for inter-National Assembly work are being made;

f. The steps proposed by Britain for obtaining news, photographs, etc., are fully approved and co-operation is assured;

g. The obligation of the Egyptian NSA to send money to our Africa Fund, and for us to administer it without reservation, fully accepted;

h. Additional help for the Sabrís is forthcoming;

i. The Townshend Fund contributions are to be continued;

j. Eagerness for full co-operation in the Africa Conference was obvious and there is promise of a good Egyptian attendance if the situation permits;

k. The National, as well as the local Cairo Youth Committees, are united in determination to stimulate the pioneer spirit, to give leadership in pioneering, to help in actively supporting the whole Africa project, to arouse nation-wide consciousness of the significance of the project, and to help in vigorously prosecuting the Five Year Plan.

7. As I was writing this the NSA Secretary came to the hotel. He was full of good news and enthusiasm. Apparently after we left, the 19 Day Feast continued and the following results were reported:

l. Five pioneer offers were received;

m. The local youth committee had a special meeting and decided to hold a large youth meeting on the following Friday to stimulate youth activity and pioneering;

n. The National Youth Committee asked the NSA to give them guidance and instruction with regard to pioneering, and offered to spend their summer holidays visiting the various centres in Egypt to arouse the enthusiasm of all the youth.

o. Some of the fathers asked how their sons could best serve the Faith;

p. Youth in government service will try to arrange to transfer to goal towns and even to goal countries.

q. A delegation from the local assembly of Mehalla-Kubra had come to meet the Cairo members of the National Assembly (who form the Executive Committee of the NSA) with the request that their local assembly be disbanded. Apparently this unwise assembly had challenged the Katib-u'l-Jom'eh to come and investigate the Faith. This had angered him and he had called on the populace to arise against the believers. They were now worried and wanted the whole thing to die down. After attending the 19 Day Feast, however, they were filled with new life and spirit, withdrew all requests for disbandment and asked to go back to serve the Cause as never before;

r. At an even later hour, two believers, one the son of the NSA chairman and the other a tutor of Arabic, Mr Azzawi, came to us at the hotel – the former to ask what more he could do to serve the Cause, the latter to discuss aspects of pioneering, both with regard to his own pioneering, possibly in Tripoli, and to discuss pioneer techniques and methods of working out pioneer projects which we had developed during the Six Year Plan; all spoke of the new spirit in the community.

8. A report of our visit is to be sent by the Egyptian NSA to you, possibly to the other co-operating assemblies and to the Guardian.

9. A number of believers in Cairo were keenly interested in East and West Africa – a session of the Feast gave an opportunity for me to be questioned closely on the conditions, languages, religions, possible work for Egyptians, etc.

10. It is only the need for the Executive Committee, which met with us, to present a report to the full NSA meeting in early July, and the receipt of the Guardian's clarification of our respective responsibilities, that restrains a believer from commencing active expression of the thoughts energising any of them, and there is a readiness on the part of the NSA sub-committee (6 members) to go ahead on the basis of their present interpretation. This is, that the new countries given to Persia, Egypt and India merely extend the original project, and that whilst the initiative for pioneering in their respective goal countries rests primarily with the countries concerned, the over-all guidance and initiative rest with Britain.

11. I must at this point report the amazing, thrilling, inspired talks and discussions conducted by 'Alí Nakhjavání. His devotion, vision and eloquence have been largely responsible for what has been done here. A providential visit to the National Archives a few minutes before we joined the Feast resulted in our finding a letter from the Guardian in Arabic to Egypt dated 2 May 1933, in which he spoke of the particular rôle the Youth should play, especially in the pioneering work in other countries in Africa. Permission was given for him to use this in his talk, and he did so with gratifying success. He also pointed out that although very few of the British and American believers, especially the NSA and national committee members, had met the Guardian yet they had accomplished great things. What must not be expected of a community that has such a high proportion of believers who have met him – almost 50 per cent of those present had had the privilege. He also addressed himself to the women, and how the eyes of the Bahá'í World were now on them.

12. Resulting from all these consultations I began to get a picture of the possibilities of our inter-National Assembly co-operation. I would like to summarise this picture, in case you care to use it as a basis for a plan. Much has naturally come from the discussions we had before we left England, but I do not believe it was actually formulated.

INTER-NATIONAL ASSEMBLY AFRICA CAMPAIGN

a. All participating Assemblies will send pioneers to the countries assigned to them, financing them if necessary and, when possible, calling on the Africa Fund when it is not. Openings in goal countries not specifically given to them will not be overlooked;

b. All participating Assemblies should contribute to the Central Africa

Fund, which will be controlled, expended and accounted-for by Britain. Financial assistance by participating countries to their own pioneers going to their designated goal countries might be debited and credited to this Fund without actual transfer of cash. Financial support of their own pioneers, however, will not fully disburse their obligations to the Africa Fund.

c. Britain would:

   i. Co-ordinate pioneer activities, indicating to all participating countries the specific needs as these change from time to time.
   ii. Guide all pioneers and groups in the goal countries.
   iii. Collect, collate, summarise and despatch to all centres the news, etc., from all centres, probably in the expanded 'Africa News'.
   iv. Stimulate, 'fan the zeal' etc., of all centres and assemblies by correspondence, the organisation of personal visits, and the use of travelling teachers from any country.
   v. Joint consultation of some members of all participating assemblies in the not too distant future is essential. (Possibly using Cairo for this).
   vi. Participating assemblies send reports of their activities to Britain, who will collate them and render a quarterly report to each NSA in addition to the 'Africa News', which will be published monthly in Britain.

d. Whilst Britain would continue to produce literature, other assemblies might help – e.g. Egypt has some pamphlets in Arabic, but needs a simple introductory pamphlet for translation into Arabic.

e. (Our new English manuscript might be a basis for such a one, please send one or two copies.)

f. Also, some time ago, the Egyptian NSA asked the Addis Ababa Bahá'ís to produce a pamphlet in Somali: they are now following this up.

g. Again, they believe they can get a good quality pamphlet printed much cheaper than in England, in spite of the difficulties of proof-reading, and they are investigating this.

DAR-ES-SALAAM

We did not stop in Nairobi to meet Marguerite Preston but arrived in Dar-es-Salaam on 28 June, where we contacted Jalál Nakhjavání and were taken to a typical, medium-priced hotel – a cluster of huts round a central main building. There we planned to wait while we checked our immigration/entry permits for several East African countries, awaited mail from London, as well as awaited guidance from the Africa Committee on which country we should try to settle in, with the possibility that the Bananís/Nakhjavánís might go to one country and I to another. The Banání family purchased a car and explored the possibility of business in Dar-es-Salaam.

FIRST AFRICAN BELIEVER TWO YEAR PLAN

On the day after our arrival, an event occurred which later turned out to be very significant. We were taken by Jalál to a solicitor with whom he had become friendly to examine the legal implications of the Persian pioneers and settlement in an East African territory, and from that office we were to go to the Immigration Office. As Jalál had to go elsewhere on business, the solicitor sent his African clerk with us to show us the way to the appropriate government building. After a few minutes' of walking and speaking with the clerk, I suddenly said to him, 'What would you say if I told you that Christ had returned?' He stopped dead and, with a frightening solemnity, said, 'Has he?' I then introduced the Faith to him and we carried on our short journey.

He was Dudley Smith Kutendele from Nyassaland, and he became the first African believer in Tanganyika. He later returned to Zombe, Nyassaland. During the time he was in Zombe a report was received in London that there were some troubles there and that Dudley was in prison. The British National Spiritual Assembly wrote to the government, who replied that they had no record of the imprisonment of Dudley so they wrote a second letter which was copied to the Guardian on 27 January 1954. It was subsequently reported in *Africa News*, Africa Edition N°. 12, that Dudley had settled in Limbe and was in touch with the new pioneer there, Enayat Soheili.

The resident immigration official in Dar-es-Salaam was a Parsee from Bombay and greeted the Persians warmly. He made it plain that there would be few difficulties. With the assurances given to him by 'Alí that, as a sales representative of Jalál and of some English firms, he said that I would have no problems in Tanganyika, Kenya or Uganda. This I conveyed in a letter to the Guardian of 5 July:[107]

> *Beloved Guardian,*
>
> A new situation has developed here. The husband of Mrs Preston has died suddenly.

[107] Unpublished letter (personal archives).

I am writing this news for two reasons which seem to me to be important, otherwise I would not further add to the many questions put to you recently:

1. Mrs Preston will be deeply grieved – she and her husband were so very happy together and full of plans – he to help the African, she to serve the Cause. Now, just as her three children are old enough to give her a little more freedom, this apparent tragedy happens. She hoped that he would soon accept the Faith, so now that he has passed away so early in life (39) and not yet a Bahá'í, will be added pain. I do not yet know how she has reacted to all this, but I deeply feel that she will be grateful for your prayers. Her present address is Muthaiga Country Club, Nairobi, Kenya.

2. After a short talk with her brother this afternoon, we both agreed that it is highly probable that, after settling her affairs here, she will return to England.

This is not at all certain and I have advised the Africa Committee by cable. The Banánís, Nakhjavánís and myself are standing ready to go anywhere.

Dar-es-Salaam will be 8 strong without us (+ 4 contacts);
Nyasaland will present many difficulties;
Uganda will be easy;
Nairobi (if Kenya now comes into the picture) will be easy, and by far the most desirable, both as a centre of Bahá'í activity and for business.

We have asked the committee for advice by cable.

With loving devotion, Philip.

Before he received this letter, on 4 July, he cabled[108] the National Spiritual Assembly that the settlement of the Banánís/Nakhjavánís was left to their discretion and we were all asked to go to Uganda. Mr Banání decided that they would buy a car and travel by boat from Dar-es-Salaam to Mombasa, and then by train to Nairobi. I was to put the car on the train to Dodoma and drive it to Nairobi, where we would all meet at a known hotel and drive on to Uganda – at that time neither 'Alí nor Violette could drive.

While this was taking place there had been some panic in the hotel. Apparently a man was ill and almost in a coma and the management did not know what to do. As an officer in the RAMC (retired) I was asked to

[108] Effendi, S. (1981). The Unfolding Destiny of the British Bahá'í Community: The Messages from the Guardian of the Bahá'í Faith to the Bahá'ís of the British Isles. London, Bahá'í Publishing Trust., p. 266.

see the man. He was shaking with ague, had a very high temperature, and was lying in dirty, wet sheets. It was such a typical malaria that I gave him a large dose of quinine and told the staff to provide him with large quantities of water to drink. I began to work on him with ice bags and cold water to bathe him to get his temperature down. In the evening he had dry sheets, his temperature was considerably reduced and he had a comfortable night. By the next day he was well on the way to recovery from that bout; it must have been almost over when I was called in but I was regarded by the man and the hotel staff almost as a miracle worker.

On arrival in Dar-es-Salaam I had sent a cable to mother with the long letter to London mentioned above, several letters to friends, followed by three to the Guardian. From mother three letters were sent to PO Box 1058, Dar-es-Salaam, dated 3, 12 and 18 July (the last one arrived after I left and was forwarded to Kampala).[109] These were full of love and concern that I looked after myself properly. In the first one she wrote that everyone there had been complaining about the heat but she had not felt it – 'I must be getting tough ready to come out to you'! A newsy letter dated 12 July concluded, 'I am always praying for you'.[110]

In the letter dated 18 June she asked me not to send her any parcels, adding, 'My dear you should not spend your money on these things until you have got yourself settled and fitted up with all you need'.[111] She concluded:

> Now my darling I want to wish you all the best for your birthday. I do hope you will get this on the day. I shall be thinking of you my dear and looking forward to the time when I can *say* 'Many Happy Returns of the Day'

To the very end of her life she was longing to pioneer to Africa, but as she wrote these letters she must have known that it was not to be.

On 8 July, Ursula Newman wrote, shortly before she married Dr Mehdi Samandarí, that she had been at a gathering at Liverpool Station to send off Hassan and Isobel Sabrí on their journey to pioneer to East Africa. She wrote:[112]

> As I am a very odd and unexpected substitute for you on the NSA I have had the privilege of reading your exciting report on the meetings in Egypt. I should think you and dear Ali would make a grand team. Our period of suspense happily ended with a cable

[109] Unpublished letters (personal archives).
[110] Ibid.
[111] Ibid.
[112] Ibid.

> from the Beloved Guardian to Mehdi's father, approving of our marriage....

Before the Bananís/Nakhjavánís left Dar-es-Salaam for the boat, a photograph was taken of we five Uganda pioneers (with the Nakhjavání's little daughter Bahíyyih), and the five Dar-es-Salaam pioneers: Jalál and Darakshandy Nakhjavání (with their daughters Mina and Hoda), Farshid Naimi (Darakshandy's brother), Thomas Hansford (from the Isle of Man) and Mr M. Thomas (from India).

THE JOURNEY NORTH

A Morris Austin station wagon was bought and the Persian pioneers were taken to the boat for their trip to Mombasa. The car was loaded onto the train, but just before leaving, word was received that the National Spiritual Assembly had cabled the Guardian asking if they could 'reinforce Kenya' and they cabled me asking me to extend what help I could to Marguerite since her husband had passed away. The Guardian replied, 'Grieve passing Preston. Assure wife loving prayers. Approve reinforce Kenya.'[113] It was on that train journey that I met a civil engineer who was working in Tanganyika – John Firman – and we talked through most of the night about the Faith. By the time we reached Dodoma, he had expressed his acceptance of the Faith and we parted, not to meet again for some years, when he was posted to Kampala.

I made my way to the hotel in Nairobi – I seem to remember it being 'The New Stanley' – telephoned Marguerite in Sotik, Kakamega, and decided, in the light of the National Spiritual Assembly's cable, to extend every help to her, not waiting for the Persian pioneers, but going to Sotik and later meeting the pioneers at the hotel in Nakuru on Lake Victoria. I therefore left a letter explaining everything to them and asked them to take the next train to Nakuru. I must confess that to this day (written in 1993) it seems to me to have been the natural thing to do: to fulfil the wishes of the National Assembly and to suggest that instead of having all the hassle of getting off the train, getting taxis to the hotel, rebooking on the train and catching the next one, it would be preferable to remain on the train right through to Nakuru. It was not until we eventually reached Kampala that I learned how much I had upset the Persians, and particularly Mr Banání, firstly that I should change all their plans without any consultation, putting them to the extra expense of fares from Nairobi to Nakuru and, secondly,

[113] Effendi, S. (1981). The Unfolding Destiny of the British Bahá'í Community: The Messages from the Guardian of the Bahá'í Faith to the Bahá'ís of the British Isles. London, Bahá'í Publishing Trust., p. 266.

taking his car without his express permission.

As it happened, I was almost in Sotik when driving on a typical unmade Kenya road in the tea country that a large stone knocked a hole in the lowest part of the car – the under-engine cover – and the oil leaked out. Being an alloy, it could not be welded and I had great difficulty, after reaching Marguerite's farm, in getting it repaired. Fortunately, no permanent damage was done, but it was yet another 'black mark' against me which Ali dare not explain immediately to Mr Banání, but had to wait until he was in a relaxed mood after reaching our destination.

We were to be re-united at the end of July and so I arranged a 'Feast' for us to celebrate together on 1 August at the Nakuru Hotel for which Marguerite would join us. It was a joyous occasion and we left Nakuru early on the morning of the 2 August.

We reached the Kenya/Uganda border at Busia, completed the minor formalities, and crossed into our pioneer country, Uganda, at noon on the 2nd of August 1951. It was an emotional moment.

On reaching Jinja, en route to Kampala, we stayed for a rest at a spot overlooking the Owen Falls, where a plaque gave a brief history recording the date of Owen's 'discovery' of the falls which bear his name. About two years later I was to witness completion of the dam built just below those falls and, as the water rose, see them covered forever and become part of the extended Lake Victoria.

When we drove on to Kampala and first caught a view of the town from a high point on the road, it looked so beautiful that we caught our breath. We stopped to say a prayer and all felt: 'This is our home'.

We drove around to the centre of the town and stopped at the imposing 'Imperial Hotel' and booked in there for a few nights.

That same evening I saw an Englishman in a Scout uniform, and on entering into conversation with him learned, to my astonishment, that he was the one who had actually taken the job for which I had applied without success. He told me of a special camp for Scouters (Scout Masters) at a place on the side of Lake Victoria called Kazi, and invited me to spend a night with them and give some demonstrations of first aid.

Mr Banání kindly allowed me to use the car; I went to Kazi and in the evening went along to a tent where a number of Scouters were having a 'get together'. They asked about the reason for my visit to Kampala and I was able to introduce the Faith to them. Two of them appeared to be quite interested and one readily accepted my invitation to visit me and meet my friends at the Imperial Hotel. The other one invited me to meet him at a cricket match in the Kampala Sports Stadium on the following afternoon.

On returning to the hotel I found it buzzing with activity – the Omukama of Bunyoro was to visit. He was one of the four hereditary 'kings' of the major Bantu tribes of Uganda.

This was significant for two reasons:

(a) he was an absolute monarch of his tribe and

(b) normally black 'guests' did not come into the Imperial.

During the course of the evening, we met with one of his ministers and introduced the Faith to him. Subsequently a District Scoutmaster from the camp, a Muganda, came on several occasions to meet us at the Imperial, but it must have been the 'glamour' of the venue which was the attraction, as he did not follow up his studies of the Faith, particularly after the pioneers moved out of the Imperial.

CONTACT WITH THE FIRST AFRICAN LATER TO REGISTER AS A BAHÁ'Í

The story of the other Scouter is more significant. As invited, I went to the cricket match and enquired about this man; it appeared that, as his side was fielding, he could not leave the game for some time. I decided to wait and, after a short while, a young man came to ask me what I was doing there – it was very unusual for a European to be sitting watching an African game of cricket. He was immediately interested in my reason for waiting and when he heard the Scouter's name he said, 'He is my brother'. Whether this was said in the usual connotation of his being a close relative or his actual blood brother I did not discover, but this young chap became very interested. His name was Fred Bigabwa and he became the first African to accept the Faith in Uganda, the first of his tribe (the Batoro) and, later, the only Mutoro on the first Spiritual Assembly of Kampala. His brother never followed up our initial contact. Fred's sister was married to Crispin Kajubi, a Muganda, who subsequently became the first of his tribe to accept the Faith.

After becoming Bahá'ís Fred and Crispin became great propagators of the Faith and would bring many friends and their wives to the weekly meetings; there was also a regular and growing body of early morning students.

The British National Spiritual Assembly cabled the Guardian on 18 December that they had enrolled and he replied immediately on 19 December:[114] 'Delighted. Assure them fervent prayers hearty welcome Bahá'í fold.'

[114] Ibid., p. 275.

MY APPOINTMENT WITHIN THE UGANDA MEDICAL SERVICE

It had been suggested by the Scout Commissioner that, with my interests in promoting the best interests of the African, I might be able to find employment in the Government's Community Development Department. So, after reporting to the Immigration Officer, another Parsee and the Honorary Consul for Goa, I went along to see the Head of that Department in Kampala.

I took with me a résumé which had been duplicated in England and, after studying it, he suggested that, with my Army experience as an officer in the Royal Army Medical Corps and the experience I had had as Commanding Officer of a Hygiene Unit in Kenya at the end of the war, my services might be more appreciated by the Health Department of the Uganda Medical Services. This resulted in an interview a few days later, when I learnt that an officer who had been appointed from the collapsing 'Groundnut Scheme' of Central South Africa to a post as 'sanitary overseer' with the Uganda Medical Department, had not turned up and the government had received no word of explanation or apology from him, so his post would be vacant. It was felt to be too inferior a post for a retired captain of the RAMC, but they would offer it to me if I wished.

Although I was very excited at being offered any kind of employment, particularly after only a week in the country, and at a salary which was much higher than I had expected, with the provision of housing and a special low interest loan to buy a car, I pretended 'hard to get' and asked for a little time to think it over and to see how soon I would be able to 'wind up my business affairs'. The suggested post would be available in early October.

All the pioneers thought that a wonderful door had opened so I went around the town to try to book some orders for Mr Norton. After another week or so, I telephoned Mr Hines, the Head of the Department in which I would be employed. I told him that I was in a position to wind up my affairs and would be ready to start work before October, even if it meant my working without salary for a month or so while I became acquainted with my job.

In the meantime the Persian pioneers had decided to move out to a nearby, much less expensive hotel, the Speke but, to maintain a good image, I decided to stay on at the Imperial. It was to this address that, after agreeing that I could start work on 1 September, Mr Hines wrote on the 28th of August formally offering me a 'temporary appointment' as sanitary overseer, initially in Masaka, about 90 miles from Kampala. The appointment would be on the basis of one month's notice on either side until they had had some experience of my work, at which point 'more permanent employment' would be considered. There would be no overseas leave attached to this contract, but after 12 months' service, I would be entitled to 18 days local leave per annum.

It was during the euphoria of these days that I received a sad letter from my brother, Jack. To illustrate the strong feelings he had on my pioneer move and the effect it had on me, I will quote it in full:[115]

> *Dear Phil,*
>
> This, I think, is going to be the most difficult letter to write in my life and it is devoted entirely to our Mother. As you know when you left her she was fine and recovering her strength slowly but surely every day. She was happy in the thought that we were both (all she had in the world) close to her and seeing her every day.
>
> Well, you went away and *instantly* she began to lose her appetite, her weight and her whole outlook seemed to be gloomy. After a week or so she sent for the doctor who said he could do nothing for her and suggested St Luke's (Hospital). After being in there a week I had a few words with the sister who said there was nothing they could do to get her better. Phil, she is worrying and fretting about your being away and she can't come to you. She says 'Tell Phil goodbye for me'. Oh lad, this is awful, I never thought I should have to put that down on paper. She was doing so nicely in her little flat and if only you could have got a job here if only as long as she lived and then gone out there she would be enjoying her remaining few years instead of what I think may be only a *few weeks or days* now.
>
> Phil, I feel bitter against your faith because it has been the cause of splitting us up and when a woman of mother's age has to say goodbye to her son I think it is a *crime* not religion.
>
> I know it's too late to even think of our being together now at the end (which I feel is very near) but you can rest assured that we will do everything in our power to give mother every comfort. I can't write any more Phil, so please reply at your earliest.
>
> *Jack*

While I could sympathise with his reaction, as he had no particular faith, it was not until after mother died that I was able to put on one side all

[115] Unpublished letter (personal archives).

that he wrote in this letter of 13 August 1951. I received it on 18 August and I cabled her in hospital:[116]

> Commencing excellent job UGANDA GOVERNMENT two weeks time, good salary. Many Friends, contacts, only need news your recovery complete my happiness.
>
> *Deepest love always, Philip*

To which she replied on 27 August, 'Trying hard to get well – *Mother*'.

I also cabled the Guardian:[117]

> Just received news Mother desperately ill family condemning me leaving her. Humbly beseech prayers. Hoping commence work Uganda Government early September.
>
> *Loving loyalty*

Soon after arriving in Kampala I received a letter from Ursula Newman, who had replaced me on the National Spiritual Assembly in June, saying that she was to marry Dr Mehdi Samandarí:[118]

> *Dear Philip,*
>
> Alláh'u'Abhá! It is most exciting to think of the gathering of Bahá'ís in Tanganyika, the formation of the first group in the plan and election of officers.
>
> On Friday a crowd of us met at Liverpool Street to send the Sabrí's off on their journey – Marian Little was there in great form.
>
> I am in London for a Summer School Committee meeting. I somehow feel that the discussions on Africa at this year's school will have more relation to reality than in the past, because we shall have been fed with some solid matter from the pioneers.
>
> Only one thing saddened the gathering at Liverpool Street and that was the shocking news about poor Terence (Preston). It is very difficult to understand why poor Marguerite should have to endure this terrible loss just as she was entering into active service for the Cause in Africa.
>
> As I am a very odd and unexpected substitute for you on the NSA I have had the privilege of reading your exciting report on the meetings in Egypt. I should think you and dear Ali would make a grand team.
>
> Our period of suspense happily ended with a cable from the beloved Guardian to Mehdi's father, approving of our marriage – so now we

[116] Unpublished letter (personal archives).
[117] Unpublished cable (personal archives).
[118] Unpublished letter (personal archives).

are going ahead and making our plans. July 28 (Saturday) may be the day. There has been a great outbreak of marriages this year! Dr Afnán and Shomais are getting married at Summer School.

The Africa Committee is now in session – somehow your connection with it and your presence in Africa now have brought the two much closer together.

This is just a little note to add to Mehdi's letter to join in sending loving greetings and prayers for great conquests in new lands.

Dear old Philip – we shall all miss you here very much, but yet we feel in close touch with you and shall watch for exciting news.

Deepest love, Ursula

Life in Kampala during August was hectic. We had to get to know the town, settle our immigration formalities, look into the accommodation situation, make immediate plans for receiving mail, arrange driving lessons and obtain licences for 'Alí (and later Violette), for me to find a job and, above all, to decide how we should pursue teaching the local people and cultivating the public image we wished to establish.

We first obtained an immediate mailing address – 'Pioneering Private Bag' – which necessitated one of us, usually 'Alí, visiting the post office daily.

Just as I received my offer of employment from the Uganda Protectorate Medical Department, the Guardian was writing an astonishing letter to me – it was sent on to me soon after my arrival in Masaka.

The Guardian answered several questions I had asked in my letter written to him from Egypt but posted on arrival in Dar-es-Salaam – his comments on our visit to Geneva were illuminating but his references to my mother were very moving and, reading between the lines, I felt he did not really feel that she would live to join me. He then 'cherished' the hope, that I may 'prove to be a spiritual Stanley of Africa'![119] I immediately tried to find out more about Stanley and didn't particularly like what I read about him, but took heart from the exact words he wrote – 'a spiritual Stanley'. Looking back it may have been a reference to what I do not think I had mentioned to him, as I did not then know the outcome. This was my 'discovery', not of a Livingstone, but of the first Africans to accept the Faith in Tanganyika and Uganda, and of John Firman, who is still actively serving the Faith almost half a century after that train journey to Dodoma.

It was the postscript in the Guardian's own handwriting which was most humbling. I quote that letter, dated 30 August 1951, in full (this is the

[119] Unpublished letter (personal archives).

first letter I received in which the part written by Rúḥíyyih Khánum was typed):[120]

Dear Bahá'í Brother,

Your letters dated June 8 and 28, July 5 and 17, with enclosures, have been received, and the beloved Guardian has instructed me to answer you on his behalf. I am also enclosing two receipts.

He was very sorry to hear of the sudden death of Mr Preston – a great blow for his poor wife. She will need the love and help of the friends in Africa very much at present.

Regarding the question you asked about funds for the Shrine being sent from Egypt: the friends must not do anything illegal; if they can remit via England legally, they can do so, otherwise they should let it accumulate in Egypt for the present.

You may mail him the reports from Egypt.

He feels you and Mr Nakhjavání should encourage the Persian boys in Geneva. All he ever asks of the friends is to be true Bahá'ís, and if the Persian students would thoughtfully grasp his instructions regarding the administrative relation of believers in the goal countries to the ETC and the American NSA the trouble would no doubt not have arisen. These students have a high responsibility; the western Bahá'ís look to the Persians and they should, instead of being proud and often disputatious, show a spirit of loving consideration and a submission to the proper administrative authority. Needless to say they should exemplify the Bahá'í life – which, alas, many of them did not.

He was very sorry to hear your dear mother is ill. She has truly shown an exemplary Bahá'í spirit in every way and it is easy to see a lot of your own characteristics of faith and courage come from this fine woman. You have every reason to be proud of her! He trusts, and is praying, she may recover and later join you. But whatever happens, her reward at the hands of the true Beloved is certainly assured. He wishes more of the Bahá'ís would arise to such heights of devotion and sacrifice.

The progress being made in Africa is truly miraculous, as if a special benediction from on High is being extended to this work. Please give his love to the devoted Bananís and tell them the services they are rendering are imperishable and deeply appreciated by him.

He feels sure that the work in Uganda will now go forward rapidly.

[120] Ibid.

1928: Philip with his mother, Lizzie, and father, Herbert

1936 (circa): Philip as King's Scout

1945, June: Philip in Alexandria, with Alí Rushdi (left) and Anissa Abbas and Abdu'l Majid

1946, February: Philip at Lake Naivasha, Kenya

1946, June: Philip with Suez Bahá'ís

1946, May: Philip in Haifa

1946, May: Philip in Akka

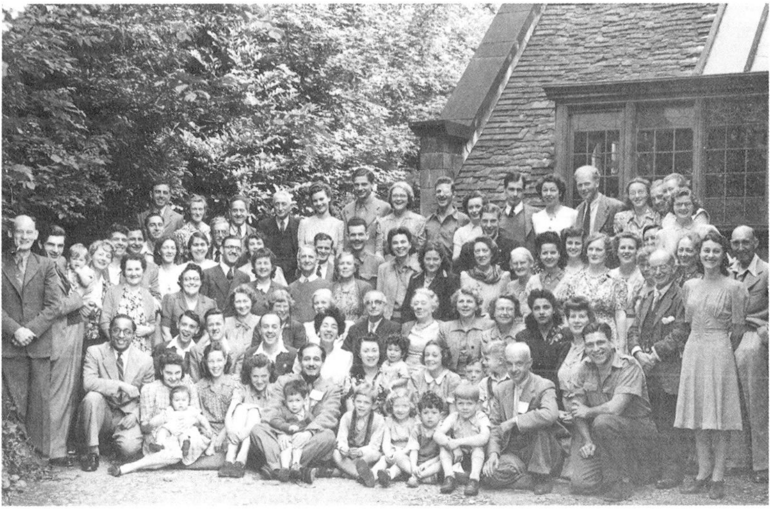

1947: Summer School, Matlock Bath. Philip extreme right at front, Hasan Balyúzi centre row, Hassan Sabrí on extreme left; John Ferraby with baby Brigitte, second left standing

1949: Philip with his mother, Lizzie, in the garden of their home

1949: Ashover Summer School. Philip 2nd left, standing. Seated front row: Hasan Balyúzi, centre; Lizzie Hainsworth, 10th from right; Clare Gung, 5th from right. Back row: John Ferraby, 2nd from left; Ted Cardell, 5th from left

1949: Teaching Conference Manchester. Philip back row, left of centre: seated floor; Hasan Balyúzi, centre (dark suit); John Ferraby third from right. seated chairs: Betty Goode, 4th from left; Clare Gung 7th from left

1951: 29th NSA of the Bahá'ís of the British Isles. l – r: Philip Hainsworth, Hasan Balyúzi, Dorothy and John Ferraby, Connie Langton Davies, Dick Backwell, Zeine Nuradin Zeine, David and Marion Hofman

1952 (circa): Bahá'ís of Kobwin – Oloro Epyeru, seated end right; later elected to NSA

1952, April: First LSA of the Bahá'ís of Kampala:
Seated l – r: Samiyyih Banání, Músá Banání, Violette Nakhjavani
Standing l – r: Philip Hainsworth, Krispin Kajubi, Enoch Olinga, Alí Nakhjavani, Peter Musoke, Fred Bigabwa

1953: Kampala Conference. Meeting with Hands of the Cause in tent at 4 Kagera Road: Músá Banání, Leroy Ioas, Dorothy Baker, Horace Holley, Dhikru'lláh Khádem, Tarázu'lláh Samandarí, 'Alí-Akhbar Furútan, Valíyu'lláh Varghá, General Alá'í and Mason Remey

1954,15 August: Philip with Gerhard Bender at a meeting in Eslingen, Germany, close to the site where 'Abdu'l-Bahá spoke in 1913. l-r Fazollah Namdar, Gerhard Bender, Philip and Ben Levy

1955: Working on simulium damnosum control

1956: Wedding of Philip and Lois: Hasan Balyúzí, seated centre, conducted the ceremony. David Hofman reads the telegrams

1956: First NSA of Central and East Africa. Left to right; Hassan Sabrí, Philip Hainsworth, Aziz Yazdi, Jalal Nakhjávaní, Alí Nakhjávaní; seated l-r Max Kanyerezi, Tito Wanantutzi, Oloro Epyeru and Sylvester Okurut

1957: Philip on safari

1957, July: Kampala community

1957, September: On safari past the Equator!

1957, October: Constructing the borehole at the Kampala Temple site (Philip took the photograph)

1958, January: Dedication of Temple site. 'Amatu'l-Baha Rúhíyyih Khanum with Hand of the Cause Músá Banání

1959, May: Temple construction. Philip on the first roof; Philip, Lois, Richard and (almost) Zarin on the lip of the dome. Philip climbed up carrying Richard and the photographic equipment, then set the camera to automatic for this picture

1958: Philip and Lois on safari

1959, October: Kampala railway station - off to England on leave. Adieux from Samiyyih and Músá Banání and Mary and Rex Collinon; thence by train to Mombasa to board the Union Castle

Uganda Medical Department, Entomology section.
European officers l-r Geoff Ealden, George Barney, Philip with their colleagues

1961, January: Temple dedication - Amatu'l-Bahá Rúhíyyih Khanum speaking. Philip, in the choir, seated behind her

1961: Rúhíyyih Khanum consulting with Temple Dedication Committee

1961: Rúhíyyih Khanum speaking at the Temple Dedication conference at Makerere University, Kampala

1962: Visit to Tanga to see Alan and Mary Elston: their houseboy, John and our dog, Rajah also in picture

1963: Damali, the Nabagereka of Buganda, with Lois, her mother, Richard and Zarin

1963: Philip outside our Kampala home with Richard and Zarin

1963: Dalston Hall. Philip making a plea for travel teachers

1963: Rúhíyyih Khanum opening the First International Congress, Royal Albert Hall, London. Hand of the Cause William Sears and Philip Hainsworth were the two keynote speakers

1965: Our family just before our departure from Uganda

1976: Conference in Canterbury on the 40th anniversary of the founding of the World Congress of Faiths. Philip and Douglas Martin represented the Bahá'í International Community

1976: A small group of the British contingent at the Paris International Conference (Philip and Lois at left, towards the back)

1987: Manchester Youth Conference. Philip 4th from left, front row; then Lois, Charles and Yvonne Macdonald, Hand of the Cause Ugo Giachery, Guilda Walker

1988, May, Haifa: UK NSA delegates at International Convention. l – r Ridvan Moqbel, Simon Mortimore, Iain Palin, Jan Mughrabi, Roger Prentice, Philip Hainsworth, Hugh Adamson, Wendi Momen, Charles Macdonald

1954: Philip teaching Progressive Revelation

1965: Outside the Temple, standing: Philip; Mary and Rex Collison. Seated: Ayah Mary, Richard, Zarin, Lois, Mr Azemikah (Congo pioneer), Samiyyih Banání, Noushin Faroumand

1969: Burnley. Cleasby wedding

1972: Leeds in the garden of our home

1976: Attending the double wedding of Gita and Neeta Ghandi to Roger Kingdon and Parto Forouhi

1981: Chigwell Youth Conference

1985, December: at the Dedication of the Indian Temple

1987: Talking on 'Bahá'í Focus on Peace', one of the books he wrote

1988, May: Haifa. UK NSA members, with British Bahá'ís serving at the World Centre, in the home of George Bowers, seated floor second from left; Mark Hellaby, Arabic scholar, seated centre; Elsie Bowers standing second left; Ian Semple, centre back row. First row seated – David Hofman centre; Marion Hofman second from right

1991: Conference in Northern Ireland

1993, Haifa: International Convention. Consulting with Alí Na<u>kh</u>jávaní

1994, 7 August: Philip escorting Amatu'l-Baha Rúhíyyih <u>Kh</u>anum into the Great Room at Grosvenor House, London to a national meeting with UK Bahá'ís

1998: In the driveway of our home, Morants Court

1999: Surprise 80th birthday party arranged by Zarin (centre); Ron Batchelor in the background; Erfan and Iqan's heads in the foreground!

1999: The car stuck in the mud after a visit to the Temple. Philip insisted upon helping to push!

2001, January: Philip and Lois at the wedding of Michael and Katherine (née Lee); with Richard and Corinne (née Kent) and their children Arwyn, Reissa and Melissa; Zarin and her husband, Soroush Fadaei, and their children Iman, Anisa, Erfan and Iqan

2001: At the home of George Olinga, Tilling, Uganda: Lois, Philip, Alí, Violette

The news from Dar is wonderful, too.

Your eager spirit has led you back to Africa and he cherishes the hope that you may prove to be a spiritual Stanley of Africa.

His loving prayers are with you,

With Bahá'í love.

P.S. The racial question all over Africa is very acute, but, while being wise and tactful, the believers must realise that their standard is far from that of the white colonials. They have not gone there to uphold the white man's supremacy, but to give the Cause of God to, primarily, the black man whose home is Africa.

In Shoghi Effendi's handwriting:

Dear and prized co-worker,

The work you have achieved since your departure from the Holy Land, in the service of our beloved Faith, evokes, through its range and quality, my profound admiration and heartfelt gratitude. The services you are now rendering in Africa, ennoble and enrich this record of notable achievements. You are often in my thoughts and prayers, and I cherish the brightest hopes for your future activities, and will continue to pray from the depths of my heart for your dear self as well as for your dear mother.

Your true and grateful brother,

Shoghi.

At the same time, he cabled my mother on 30 August 1951:[121]

Appreciate self sacrifice loving prayers recovery – *Shoghi.*

On 2 September Jack wrote:[122]

Dear Phil,

I have just got back from hospital and have left mother very weak. In the sister's opinion she is sinking very fast and we can go in to see her any time which I think is a very bad sign. I'm afraid this is the end of her Phil and we have all done our very best to comfort her and take her everything she asked for. The Nortons have proposed for her to be nursed privately but mother says she is comfortable and desires to remain where she is. Mrs Norton and Mrs Stone called to see her yesterday and give her a cable from 'Shoghi' I think they said the Guardian. This seemed to buck her up for a time but today she is lot weaker. I took her 6 eggs and asked for them to be given to her beaten up in milk. That's one way to get

[121] Unpublished cable (personal archives).
[122] Unpublished letter (personal archives).

food into her. I can't say any more but I'll go again tomorrow and let you know.

Jack

I received it very quickly in Masaka where I was being initiated into the work of a Health Office. About this time, I received a letter from Ugo and Angelina Giachery, dated 24 August and written in Sweden:[123]

Dear Philip,

Your dear letter of 6 August has been forwarded to us here where we are spending a few days before going to the Conference which shall take place in Scheveningen, Holland. The Italian authorities, observient to the Pope, had denied the permit to hold it in Rome. Perhaps by next year we shall be able to do so.

The joint letter we sent to the Guardian from Rome, was received by him and I am sending copy of his answer to Ali. All the news you give us on your activities since you left Rome are most elating and we shall share your letter with the Friends in Rome upon our return there, as most of them still remember you and the other dear pioneer with great admiration and have often enquired about you and your welfare.

Right after you left I wrote to Mr and Mrs Norton to give a brief account of your visit in Rome and asking them to convey the information to your dear mother. We hope she is better and does not miss you too much (who cannot miss you?)....

The photos I took in our terrace are quite good I shall send them to you upon our return to Rome. I am sorry I did not send it before leaving but I had too much work before the date set for our departure that I had hardly any time for rest. We had to secure some special export licenses for iron work to be shipped to Haifa and prepare for a shipment of 120 tons of carved stone for the Shrine. Now all this material is safely in Haifa. Please write to us from time to time and let us hear of your progress.

With a strong and brotherly hug, affectionately yours,

Ugo Giachery

Dear Philip

We were so happy to hear from you. In Rome we always speak of your visit with great love and happy thoughts. We shall remember you all at the conference in Holland and you will be remembered in our prayers, *love to you all, Angelina R Giachery*

[123] Unpublished letter (personal archives).

BEING A MEMBER OF THE KAMPALA COMMUNITY BUT NOT LIVING THERE!

The Bahá'ís of Kampala received a copy of a letter from the Guardian to the Bahá'ís of Dar-es-Salaam and when we all met on the first weekend after I had settled in Masaka, we agreed to write to him ourselves. Here are those letters and the exciting reply we had from him. From the Guardian, dated 27 July 1951, to the Bahá'ís of Dar-es-Salaam:[124]

Dear Bahá'í Friends,

Your letter made our beloved Guardian very happy. His thoughts – and hopes – are constantly focused these days on the wonderful work opening up in Africa, and he rejoiced to see so many of you united there in Tanganyika.

Truly this Cause moves forward propelled by forces more than we can see or grasp; God has surely raised you up and given you this blessed privilege, this unique privilege, of kindling the Light of His Faith there and writing your name in history.

How significant that the first group to be formed in the heart of Africa is composed of believers from the East and the West, united, working side by side to bring the Message of the Blessed Beauty to one of the great waiting races of the world, hitherto oppressed and disregarded, but now being offered the waters of life and a wonderful future.

You may be sure your activities will be supported by his special and fervent prayers, and that he awaits with keen interest news of every new development in your work.

While being wise and tactful you should, however, never lose sight of the fact that it is to the African peoples, primarily, that your mission is addressed. To bring them into our world-wide brotherhood is your duty and privilege.

With warm Bahá'í love,

R. Rabbání.

In the handwriting of the Guardian:

Dear and valued co-workers,

I was so pleased to receive your letter and am greatly encouraged by your exemplary and magnificent response. You have indeed set a noble example, and the record of your services will, I trust, enrich the annals of the Faith. Persevere in your labours, and rest assured

[124] Ibid.

that the Beloved will watch over you and sustain and guide you in your historic and highly meritorious activities.

Your true and grateful brother,

Shoghi

To the Guardian from the Kampala Group, dated 9 September 1951:[125]

To our well beloved Guardian,

With trembling hands and hearts, fully conscious of our shortcomings and weaknesses, ashamed of ourselves, our immature thoughts and actions, yet clinging fast unto our Guardian's loving bounty, we submit these few lines, fervently hoping they may be acceptable in his presence.

It is now about five weeks since our party arrived in Uganda. Your telegraphic message of infinite love and kind comfort, addressed to our party through London, joined our hearts in humble thanksgiving and praise.

Your letter to the Dar-es-Salaam Bahá'í Group has been read and re-read, and we are trying to realise its implications, and make it the key to our teaching activity.

We are happy to report that the Immigration Board of Uganda has approved the entry permit of the Banánís and Nakhjavánís. The actual permits are to be delivered to them after a few formalities have been complied with.

Philip has entered Government Service and is stationed at Masaka, some 85 miles away. His position with regards to our group is before the Africa Committee. He hopes to join us for Feasts, and on occasional weekends.

So far, contact has been established with three Africans and literature has been given to them. The Faith has been discussed with a few Indians and Europeans.

Our humble efforts are worthless and fruitless should they be deprived of the Divine confirmations of the Abhá Kingdom. May the Guardian's prayers and kind love ever continue to surround us, solve our problems, remove our difficulties and lead us to the heights of true selfless servitude and the good pleasure of the Beloved's heart.

In His service,

Músá Banání; Samiheh Banání; Philip Hainsworth; 'Alí Nakhjavání; Violette Nakhjavání (Full signatures of all members)

[125] Unpublished letter (personal archives).

The Guardian replied on 2 October:[126]

Dear Bahá'í Friends,

Your letter of 9 September brought great joy to the heart of our beloved Guardian.

He was particularly pleased to see you have been granted visas to remain there, and also to hear dear Philip has got a job, which he hopes will make things easier for him, and also release funds for the support of other pioneers.

The Guardian attaches the greatest importance to your presence in Uganda, and feels that your group, and the prospect of an Assembly in Tanganyika, have now firmly established the opening phase of the African work, so important, and so evidently blessed from on High.

His thoughts and prayers are constantly with you all, and the historic services you are rendering are deeply appreciated by him, and by all the Bahá'ís in East and West.

He feels sure you will be successful, and is eager to receive news of the progress of your work.

With Bahá'í love, R Rabbání

In the handwriting of the Guardian:

May the spirit of Bahá'u'lláh sustain and overshadow you always, aid you to extend steadily the range of your historic and exemplary activities and services, consolidate your splendid achievements, and enrich the annals of our glorious Faith, now entering upon so important a state in its evolution in the African continent.

Your true and grateful bother, Shoghi.

On 8 September, I received a cable from Arthur Norton confirming Jack's fears written on 3 September:[127]

Mother hospital rapidly sinking. Realises and resigned. Cable farewell message 'Tolerance' Will convey.'

To which I replied:[128]

Deeply sorrowing earthly separation but confident our love transcends human frailties. You Dad will continue great work. All my love, Darling. Arthur please advance brother twenty pounds will send cheque,

Love, Philip.

[126] Ibid.
[127] Unpublished cable (personal archives).
[128] Ibid.

On 21 September, I received the final news:[129]

> Darling Mother passed Abhá Kingdom 10.10 pm Nineteenth, Jack, Marian, Arthur present perfect ending.
>
> *Love.*

This news was followed by a report actually posted just before she passed away by Marian and Arthur Norton. In this letter dated 19 September, they refer to an air letter sent two days earlier, which I did not receive:[130]

> *My dear Philip,*
>
> I confirm my air letter to you dated 17 September, and I am writing you again quickly as I want you to be kept up to date with the condition of your dear Mother. After posting your letter on Monday (17th inst.) Marion and I went to St. Luke's Hospital and we spent three and a half hours at your Mother's bedside, leaving only when she appeared to be sleeping. Your brother was also there part of the time. We read prayers to her, and tried to give her all the comfort and help in our power. I have never met such a brave soul. She is patient, resigned, and happy. Marion supplied her some time ago with a large bottle of lavender water, and she loves to have this on her forehead and neck. Every time Marion puts this on she says: 'Isn't it lovely'. It is only with great difficulty she carries on any conversation, but she is perfectly conscious, and knows every word we say. Last night (Tuesday) I went alone to see her, as Marion was prevented at the last moment from going owing to something in connection with her own Mother. I stayed at the hospital for about an hour. Your brother was present all the time. I read her four prayers, and your brother was about to leave the bedside, but your Mother asked him to stay and hear the prayers. I have just telephoned the hospital (8.30 am today Wednesday) and was told she did not have a good night, and seems weaker again. I was told last night at the hospital the Dr. says she has cancer of the blood stream. I try and make notes of what she says from time to time. Last night she said 'How is Philip' I said he is well and happy. She then said what is he doing. I told her you were doing medical work and of course I said he is doing pioneering for the Faith. She said 'Yes, I know'. On Monday evening she looked at Marion and I, and said 'I do love you'. Also on Monday evening she said 'Give my love to Philip' and tell him not to let go of Jack. On looking at my

[129] Ibid.
[130] Unpublished letter (personal archives).

notes the exact words were 'Tell Philip I love him'.... Your brother asked me last night if he could call at my office to collect the Twenty pounds you asked me to advance him. I said I could not hand him this money unless, and until something happens to your Mother. I trust these are your wishes. Well Philip I have tried to give you a clear picture of the situation up to today. I shall, or both of us will go again tonight to the hospital, as she always looks forward to our coming. We have left our telephone number at the hospital in case we are wanted either during the day or night. Rest assured we would go immediately. She is so weak she might pass away any time, or last some days. She is a lady of the first order, and everyone knows in the hospital ward she is a Bahá'í. Last night I had a long talk with the head nurse who wanted to know about the Faith. I asked your Mother last night if she was happy. She said 'Oh yes'. When her passing does come, she will leave us with a picture of serenity, happiness and joy. I told her she would be welcomed in the Abhá Kingdom, and she replied 'Yes, I know'.

Love from

Marion and Arthur.

On 20 September, Jack wrote:[131]

As you will know by Mr Norton's cable, Mother passed on last night. She died beautifully, no pain at all and I was with her. She whispered 'Jack' faintly and put her hand on my head and that was the end. I have been with (her) every day, some days all afternoon and until late at night and she has had *every* attention.

So now we have to carry out her last wish, A Bahá'í funeral. I have arranged with Mr Norton and we have fixed up for Monday, the service in our house, interment at Undercliffe and then a short meeting at the Centre. 'Just like Bert's' [our father] that is what she wanted.

I am enclosing a note which she gave me four days ago, also a form from the Registrar which you must sign where marked and return to me as soon as possible. I shall take this back to the Registrar who will then issue a Death Cert, this to be sent to you enabling you to draw your insurance. I understand from the Refuge Co that you authorise me to draw the money or you can do it yourself. Let me know which you decide to do.

I'll write after the funeral.

Cheerio, Jack.

[131] Unpublished letter (personal archives).

On 9 September, I received a letter from Lotfu'lláh Hakím in reply to mine sent during our first week in Kampala:[132]

> *Very dear Bahá'í Brother Philip,*
>
> Your loving and most welcome letter of 6 August was received sometime ago for which I thank you very deeply. Your letter has been shared with the dear friends here and all were very much interested in all your news and experiences in your wonderful pioneering. They all wished to be very heartily remembered to you and the dear friends there.
>
> I am happy to say the beloved Guardian is keeping well and as active as ever and so is dear Rúḥíyyih Khánum.
>
> The sweet memory of those happy days that I used to hear from you while in England or Scotland is still very fresh with me and when ever I visit the Holy Shrines I remember you and pray that you may always be well and happy and prosperous in your services in the Path of the Cause of God. In fact those days spent with the dear friends in British Isles and their love and kindnesses will never be forgotten. Those times are very precious to me. And now that you are pioneering as a most wonderful soldier of Bahá'u'lláh you may be sure you will not be forgotten. This morning while visiting the Holy Shine of the Báb I thought of you, Claire Gung, Nakhjavánís and the Banánís and prayed for your welfare and happiness.
>
> I am happy to say that the scaffolding of the star (base of the octagon) with its cement casting of the Shrine is over and now they are going to begin the construction of the octagon which is the next step. They are now preparing and in a couple of days or so they will begin the construction. All the materials such as cut stone window frames, doors and etc. for the octagon that the beloved (Guardian) had ordered from Italy have arrived and are ready to be used. It is most wonderful notwithstanding so much that the beloved Guardian has to do he sees to every little detail of the construction as well. It is really a miracle.
>
> The Holy Shrine and the Bahá'í gardens have become very popular here. Continually tourists and people of almost all nationalities come and visit the hallowed place on Mt. Carmel. The reporters and photographic recorders of different papers throughout the world come and take series of photos of different parts of the Shrine, gardens, terraces and etc. They all marvel at the beauty and hallowedness of the place. We (the Bahá'ís all over the Bahá'í

[132] Unpublished letter (personal archives).

world) owe all of it to the beloved Guardian. He is continually adding to the beauty of the Cause. We should be very grateful to Bahá'u'lláh and 'Abdu'l Bahá for this most wonderful Guardian.

I sincerely trust and hope that you are all well settled by now and are happy with your work and conditions there. I hope the Bananís and Nakhjavánís have been able to get extension of visa for their stay. Should you see or write to any of them and to Claire Gung please remember me very kindly to them.

I hear the dear friends have had a most wonderful Summer School this year at Hull. How I wish we (you and I) were there as well. I am looking forward to hear in detail of the Summer School also of the Teaching Conference in Europe.

Millie and Mason have not yet returned. We hope they will come soon. All the friends here join me with warmest Bahá'í love and all good wishes to you and the pioneer friends in Africa.

Yours in His Service,

Lotfullah.

I was able to cable the news of my mother's passing to the Guardian and he replied on 26 September:[133]

Deepest loving sympathy ardently praying soul mother Kingdom, *Shoghi.*

There is a most moving story about something that happened during the last few hours of mother's life that I learned later. As was reported, she was so weak that she had to be fed, but she was radiant when she was awake and as someone remarked 'appeared to be pure spirit'. Suddenly, the nurse reported, she sat up in bed and demanded pen and paper. For many days she had not been able to move unaided but then she actually sat up and spoke with great clarity and strength.

In one envelope she put a note, addressed it 'My Will', and addressed the other 'To be sent to Philip when I am gone'.

The will was simple – the special letter more than compensated for what Jack had written so many weeks before:[134]

Dear Philip,

Don't let anyone tell you that it was you going away that made me ill it was not so. Its just the old body that's done its job but love the spirit is still bright and alive now love I want to thank you for those six happy years you have given me for Philip I never thought ever

[133] Unpublished cable (personal archives).
[134] Unpublished letter (personal archives).

to be able to see all the places and mix with all the friends. Thank you love now my darling this must be good bye and God bless you.
Mother

Jack and Annice have been so good to me.

On 26 September Rúḥíyyih Khánum wrote a most loving personal letter which reached me in Masaka and I quote it in full:[135]

Dearest Philip,

My heart goes out to you in this hour of trial. I can imagine how you feel about losing your Mother, and when you are so far from her. It takes the real spiritual stuff in us to rise to these moments in life – but you have it.

My own Mother I never saw again, as you know. But in your case, though I know it pains you just as much, you were no doubt a little prepared for it? I hope so, otherwise I know the shock is terrific. And I know you feel as I did then, that the loved one is free and in a safe place, near the Eternal Beloved. How deeply I pity people who have not this sense of continuity we have when they lose their nearest ones.

I have planned and planned to write you. You are much dearer to me than you could imagine. I admire you so much and feel so proud to see you go on and up, and not come to a standstill, as so many do! But I have given up all my own letter writing. (I hope to get back to it) My father's long illness produced a state of complete mental exhaustion, but gradually now I feel able to work and *think* a little.

The work you did in England was wonderful. (Shall you get a swelled head if I tell you what I really think?) I felt you really set the place on fire when you got back from Haifa, and you never knew how much the Guardian worried over you in Haifa, lest your own pure faith be tested by finding the family gone and the place so empty!

I always felt you would go back to Africa, and was so happy you did. Oh Philip go on putting the Cause first! So many fall by the wayside and abandon the heights for some soft little human spot to incubate in, to be just like everyone else in! I am sure one of the ways God shows His mercy to us in the next world is to blind our eyes so we will not clearly see the things we could have done, but did not. Otherwise I am sure we would go mad. There is a sentence of Bahá'u'lláh where He says: 'and if the believers had been

[135] Ibid.

occupied with that which We commanded them, now all the world would be adorned with the robe of faith'. (I am quoting from memory, so the exact wording may be incorrect but the thought is there.) He wrote it in Baghdád or Adrianople – so how much more it must apply to us today?

I think about everything can become a habit, not only alcohol and bad things! Sacrifice can become a habit, patience, indifference to danger, no doubt nobility and saintliness. It's a great help. This is a digression to express a thought I have increasingly of late years, as I see all the attachments and desires die out in me and that I no longer suffer over them! And it's become obvious pioneering becomes a habit because so many of the American 1st 7 Year Plan pioneers have become insatiable pioneers. They can barely wait for the next Plan to come out so they can start all over in a new field. It's nice to think such a comfortable law as habit works on the spiritual plane.

I envy you working in Africa. I love Africa and always wanted to go there. The Guardian is so enthusiastic about the work there. There is nothing you could have done that would have made him happier than your going out there. And I know, Philip, your dear, good Mother was proud of you and will be with you in spirit now as her tired old body never could have been on this plane. Death confers youth, and your father and mother must be very like you now. At least I like to think of it this way and feel I am right.

God bless you dear, and give you everything good in life.

Please give my love to the Bananís and Nakhjavánís.

Yours in the Faith, Rúḥíyyih

Did you know the Guardian cabled your Mother assuring her of his prayers, some time ago. I hope it reached her.

I quote from the letter I wrote on 28 September to Shoghi Effendi to try to convey some of my emotion of that particular time:[136]

Beloved Guardian,

I want to gratefully acknowledge receipt of your letter to me dated 30 August; your cables to me of 22 August and 25 September, and your cable to my mother.

I am happy to say that my brother's tone has changed a little for the better, and the latest news is that a fine Bahá'í funeral was held, followed by a meeting in the Bradford Bahá'í Centre.

Although for the last two weeks of her life mother could speak only

[136] Unpublished letter (personal archives).

with difficulty as she was existing on soda water, some three days before her passing she wrote a note, 'to be sent to Philip when I am gone'.

In addition to her weakness, mother found it extremely difficult to write a letter even when she was much younger, so she certainly showed the courage you wrote about, right to the end. On the morning of her death, Arthur Norton, who was with her daily and kept me fully 'in the picture', wrote, 'When her passing does come, she will leave with us a picture of serenity, happiness and joy.'

All this has been a great relief to me, and especially your letter, which contained such a wonderful paragraph about her, and which actually reached me but an hour after the cable giving me the news of her death.

It seems strange that, now I have a job and a house, and every chance of an entry permit for her, she should pass on to greater work, but I am sure she will now be able to do that which her frailties would not permit on this earth, and I only hope and pray that she and Dad will be able to work together. Oh but she longed to come to Africa, and my only regret is that she could not 'make it' in time. Perhaps, had it been possible for me to get here earlier, i.e. when you first urged Hassan Sabrí and I to go, I might have been able to arrange for her to come. Still, I feel more and more that if one's intentions are good, and one does all one can in the service of the Cause, His Will be done, even though it does not always seem understandable at first.

I am here on probation for six months. If I prove satisfactory, and if I still wish to remain with the Medical Department, I shall be offered a 33 months' contract, commencing from the day my temporary employment started – i.e. 1 September 1951. At the moment the custom is for this service to be terminated by six months' leave in England with full pay. Before long, however, it may be changed to a 3 months' leave at the end of 18 months, and the other 3 months at the end of the tour. In the second system, the Africa Conference would come in the middle of my first 3 months' leave, but in any case, I will, I hope, be able to get local leave to give me about 3 weeks' holiday at the Conference time.

The Africa Committee are delighted that I have this job, for it will enable me to pay off the debts still remaining; it will give me a career; it may lead to some position of importance in the future; it solves the two great problems of housing and immigration and gives good leave and reasonable salary.

But, beloved Guardian, it is a big change for one who, during the past 5 years, has been absolutely free to serve the Cause whenever and wherever he was needed. I like my work, it is useful, beneficial to the people and puts me in touch with the Africans.

But I did not come to Africa to make a career, make money or get good holidays, and if I am to keep the job, I shall have to tread very carefully during this probation period.

At the moment I am pursuing the policy of getting to know my job thoroughly during the day, and working until dark, in my house and garden, to, (a) make it presentable for when I am free to invite people and (b) to grow vegetables to cut down expenses. All this is enjoyable, but it is not directly teaching the Cause, and at the moment I have no idea where or when the 'openings' will come. I feel that so much of our two years has gone already and we have hardly made a start in Uganda.

I therefore humbly offer my sincere gratitude for your loving prayers, I feel very conscious at the moment that though I do not deserve them, I need them very much.

It was a great pleasure to learn from Dr Hakim that you are keeping well – I often wonder which I yearn for most, news of the Cause in Haifa, or news of its dearly loved Guardian.

With constant devotion and gratitude in His Service, Philip.

PS Papers from Egypt NSA enclosed also in separate envelopes.

It was so strange, living in Masaka and only in touch with the other pioneers by letter. It was impossible to 'consult' and I deeply regret that I did not keep copies of the letters we exchanged. Whenever I could, I drove down to Kampala – to have some meetings, to participate in the teaching work, and to straighten out some little point or other which seemed to have become a cause of difference. We appeared to look at things so differently and yet we had such a loving relationship when we met.

Among the many letters I had written from Kampala was one to the chairman of the Canadian National Spiritual Assembly, John Robarts (later a Hand of the Cause), and he replied on 14 September:[137]

Philip, my trusty companion of the Six Year Plan,

What a thrill it was to receive your letter! It arrived at Louhelen and I read parts of it out at one of the sessions and everybody was delighted to receive word direct from an African pioneer.

Re-reading this letter, as I have done more than once, takes me back to those very happy days when we used to give each other progress

[137] Unpublished letter (personal archives).

reports over the telephone at the close of each day's work. I was so pleased to learn of the marriage of Ursula and Mehdi, and of Isobel and Hassan. I only await news of your signing somebody up and wonder if it will be a nice little African girl.

Yes, we are becoming concerned over the fact that we have only eighteen months of our five years to go and there is so much to be done. Perhaps you will have to come to Canada after all. Many times at our NSA meetings I have drawn upon my experience in the British Isles and the methods I learned from you. We haven't a full-time Secretary and our Assemblies are so scattered – some of them being hundreds of miles from their nearest neighbour. The cost of visiting them is enormous. On the other hand, there is a wonderful spirit of dedication right across the land and we can feel the assistance that is being given to us everywhere. We know that mysterious forces are propelling this Plan forward and that somehow 1953 will come along and we shall rejoice that our task has been completed, but sometimes I think we are counting too much on those mysterious forces and not doing quite enough ourselves.

I can just see you consulting with those Persian believers you mention and you learning that virtue, Patience. It convinces me, as never before, that there is a great sense of humour operating through these mysterious forces too. If only I could drop in and see your group meeting and also to have a long chat with you. I am putting you on our Canadian Bahá'í News mailing list as a little gift in memory of old times, but only on condition that you write me again soon and tell me what goes on in Africa. I would also like to know how your mother is and what news you have of the Hofmans, the Ferrabys and in fact, all my friends of the Six Year Plan.

We shall be thinking of you often, Philip, and wishing you the greatest of success in your new field.

Sincerely yours, John A Robarts

It soon became essential for the pioneers to have their own home. Mr Banání was able to buy a house at 3 Kitante Road and the teaching work began in earnest. When we learned that the Africans went to work early every morning, immediately on getting up, it was arranged that those who were really interested would call in on the way to work. They would be provided with slices of bread and cups of sweet tea, and 'Alí would teach them the Faith. Sometimes we found that a promising 'contact' would not be coming near to Kitante Road, so 'Alí would go and do a 'milk-round' – i.e. collect in the car those who were interested and, after the tea and discussion, either take them back home or on to their work. The main emphasis of his teaching was how the Faith related to Christianity.

This illustrated an interesting phenomenon that we noted with all the African tribes we taught. If an African was educated at all, or had a name other than a tribal one, it meant that he/she had been educated at a mission school and the purpose of mission schools was to teach the Bible. This meant that the basic thinking of any educated African (except the minority who were brought up as Muslim) was based on the Bible. Even when they had later moved on to university, or had entered business or politics, and had virtually cut themselves off from their mission roots, the first questions they asked when introduced to the Faith were 'What does it say in the Bible about Hell?' (or the Resurrection, the birth of Jesus, the miracles, etc.) Or else they would ask, 'Is there anything about the Faith in the Bible?' We all became very proficient in relating our teaching to the King James Version of the Bible, which has been the basis for most translations. It was this warm hospitality and complete absence from racial prejudice that captured the hearts of the Africans (appealing to their emotions) and the satisfaction of the answers to their Biblical questions (appealing to their minds) which brought in their balanced acceptance of the Faith.

On 20 October we all met in Kampala to celebrate the Birth of the Báb, and for the first time we had a proper meeting in the home of a Muganda. The manuscript of the new African pamphlet in Luganda was read and the quality of the translation was favourably commented upon; the Words of Bahá'u'lláh had new meaning to the Baganda when heard in their own language.

In November, I had moved from Masaka to the Health Office, Jinja, in Eastern Uganda and across the Nile at Owen Falls. Here I found a large amount of work to do in malaria control, not only by dealing with mosquitoes breeding in hippo hoof prints on the golf course along the shores of Lake Victoria, but in large African housing areas such as the railway works, sugar plantations, and in ditches and fresh water drains. I developed a close relationship with the East African Fisheries Office, to which I delivered any new small fishes I discovered or snakes I captured in the swamps.

It was a 50-mile drive to Kampala and I used to go every weekend in those early days, for meetings and consultation. As when I lived in Masaka, I remained as secretary of the Kampala Group, with 'Alí as chairman.

In November, we received two publications that were very significant to us, and to me in particular.

One was the *Bahá'í Journal* N°. 93 (November 1951), which contained the news of the passing of Louis Gregory and his posthumous elevation as first Negro Hand of the Cause. We decided to hold a memorial for him on 24 November.

It also reported that at the same time as we had been holding our special 20 October meeting, a similar 'Africa Evening' had been held in Oxford attended by the first American pioneer for Africa, Mrs Ethel Stevens, just before she left for her goal town of Accra, Gold Coast.

In the same issue was a memorial paragraph for my mother and a 'Thank you' note from the Hainsworth family:[138]

> Lizzie Hainsworth
>
> With the joyful tidings of light I hail thee: rejoice'
>
> On the night of September 19th, Lizzie Fowler Hainsworth, aged 73, passed peacefully to the Abhá Kingdom after eight weeks in a Bradford Hospital. A Bahá'í since 1946, she found her greatest joy, according to her own testimony, in service to the Cause. Early in 1948, in her seventieth year, she volunteered to pioneer to Edinburgh but was sent by the NTC to Nottingham and the following year to Oxford. After the Six Year Plan she returned to strengthen the Bradford Community. Hers was the first pioneer offer for Africa at Convention, 1950, and in October of the same year our Guardian wrote to her son, Philip, 'She seems the true heroic pattern!'. During all this period of service to the Cause she loved she fought valiantly against a severe and trying illness with assurance from our beloved Guardian of his love and fervent prayers. Only a few days before her death a cable from him made her radiantly happy, 'appreciate self-sacrifice, praying your recovery'.
>
> To all who knew and loved her, her name will synonymise loving sympathy and understanding; warm hospitality, generosity and a sparkling sense of humour; deep courage and endurance. Immortal qualities and which characterised a saintly soul.
>
> The Hainsworth family and the Bradford Assembly wish to express their thanks to all those who sent letters of condolence at the passing of Mrs Hainsworth. Philip wishes to convey his special gratitude to those who have written or cabled to him in Africa messages of enquiry and condolence.

On the same page were some paragraphs from my letter from the Guardian of 30 August 1951 and a report of a letter from the private secretary of King George thanking the Bahá'ís for their prayers for his recovery.

[138] Unpublished (personal archives).

The other publication was *Africa News* N°. 1 (15 November), which was published by the Africa Committee and printed in Dar-es-Salaam. It contained the following item:

> Kampala
>
> Members of our group have made it a habit now to get up early at dawn every morning for joint prayers and chanting of Bahá'í verses. As we are still in the hotel, from fear of inconveniencing others we leave the hotel, and as we have no house, no place to go to, we simply climb in our car up this or that hill of this beautiful township.
>
> August 22 should be considered as the key date to the teaching activities in Uganda, when three African adults got together in the Resident's Lounge of the Imperial Hotel of Kampala, and where, together with Philip and Ali, Uganda had its first Bahá'í fireside meeting. The first two, after a following meeting, had to go to Fort Portal and Entebbe, where they are actually residing, but the third became the nucleus of future Bahá'í African contacts. The circle of interested contacts gradually grew in Kampala. It now arrived to about twelve Africans; this number includes two ladies as well. Every morning from 7.30 to 8.30 am at the house of one of our contacts, we have a short class at which very gradually and slowly the Bahá'í history, teachings and proofs are being given by Ali. Of these twelve contacts only four of them attend and show a deeper interest. Three times a week we have an afternoon fireside at the home of the same African who is offering his house in the mornings. In this meeting the ladies also join.
>
> To extend the circle of our contacts, members of our group have become members in two local societies who have no race discrimination and had general welfare and educational purposes.
>
> Philip Hainsworth's job as Sanitary Overseer took him for a time to Masaka and he is now in Jinja.
>
> For the memorial meeting for Louis Gregory in Kampala on 24 November we had invited Marguerite Welby (Preston) to join us for that occasion and to consult on how we may work together.

KAMPALA'S FIRST PUBLIC PROCLAMATION

The first time the Faith was publicly proclaimed in Uganda was actually by a non-Bahá'í, done on a most auspicious occasion on the first day of December. The *Bahá'í Journal* report some four months later tells the story:

> On Saturday evening, 1 December, one our contacts, who is now in

charge of the newly established all-Uganda African Social Centre in Kampala, gave a twenty-minute talk about the Bahá'í Faith and its Teachings to an audience of some 300 Africans of various tribes, including two African Kings, the Kabaka of Buganda and the Mukama of Batoro.

At the close of the programme conducted as part of the Young Christian Conference, during a period when the floor was free for anyone to say anything thought to be of interest to the audience, he presented the Faith quite objectively and without adding his own personal feelings.

ANNOUNCEMENT OF FIRST INTERCONTINENTAL AFRICA CONFERENCE 1953

On 30 November, the Guardian announced to all National Spiritual Assemblies in the Bahá'í world 'momentous' plans for 'Great Jubilee commemorating the termination Bábí Dispensation and the birth Bahá'u'lláh's Revelation Síyáh Chál'. These included the convocation of four intercontinental Bahá'í teaching conferences, beginning with the Africa Conference in Spring 1953. On 24 December he released his most staggering message to date, an announcement of six major developments followed by the appointment, for the first time in the lifetime of the individual believers concerned, of twelve living Hands of the Cause: three each in the Holy Land, Europe, Persia and America. George Townshend, Herman Grossman and Ugo Giachery were the three for Europe, and all nine outside the Holy Land were urged to attend all four of the intercontinental conferences.

George Townshend and I had exchanged sporadic correspondence since I first went to Northern Ireland in 1940, and we had become closely associated during the time in 1947 when I helped him move into Dublin, and subsequently at the British summer school. When he was appointed as a Hand of the Cause, I cabled him my congratulations. He replied in typical vein on 10 January 1952:[139]

> *Dear Philip,*
>
> How good of you to send me a cable of congratulation all the way from Africa: and such a warm enheartening cable, too. It is very

[139] Unpublished letter (personal archives).

much appreciated. I feel still overawed by the news and the change of prospect; it penetrates very deep.

Last night at a meeting of the Bahá'í Community here I heard the full glad tidings of visits next year to the Big Conference. So I may before long meet you in Africa and see your new moustache and shake hands with you under a palm tree. Cheerio.

Ever, George Townshend.

On 26 December, the Guardian announced that pilgrimage was to recommence and 'Alí and I decided to put as much pressure on Mr Banání as possible to be among the first to go. He agreed and we worked out a plan. We were aware that the Guardian would visit the Shrine of the Báb on certain days at about 4.00 p.m. and we asked Mr Banání if he would tell the Guardian of the growth of the Faith, of our contacts and that we were now seven in Kampala.

A third African, a Muganda, Peter Musoke, had expressed his acceptance so we needed only one other declaration to be able to be sure of an Assembly by Ridván. Mr Banání was asked to say that on the Sunday afternoon after his arrival we would arrange a meeting of all our contacts and beseech the Guardian to say special prayers for Kampala on that occasion, so we could feel the spiritual link.

In the meantime, we were all thinking of the mammoth task which would face us in little more than a year – the organisation of the first 'All-Africa Teaching Conference'. As early as January 1951 the Guardian had unfolded some plans for a conference to be held in Africa. In April he had stated it should be held 'during the Centenary of the Birth of Bahá'u'lláh's prophetic mission' (1953) and in August further advised that it should be held between January and March of that year. By the end of November we had learned from the Africa Committee that:[140]

- The conference would be held in Uganda;
- The British National Spiritual Assembly was the 'consultative body for all African territories and for the planning of the Africa Conference';
- The ideal would be to have at least one Bahá'í from every territory in Africa which had been opened to the Faith attend the conference. The number of territories even at that time stood at 25.

Indeed 1951 had been a most eventful year, ranking perhaps with 1946 as the two most significant in my life. Looking back it is almost frightening to see how inter-related some events had become and helped to weave the pattern of my life.

If my father had not been an invalid and I had not had a very sickly

[140] Unpublished notes (personal archives).

childhood, I might never had had the great yearning to 'be different', to be 'better than the other chap' in my early life.

Had I not developed this competitive side to my ego I would not have gained so many badges as a Scout.

And had I not been such an ambitious Scout, I would not have gone to the Coronation of King George and would not have had the glimpse of the universality of Scouting nor have been so prepared to accept the Faith so readily a year later.

And of course had I not been a Bahá'í I would not have gone into the RAMC or had the ambition to become a commissioned officer.

If I had not I not gone to Kenya in the RAMC I might never have had the chance to go to Uganda.

If I had not come home from Italy for a commission, I would not have become acquainted with the Six Year Plan and opened Norwich to the Faith, nor would I have had the experience of going to Egypt and Kenya and later to visit Haifa and meet the Guardian.

The year 1952 started wonderfully with the letter from the Guardian dated 1 January addressed to the Kampala Bahá'í Group, as follows:[141]

> *Dear Bahá'í Friends,*
>
> Your letter of 3 December with report for November enclosed, reached the beloved Guardian; as well as the photograph showing the participants in the Louis Gregory Memorial Meeting; and he has instructed me to write you on his behalf.
>
> Your news thrilled him; and when he saw the faces of the two first African Bahá'ís resulting from this great African Teaching Campaign, his heart was filled with joy and gratitude.
>
> The privilege you are all having of serving there is very great; however so meritorious is this service in the eyes of Bahá'u'lláh, that His bounties and blessings seem to be visibly showering upon you all.
>
> The Guardian hopes that the Africa Conference will be an outstanding success; and that by that time there will be many negro and white African Bahá'ís attending it as of right, on their own soil.
>
> Please tell the new believers that the Guardian extends his personal welcome to them into the service of the Faith of Bahá'u'lláh, and assures them that he is praying that they may render this Cause, which has been brought to them by loving and devoted hearts from overseas, great services; and that they may be the means of

[141] Ibid.

attracting many more of their countrymen to this Message, which can alone ensure the peace and brotherhood of mankind.

The Guardian's thoughts and prayers are often with you all, and he sends you all his loving greetings.

With Bahá'í love, R. Rabbání

In the handwriting of the Guardian:

May the almighty whose Faith you are promoting with such zeal, devotion and exemplary perseverance and courage, reward you abundantly for your truly meritorious, historic and valuable labours, guide and sustain you continually, and aid you to consolidate your achievements and win great and memorable victories in the service of his glorious Faith. Your true and grateful brother, Shoghi.

Quite early in 1952, there were several highly significant events: the first was that Mr and Mrs Banání went on pilgrimage and took with them a letter from the Kampala Group dated 27 January to which the Guardian replied on 6 February:[142]

Dear Bahá'í Friends,

Your letter of January 27 was received by the beloved Guardian, through the kindness of Mr and Mrs Banání.

He was most touched to receive your contribution for the Shrine of the Báb, a receipt for which I am enclosing.

It has brought the greatest joy to his heart to have these dear believers here; and he is prolonging their pilgrimage in order to discuss thoroughly with them the work being done in Uganda, and indeed, in Africa, a work to which he attaches the greatest possible importance.

A source of deep joy and satisfaction was the news of the declaration of Mr Crispin Kajubi and Mr Fred Bigabwa. He was so pleased to have photographs of them, and he has placed them in the Mansion, as the first Bahá'ís of Uganda, representative of the tribes of that country.

The Guardian feels sure that, with wisdom, dedication, tact and prayer, your Group will be able to spread this Divine Message there to peoples of all races; and lay, not only a lasting foundation for your own community, but prepare the way for the great All-Africa Conference, which will be held there in 1953, and to which the Bahá'ís all over the world are already looking forward with such eagerness.

[142] Unpublished letter (personal archives).

He assures you that you are all remembered in his loving prayers in the Holy Shrines, and that your services to the Faith are deeply appreciated.

With warm Bahá'í love, R. Rabbání.

In the handwriting of the Guardian:

May the spirit of Bahá'u'lláh powerfully sustain you in your high endeavours, aid you to extend rapidly the range of your historic and meritorious accomplishments, and lend a tremendous impetus to the onward march of our beloved Faith in that vast and promising continent.

Your true brother, Shoghi.

THE GUARDIAN ENCOURAGES MY SERVICE IN THE GOVERNMENT

On 6 February, the Guardian wrote to me through his secretary:[143]

Dear Bahá'í Brother,

Your letter of January 23rd has reached the beloved Guardian; and he has instructed me to answer you on his behalf.

He feels that you should by all means continue your government service, unless some better field of activity, with even more financial security attached, should turn up. As long as the Government does not object to your Bahá'í activities in your spare time, it would seem it adds prestige to the Cause, to have an active member of it an official.

He considers that you have no grounds whatsoever for feeling discouraged or discontented with yourself. He personally is well pleased with you and what you have accomplished, and confident of what you will accomplish in the days to come. He urges you to go forward with a happy and reassured heart; and he very deeply appreciates your spirit and your services.

With warm Bahá'í love, R. Rabbání

PS. The Egyptian papers were received.

In the Guardian's handwriting:

May the Beloved, whose Cause you serve with such perseverance, ability and devotion, abundantly reward you for your highly

[143] Unpublished letter (personal archives).

meritorious labours and aid you to enrich continually the record of your splendid services,

Your true and grateful brother, Shoghi.

The British National Spiritual Assembly had advised the Guardian that on 16 February Marguerite Preston and her son Adrian, on leaving Britain by aeroplane, 'full of plans for Bahá'í activity in Kenya', had both been killed in an air crash, to which he had replied: 'Grieve tragic loss praying fervently behalf departed.'[144]

The National Spiritual Assembly had then asked the Guardian that as the death of Marguerite had left only pioneer Ted Cardell in Kenya, should they now build up Kenya (though it was not a part of the Two Year Plan) and should they encourage efforts to form assemblies in Kampala and Dar-es-Salaam. On 29 February, he replied: 'Advise build up Kenya. Urge formation Assemblies Kampala, Dar-es-Salaam.'[145]

MÚSÁ BANÁNÍ APPOINTED HAND OF THE CAUSE OF GOD

While on pilgrimage, Mr Banání was made a Hand of the Cause. This was announced to the Bahá'í world on 29 February 1952 with the news that he must purchase a building that would be used as a local Ḥaẓíratu'l-Quds by the first local Assembly to be formed in the heart of Africa and would 'be regarded nucleus national administrative headquarters Faith destined arise morrow formation National Spiritual Assembly Central, Eastern territories African Continent.'

In the March edition of the *Bahá'í Journal*, which contained all this news, we found an illuminating letter from the Guardian to the Canadian National Spiritual Assembly 30 October 1951 which said:[146]

> In order to establish this (the establishment of new assemblies and groups), the entire Canadian Community will have to rise to a new level of activity, conscience and sacrifice, just as did the British Bahá'í Community during their Six-Year Plan. Their success is perhaps one of the most remarkable ever achieved in the Bahá'í world because they were few in number, run down in health from

[144] Effendi, S. (1981). The Unfolding Destiny of the British Bahá'í Community: The Messages from the Guardian of the Bahá'í Faith to the Bahá'ís of the British Isles. London, Bahá'í Publishing Trust., p. 277.
[145] Ibid.
[146] Effendi, S. (1965). Messages to Canada (1923-1957). Toronto, Ont., National Spiritual Assembly of the Bahá'ís of Canada., p. 24.

> the long years of suffering during the war, and poor in financial resources. Their determination, dedication and moral stamina, however, carried them through, and Bahá'u'lláh gave them the victory. He will give the same victory to everyone who shows the same characteristics. Success breeds success, and the same Community, now rightfully proud and conscious of its importance, is carrying on its African work in a brilliant manner. The Canadian Bahá'ís, more prosperous, less restricted, and equally capable, can accomplish just as much if they unitedly determine so to do.

It came as a great surprise to us and made us all feel humbly grateful to learn from a cable from the Guardian to the National Assembly that our efforts in Uganda were actually helping the home front.[147] The Guardian had also sent a soul-stirring appeal to all members of the British Bahá'í community dated 12 March 1952:[148]

> Owing rapid progress Africa Campaign, advise concentration consolidation home front. Appeal united, renewed, vigorous efforts. Praying fervently success.

ENOCH OLINGA ACCEPTS THE FAITH

The meeting in Kampala called as planned with Mr Banání before he went on pilgrimage, had what transpired to be an outstanding result, though at the time it was not considered particularly significant. The event is etched very clearly in my mind, though the 'official history' of the Faith has recorded a slightly different sequence of events. I must record it as my memory serves me for it is so vivid. My memory appears to have been later confirmed in a letter to me from Enoch Olinga in September 1954 in which he refers to my 'spiritual grandchildren'.

Not as many people turned up at the meeting in February as had been expected. 'Alí was sitting in his usual place for those meetings – facing the windows on the outside wall of the sitting room. I was near the door to let in late-comers and Violette was serving tea as people came in. 'Alí was giving the talk and, as previously planned, I was ready to take anyone who indicated their acceptance of Bahá'u'lláh to a small bedroom to introduce him or her to the Will and Testament of 'Abdu'l-Bahá. We were very conscious that as we had two registered African Bahá'ís and another, Peter Musoke, had indicated his acceptance, we only needed one more

[147] Unpublished cable (personal archives).
[148] Effendi, S. (1981). The Unfolding Destiny of the British Bahá'í Community: The Messages from the Guardian of the Bahá'í Faith to the Bahá'ís of the British Isles. London, Bahá'í Publishing Trust., p. 278.

declaration to guarantee an assembly for Ridván. When one young man indicated his interest, I took him to the other room and explained the significance of the Covenant and the Guardian, and went over with him the outline of the Will and Testament. He loved what he heard and assured me that he would express in writing his 'declaration of acceptance of Bahá'u'lláh'. My memory is that the letter was brought in during the following week, when I was in Jinja and that my explanation of the Covenant was in the late afternoon of the special meeting. 'Alí recalls that my explanation of the Covenant did not take place at the meeting called to synchronise with the Guardian's prayers for us with Mr Banání, but on the occasion of his bringing the letter (at which time I was in Jinja). The man was Enoch Olinga, later to be Knight of Bahá'u'lláh for the British Cameroon, to be later designated on 15 October 1953 as Abúl Futuh, (Father of Victories) and appointed in October 1957 as the second negro Hand of the Cause.

FORMATION OF KAMPALA ASSEMBLY

The Ḥaẓíratu'l-Quds we purchased at a cost of £5,500 was located at 4 Kagera Road, about ten minutes walk from the Bananís' house (3 Kitante Road). We decided to ask our new pioneers from America, Rex and Mary Collison, to be its first caretakers when they arrived in April.

Although Peter Musoke had expressed his acceptance of the Faith long before Ridván, he seemed to have little understanding of the significance of the occasion and was working out of Kampala on the day of the formation of the Assembly. We had to rush out in the car to find him for that important occasion.

From that meeting on 21 April the new Assembly sent a message to the British Convention:[149]

> From Kampala, Uganda, the scene of the forthcoming first inter-continental Conference, the residence of the Hand of the Cause for Africa, the town already witnessing the formation of one of the first two African Spiritual Assemblies under the Two Year Plan, the site of the first Ḥaẓíratu'l-Quds in the heart of this Continent, and the future seat of the contemplated Central and East African National Assembly, we, a handful of Bahá'u'lláh's servants, unworthily instrumental in the establishment of the first Bahá'í administrative cornerstone in Uganda, wish to send through your NSA and each one of you, to all the rank and file of

[149] Unpublished letter (personal archives).

> believers in that land, our infinite gratitude for all the co-operation and contributions they have been making in these passing months, without which what has been achieved could hardly have been accomplished, towards the speedy development of the African project.
>
> May we request you all to have special prayers for the successful discharge of our tasks, the consolidation and extension of our work, and the winning of the good pleasure of our dearly-beloved, our cherished and revered Guardian's heart.
>
> *With loving Ridván greetings, Músá Banání, Samiheh Banání, Fred Bigabwa, Enoch Olinga, Crispin Kajubi, Violette Nakhjavání, Philip Hainsworth, Peter Musoke, 'Alí Nakhjavání.*

Then a cable was sent from the British Convention to the Guardian:[150]

> Convention expresses gratitude, pledges humble loyalty beloved Guardian, seeks prayers that British Bahá'í community, in dealing with tasks confronting it, especially Africa, Consolidation, may with ever deepening unity, detachment, go forward under his indomitable leadership.

And on 29 April the Guardian replied:[151]

> Deeply touched pledge British Bahá'í Community. Congratulate valiant members marvellous progress Africa Campaign, consolidation home front. Owing attainment objectives, advise concentrate Nairobi, aiming establishment Assembly leading, promising centre British territories heart East African Continent. Fervently praying still greater victories.
>
> *Loving Gratitude.*

So Nairobi became a subsidiary goal of the Two Year Plan, bringing together all the East African territories of Kenya, Tanganyika, Uganda and Zanzibar.

MY CONFIRMATION AS A UGANDA CIVIL SERVANT

I was living a very full and exciting life in those early days in Jinja. Not only was my work most interesting, but the close contact I needed to

[150] Ibid.

[151] Effendi, S. (1981). The Unfolding Destiny of the British Bahá'í Community: The Messages from the Guardian of the Bahá'í Faith to the Bahá'ís of the British Isles. London, Bahá'í Publishing Trust., p. 279.

maintain with the mainstream Bahá'í activity in Kampala initially took me there every weekend. There we were kept informed of other developments in East Africa and even further afield, as more pioneers were responding to the pioneer call for Africa. Things were moving so fast in Kampala that I occasionally felt left out and had to get there to catch up and do my work as secretary.

It must have been in late 1951 that I drafted a brief letter to the Guardian. The rough draft reads:[152]

> *Beloved Guardian,*
>
> Many things have happened since my letter to you of 28 September written from Masaka. Due largely to the wonderful, tireless and devoted efforts of 'Alí Nakhjavání and the shining example and hospitality of the dear Banánís, the work has made progress and the pattern of teaching seems to be clearer. Doubts about the wisdom of Government service as indicated in my letter of 28 September are still with me however, and my contract is still pending. So far the Head of my Department is highly satisfied with my work, and permission has been granted to take part in the Conference and to take the Bahá'í Holy Days from my local leave. Dearly loved Guardian, so many of my weaknesses and imperfections have become manifest in this pioneering venture, that all I feel I can do now is to humbly beg your prayers that I may become worthy of the privilege of serving in this country and assure you of my loving devotion in His name.

Having completed my six months' trial with the Uganda Protectorate, I was confirmed in my appointment, and on 19 March 1952 I signed an agreement which converted my local terms of employment to a full local contract with HM Government, with home leave entitlement.

I worked quite hard in my job as sanitary overseer. The man from whom I had taken over the position was an old boy who had been in the country for many years and had actually retired when I got there. The job was mainly malaria and yellow fever control, but there were no guidelines and I had to make the job myself. I initiated several new procedures and began to know all my many workers and their various foibles. The government's senior medical entomologist came to Jinja to establish a system for pouring DDT into the River Nile, at its source in the dam at Owen Falls, and I helped. The dam was in the process of construction and it shortened the Nile by half a mile and lengthened Lake Victoria.

[152] Unpublished letter (personal archives).

My work was duly appreciated, and on 28 August 1952, the Director of Medical Services wrote me a personal letter of appreciation of my work. About that same time, we had a visit to the dam from Princess Elizabeth, and I was very busy trying to ensure that the various biting insects were under control so she would not be bitten. Soon after her visit, her father died and she became Queen.

The senior entomologist of the Uganda Medical Department, George R Barnley, visited Jinja to see what arrangements could be made to install massive drains of special oil on the Owen Falls Dam which was in the course of construction.

The plan was that once the dam was closed and the waters rose, George and his assistant, Mike Prentice, would obtain the figures for cubic metres of water per minute that flowed through one sluice when opened. Into that sluice they would run a sufficient number of gallons of the oil, mixed with an emulsion of DDT, to give, over a period of half an hour, a one part in ten million dose of the DDT – this being sufficient to kill all the larval stages of simulium damnosum breeding in the 60 miles of rapids of the River Nile from its source at the Owen Falls Dam to the Murchison Falls in the northern Game Park. S. Damnosum (called 'mbwa' locally) was a small black gnat, a notorious biting fly that carried the disease onchocerciasis (river blindness) and was breeding in all the 'white water' of these rapids. The operation was highly successful and the 'dosing' of the Nile was carried out at fixed intervals for about a year. George won an OBE for this work and I received a letter of commendation for the help I had given.

George had, during his visits to Jinja, seen the work I had done in the field of malaria control and was so impressed that he began to press the government for me to be transferred from the Health Department to his Vector Control Division in Kampala.

DEVELOPMENTS CENTRAL & EAST AFRICA

The following significant developments took place during the months following the election of the Assembly, though they are not recorded necessarily in chronological order.

I sent some photographs I had taken to the Guardian and he wrote on 24 May 1954:[153]

Dear Bahá'í Brother:

The beloved Guardian thanks you for the photographs you sent in

[153] Unpublished letter (personal archives).

your letter of March 25th, which he was very interested to see.

He was delighted with the progress of the work in Uganda, and he hopes that, now the Africa Committee is going to give more support to Kenya, and to dear Ted Cardell, we will find that he is getting on as well in Nairobi as you are in Kampala! Your work and you yourself, are very dear to his heart.

With loving greetings, R. Rabbání

In the Guardian's handwriting:

May the Beloved whose Cause you are serving with such a devotion, zeal, ability and perseverance, reward, bless, and sustain you and enable you to continually enrich the record of your splendid services to His Faith,
Your true and grateful brother, Shoghi

Several historical photographs were taken during April, one of the new Kampala Assembly, one of the pioneers and one of the four African members. The Guardian placed them in the Mansion of Bahjí. In fact, these photographs have an honoured place by the head of the bed where he slept when staying in Bahjí.

PASSING OF HAND OF THE CAUSE OF GOD SUTHERLAND MAXWELL

I had written to Rúḥíyyih Khánum on learning of the passing of her father, Sutherland Maxwell, and received her reply on 10 May 1952:[154]

Dear Philip,

Thank you so much for your lovely letter of April 21st – it was much appreciated, I assure you, not only because of your understanding, but because I like hearing from you.

I naturally will be missing Daddy, and all the philosophising in the world does not take away the ache of separation. However, I am deeply grateful to God for all his mercies to my family; and this far offsets the feeling of loneliness.

It is lovely to have Ted here, only I wish you were with him. You are very close to us Philip, and I don't see any reason why you shouldn't come on another pilgrimage – what's the matter with you? We are so happy over the progress being made in Africa. It just seems to me like a vision, and I can barely realise it is a fact.

[154] Ibid.

Please give my warmest love to the Banánís, and to all the friends there. I was so happy to hear the Vice Chairman is a Ugandan – that's a step in the right direction.

As you can imagine, both the beloved Guardian and I are tired from a long hard winter.

I must go now, as I have a lot to do.

With warm Bahá'í love, Rúḥíyyih

IMPACT ENOCH OLINGA'S DECLARATION

The acceptance of the Faith by Enoch had caused a great stir among his contemporaries. He was a translator and broadcaster for Uganda Radio as an employee of the Uganda Education Department and was well known as 'one of the boys' – drinking, gambling and often falling foul of his immediate superior in the Department, a British Overseas Civil Servant who was at the same time a leading member of an evangelistic Roman Catholic group. When he saw Enoch change his lifestyle following his acceptance of the Faith, he commissioned one of Enoch's colleagues, a solid Roman Catholic Munyoro, Peter Mutabazi, to get to work on Enoch and bring him over to Catholicism. Peter tried – he attended meetings with Enoch and before long he had to report to his mentor that not only had he failed to change Enoch's conviction, but he too had become a Bahá'í – the first Munyoro Bahá'í. Peter later pioneered to Tanganyika, became an Auxiliary Board Member and after many years of service, retired to his native Bunyoro where, although now well known as a Bahá'í, he took up employment with the Roman Catholic organisations in Hoima. He passed away in hospital in 1999.

OTHER SUCCESSES

While we felt that everything was happening around us in Kampala, news was received via the Africa Committee of other successes.

Eric Manton was a dear friend who had had a remarkable life as a hard, dedicated soldier. He had been left for dead on the battlefield in North Africa in 1943, after his unit had been almost wiped out through the defection of one of his men, but had been rescued just in time and spent about two years in hospitals. Throughout that time he had been motivated by the desire to seek out the defector and kill him. Then, in 1946 he accepted the Faith in Northampton, became a most gentle and devoted believer and had pioneered to be on the first Spiritual Assembly in

Edinburgh in 1948. With his young son, Terry, he pioneered to open Northern Rhodesia for the Faith.

Ethel Stephens was beginning to have a hearing in Kumasi on the Gold Coast and William Foster, the first pioneer from the USA to Liberia, had settled in his goal area. He had located one existing believer and there had been a new believer, making a group of three. Abbás and Shomais Afnán married in England in August 1951, had received special permission from the Guardian for Abbás to return to Persia while Shomais settled in the goal area of Ethiopia in March 1952.

Ted Cardell, pioneer to Nairobi and an isolated believer in Kenya since the death of Marguerite Preston, had been on pilgrimage towards the end of April and had been asked by the Guardian to extend his stay to make a wide photographic record of all the Holy Places. Ted had been working as a photographer for major newspaper, the East African Standard, and had established a high reputation for his photography, particularly with some unusually good pictures of the Mau Mau activities and atrocities.

NEW UGANDA BAHÁ'ÍS

By the end of May, due to the continued development of the teaching work of 'Alí, reinforced by the zeal of the African believers and the way in which the Collisons in the new Ḥaẓíratu'l-Quds began to use it for teaching, particularly in the early mornings, there were 12 believers.

One of these new believers, Max Kanyerezi, had an interesting background. His father was a very old man and he had been the seventh Muganda to be baptised a Christian (circa 1891). Max was his seventh son and became the seventh African in Uganda to accept the Faith. Max became a member of the local Spiritual Assembly of Kampala, was on the first Regional Spiritual Assembly of Central and East Africa, was appointed an Auxiliary Board Member and died in Kampala in July 1991.

Enoch Olinga and his wife, a Mugisu from near Mbale, went on annual leave to Enoch's home village in Kobwin, Teso District. There a large number of people responded warmly to the great news of a religion that had no prejudice and taught about the return of Christ. He came back to Kapala and immediately 'Alí returned with him and eventually spent several weeks there. It was also agreed that I would meet them in Mbale (the main township of the Bagisu). 'Alí immediately captivated the hearts of the Africans with his loving embrace, his sympathetic teaching and the way in which he went into their homes, ate and slept in their homes – something no white man had done before. In Teso they began to act out a play where someone represented the visiting District Commissioner or the local missionary or head of the Church of Uganda, and people had to go and wait and wait for an audience and then stand up for a brief meeting with the very superior white man. Then the scene changed and in came 'Alí, with arms outstretched and his 'Alláh'u'Abhá' and immediately sat down with them and ate their food. It should be noted that in Teso the staple diet was 'atap' – made from millet seed, ground to a coarse flour with a large, locally made type of mortar and pestle, and then made into a thick moist mass with boiling water and eaten with the hands from a common serving pot or plate. A lump is pulled off, moulded in the hand into a ball, hollowed out with the thumb and then dipped into the broth or 'mchusi' made usually from boiled chicken or groundnuts. It was an acquired taste and the atap had a consistency which, as it was chewed, appeared to be full of grit: it was widely eaten throughout the Teso District.

In the Bantu areas, Buganda, Bugisu, Busoga, Bunyoro and Toro, etc., the staple diet was a cooking banana (mutoke), while in the Northern Province, among the Lango and Acholi, it was a type of thick porridge made from maize meal (posho). Frequently meat was stewed instead of chicken. 'Alí suffered quite badly at times from this unusual diet. Though I was able to tolerate it more easily, I was not able to be away from my work, so did not spend as long on these trips as 'Alí did.

My first trips were among the Bagisu with Tito Wanantsusi, Mutambo, a veterinary assistant, and Javan Gutosi, as well as travelling to the Teso area of Palissa with Kolonerio Oule. Later I went to the Teso villages of Tilling and Kobwin in the Ngora District of Teso.

By October, we were able to report that there were 24 believers in Kampala, where some of the wives of Bahá'ís had enrolled: eight in Mbale, 67 in Teso and four in my own town of Jinja, where we established an independent group.

This led to the Africa Committee appointing a Uganda Teaching Committee of 'Alí, myself, Rex and Mary Collison and two Africans.

In the meantime, plans for the Kampala Conference of 1953 were difficult to finalise for a number of reasons.

Consultations were taking place in London between National Spiritual Assembly and Africa Committee representatives and officials in the Foreign Office, not merely regarding the holding of a conference at all (as the Mau Mau troubles were at their height in Kenya) but also about the granting of visas for the visitors expected to attend. Similar consultations were being held in Kampala with the authorities, as it was considered that Makerere University was the only site where the expected members could be accommodated for a Conference. On 25 May the Africa Committee cabled the Guardian: [155]

> Unable obtain accommodation Makerere attitude authorities doubtful. Sending report. Urgently beg prayers.

In his reply to the Committee on 4 June, he wrote through his secretary:[156]

> He was very sorry to hear from the recent cable sent him that there is a question about the Kampala Conference and whether arrangements can be made for it to be held there. Undoubtedly there is an increasingly negative attitude toward our work growing up amongst the officials, probably due to the lack of racial discrimination they are coming to realise is one of our fundamental teachings, a teaching carried into action, and not merely a pious hope.... He wishes you to keep him informed about this and the progress being made....
>
> The Guardian is very anxious that, during the coming months, the Africa Committee and the Bahá'ís should concentrate their efforts on establishing an Assembly in Kenya, and hopes that you will be able to direct pioneers to Nairobi as soon as possible.
>
> The Guardian considers that it is premature at this time to answer your question about consultation at the Africa Conference, between people from territories which will come under the jurisdiction of the East and Central Africa National Spiritual Assembly. He is so overworked and tired at the moment that he has not been able to go into the entire question of the Inter-Continental Conferences, the countries which will come under the jurisdiction of various future national bodies, etc. He hopes that he will be able, during the coming months, to do this, and if he feels it wise, will advise you by cable concerning a consultation such as you suggest, at the Conference...

In the meantime, the Africa Committee's report of 27 May was sent:[157]

> We have had a great disappointment regarding the expected booking of Makerere College. The Principal when approached in February was favourable to the idea, and throughout has remained friendly and helpful, a price had been quoted and practical arrangements discussed. The Principal said however that he could

[155] Unpublished cable (personal archives).
[156] Effendi, S. (1981). The Unfolding Destiny of the British Bahá'í Community: The Messages from the Guardian of the Bahá'í Faith to the Bahá'ís of the British Isles. London, Bahá'í Publishing Trust., p. 281.
[157] Unpublished letter (personal archives).

not finally confirm the booking until he knew that the Government would permit the Conference, but he actively helped to try and get an answer from them, and even when, after an interview which led him to say that he understood that the Government was 'not very keen on the Conference', he was told that he would probably have to accommodate a Government Conference early in 1953, he planned to manage our Conference too. This was the situation right up to May 20th. On May 21st 'Alí Nakhjavání, secretary of the Uganda Conference Sub-committee, received a letter from him cancelling the arrangement for accommodation for the reason that the domestic supervisor might be leaving.

Meanwhile the Government has taken a long time to come to a decision. The Uganda sub-committee approached the Principal Immigration Officer in January, but have heard nothing from him. In February the Colonial Office, following our interview there, wrote to the Uganda Government about the Faith, mentioning the Conference which the Colonial Office seemed to regard quite favourably. After the Principal of Makerere College had contacted the Chief Secretary's office several times, contact was made on behalf of the sub-committee and finally an answer was received which we do not consider very encouraging. We enclose a copy. It is notable that the holding of the Conference is made dependent on obtaining accommodation, for which arrangements very soon broke down. We had already written to the Chief Secretary in the name of the NSA trying to get a definite reply and have now written again asking for clarification of their letter, since it implies that the obtaining of visitors' visas will not be quick, which is contrary to the usual practice by which simple visitors' visas are given without much formality either by the East African High Commissioner here or by British Consuls abroad.

We felt that the situation is critical and that there may possibly have been some misunderstanding on the part of the Government either about the Faith or about the Conference. In an effort to achieve some change of attitude, John Ferraby, who was at school with the Governor of Uganda, has written a personal letter to him, of which we enclose a copy. We earnestly beg your continued prayers that the situation may alter and the difficulties be removed....

There followed a letter from the Guardian dated 12 June 1952 to the

British National Assembly from which a few passages are quoted:[158]

> He considers it advisable that all believers living in Africa, even those who did so before the beginning of the Plan, should have some form of credentials....
>
> Your suggestion of inaugurating the Holy Year next Ridván and continuing on until October 1953, with celebrations, meets with his approval.
>
> As regards the Africa campaign: this enterprise, so enthusiastically carried on, had been throughout this past year the greatest source of joy to the heart of the beloved Guardian. The visits of the dear Banánís and Ted Cardell, the news they brought and the general progress of the work, have made Africa seem right next door to Haifa! The formation of the Dar-es-Salaam and Kampala Assemblies was also a great satisfaction to him.
>
> He urges you to now concentrate on an Assembly for Nairobi by next April. This should not be too difficult of achievement in view of the devoted efforts of Mr Cardell and the pioneers eager to go there....
>
> The Guardian feels that although the Conference planned for Kampala is primarily a Conference and in no sense a Convention (having no delegates), there is no objection to the representatives of various NSAs who may attend meeting in separate sessions for more special and concentrated consultation. Any Hands of the Cause attending could also be included in this private discussion.
>
> He feels that now more than ever the British friends have every reason to feel proud of their accomplishments and happy over the very evident bestowals from the Throne on High. They have found, after half a century of development, scope for their abilities, and a field large enough to distinguish themselves in, and they are certainly taking advantage of it, much to the delight of the Guardian and their fellow Bahá'ís.
>
> You may be sure that he remembers you all in his prayers, and also the body of the faithful believers you serve to such good purpose....

In the 1,700-word passage that followed in the Guardian's handwriting, he not only referred to the outstanding work of the British believers but also indicated that what had been done in the Africa Campaign had made

[158] Effendi, S. (1981). The Unfolding Destiny of the British Bahá'í Community: The Messages from the Guardian of the Bahá'í Faith to the Bahá'ís of the British Isles. London, Bahá'í Publishing Trust., p. 283.

possible his change in plan, from a Third American Seven Year Plan to a World Crusade:[159]

> It may well be regarded as a befitting prelude to the official participation of this community in the Ten Year world-encircling Crusade, designed to signalise the celebration of the hundredth anniversary of the birth of Bahá'u'lláh's mission....

On 27 June, the Africa Committee reported to the Guardian that they had encouraged our Kampala Conference Committee ('Alí and myself) to try every possible line of action and asked if the Guardian would recommend they investigate other places such as Nairobi, Dar-es-Salaam or Livingstone.

The Guardian cabled:[160]

> Exert utmost effort hold Conference Kampala. If impossible approve Nairobi.

We in Kampala had been able to make a large number of reservations in Kampala hotels and we did this on faith, as the major objection from the government seemed to hinge upon accommodation. We had the brilliant idea of hiring a huge marquee that we could erect in the grounds of the house at 4 Kagera Road. This was reported to the Guardian in the Africa Committee's letter of 4 August, which also told of the first stage of the teaching work in Teso.

MY 'RELATIONSHIP' WITH NYASALAND (MALAWI)

On 14 August the Committee in London wrote to the Guardian that they had written to all participating National Spiritual Assemblies saying that their representatives should start applying for visas for the whole of East Africa for February 1953, and also advised him of the settlement of the first Dar-es-Salaam African Bahá'í – Dudley Smith Kutendele, who settled in Nyasaland with his family. Due to the hostility felt by the committee from the Colonial Office in regard to Nyasaland, the committee had told Dudley to teach only by example among his own circle of friends and to await the eventual arrival of pioneers when the official attitude had changed. It was only in 1992, exactly 40 years later, that I heard that Dudley had followed these instructions completely; he had lived and died without ever being in an active community, but had been known and respected as 'Mr. Bahá'í'. In 1992, I met in England some travelling dancers from Malawi who said

[159] Ibid., p. 283
[160] Unpublished cable (personal archives).

they had just come across the story of Dudley: he had become an isolated believer and had eventually died. They said that I was therefore the 'spiritual father' of the African Bahá'ís of Malawi!

On September 19, 1952, the Guardian replied to a letter from the Kampala Assembly:[161]

> *Dear Bahá'í Friends,*
>
> Your letter of 24 June has reached our beloved Guardian, as well as the postscript of Mr Philip Hainsworth, and he has instructed me to answer you on his behalf.
>
> He is delighted over the progress being made there, and was very relieved to hear from the Africa Committee, that the Conference plans can now go ahead smoothly. Also the reports of the work being done in outlying districts (which dear Mrs Banání has sent to Lotfullah, and which he shares with the Guardian) have caused much joy.
>
> It is wonderful to see that the African friends, having, as is their right and privilege, taken the Faith of Bahá'u'lláh to their hearts on their own, are arising to carry it to their fellow-countrymen, and are meeting with such notable success. How clearly we see that when prejudice and suspicion give way to love and confidence, the Power of God flows through and brings unexpected confirmation!
>
> He was very pleased to see you have initiated a plan of your own, but feels that any plans for translation should be worked out in close consultation with the Africa Committee. This does not mean he is averse to a new translation.
>
> Wonderful work lies ahead of your Assembly, and you may be sure he follows your activities with close interest and supports them with his loving prayers.
>
> *With warm Bahá'í love, Rúḥíyyih Rabbání*

In the Guardian's own handwriting:

> *May the Beloved whose Cause you are promoting with exemplary valour, reward you abundantly for your splendid achievements, remove every obstacle from your path, and enable you to ennoble continually the record of your unforgettable services.*
>
> *Your true and grateful brother, Shoghi*

By October, we had been able to advise the Africa Committee that Rex Collison had located a place in the United States where a large marquee could be purchased and shipped to Kampala at a little more cost than would

[161] Unpublished letter (personal archives).

be required to hire one from Nairobi. It was arranged that this should be bought and brought by a pioneer couple – Alan and May Elston.

My 'houseboy' (man servant) John, a Munyoro, and 'shamba-boy' (gardener) Munyambibi, a Munyaruanda, had both become Bahá'ís. They were essential staff for the household, as the colonial type houses were very large and had large gardens. We had regular meetings in my house with 10 – 15 people attending, most of whom had to be collected by car from the African housing estate and the railway workers' houses.

DEVELOPMENT OF UGANDA BAHÁ'Í ADMINISTRATION

An Africa Committee letter to the Guardian dated 19 September describes in some detail the return to Kampala of Enoch Olinga after his first visit home, when he returned with the first two declarations from Teso and two from Mbale. His report to the local Spiritual Assembly of Kampala was sent to the Guardian as they thought it was 'quite a historic document'.

Suggestions were made on how to issue credentials, with the newly appointed Uganda Teaching Committee being responsible for all Uganda, the local Spiritual Assembly of Dar-es-Salaam for Tanganyika and the London Committee for Kenya, the Gold Coast and any isolated believers.

Enoch's father in Kobwin had given one of his huts to the Bahá'ís as a centre and the Feast of Mashíyyat (27 September) was celebrated there with Mr Banání and the Collisons. At that time the Faith had enrolled believers from nine tribes – Ganda, Gisu, Gweru, Kabarasi, Kakamega, Luo, Soga, Teso and Toro and these included six women.

The first Teso believer from outside Kampala was Enos Epyeru. Some time after his enrolment it was learned that as secretary of a cooperative society he was also a prominent member of a militant political party – the Uganda National Congress. This information came to us on the occasion of the visit of two MPs from Britain. We immediately got in touch with Enos and explained how, as a Bahá'í, he should not belong to any political party. Immediately, he wrote resigning from the congress and sent a copy of his letter to the British District Commissioner. We were very concerned that Enos might lose his job as a result of this resignation, but were deeply impressed by his immediate acceptance of the Bahá'í position. His letter was sent to London who shared it with the Guardian.

It was not until the Guardian's letter of 4 June 1953 that he was able to deal with many of the matters presented by the Africa Committee – anything of great urgency he handled by cable. From the text of some of the letters from the Africa Committee to the Guardian it is clear that a number of such cables have been lost, as they were not available in 1979 when I edited *Unfolding Destiny.*[162]

There follow some significant extracts from that letter, written long after the Kampala Conference:[163]

> He was immensely pleased over the example shown by Enos Epyeru, in withdrawing from political affiliation, and feels that some of the African friends are showing a most exemplary spirit of devotion and loyalty. He feels that a great potential strength lies in these new African believers.
>
> No doubt your committee will be faced with problems, due to the inexperience of some of these people in administrative matters, but, through loving guidance, and the wisdom of those who are associated with them on the spot, these minor things can be satisfactorily taken care of, and the main thing, the establishment of assemblies and groups, be carried out successfully.
>
> The Guardian was indeed delighted over 'Alí Nakhjavání's trip to the Teso district. The purity of his spirit, the intensity of his devotion, and the longing in his heart to bring the Faith to his African brothers, all of which he so clearly showed forth in his actions, were no doubt the great factors which enkindled the first fires in the hearts of the believers in that land, and which have spread so swiftly and have been the cause of such joy to our beloved Guardian.
>
> PS In reading over this letter, I see that I have not done justice to the deep feeling of appreciation our beloved Guardian has for the wonderful spirit shown by Mr Banání and his wife, as well as by Philip Hainsworth and Mr and Mrs Collison. The services of all of those friends cannot be overestimated, nor those of the devoted pioneers in Kenya and Tanganyika.

PREPARATIONS FOR THE KAMPALA CONFERENCE 1953

As 1952 drew to a close, the activity intensified. I had had permission to take some leave from duty in February 1953 to enable me to attend the

[162] Effendi, S. (1981). The Unfolding Destiny of the British Bahá'í Community: The Messages from the Guardian of the Bahá'í Faith to the Bahá'ís of the British Isles. London, Bahá'í Publishing Trust.
[163] Ibid., p. 301.

conference, and an agreement that I could also take time off for the Holy Days utilising my 16 days per year 'local leave'.

The conference was to take place from 11 – 18 February 1953, the hotel bookings had been made, and the tent purchased in New York. Plans had to be made to bring the African Bahá'ís from villages as far away as Lira in Lango, north of Teso, and of course a contingent of Bahá'ís from Persia. We also knew that Richard St Barbe Baker was leaving England to lead an expedition south from North Africa, crossing the deserts, meeting Heads of State, and planning to arrive in Kampala in his Land Rover in time for the conference.

The Conference would be aimed at 'planting banner Faith remaining territories, neighbouring islands, East, South, West African Continent'.[164]

The Guardian's cable to the Bahá'í world of 8 October[165] coincided with the start of the Holy Year, which would witness the launching of a 'fate-laden, soul-stirring, decade-long, world-embracing spiritual Crusade involving simultaneous initiation twelve national Ten Year Plans'. This gave us a further impetus to make our contribution – the holding of the first of the intercontinental conferences – an outstanding success. All the Hands of the Cause who could be present would be invited to speak and take a full part in the programme. On 15 December, the Guardian announced that the Secretary General of the International Council, Leroy Ioas, would represent him and carry out a four-fold task, outlined more fully in his cable to the American National Spiritual Assembly of 5 January 1953, as follows:[166]

- Bring the portrait of the Holy Báb (a replica of one deposited beneath the dome of Wilmette Temple), the unveiling of which 'may draw newly recruited vanguard ever-swelling host Bahá'u'lláh, as well as participating visitors, itinerant teachers, settlers, closer spirit Martyr Prophet Faith, bestow everlasting benediction all gathered memorable sessions...';
- Deliver the official message from the Guardian;
- Elucidate the character and purposes of the impending global crusade;
- Rally the participants to energetic, sustained and enthusiastic prosecution of the colossal tasks ahead.

The cable opened:[167]

> Rejoice share Bahá'í communities East West thrilling reports feats

[164] Unpublished notes (personal archives).
[165] Effendi, S. (1971). Messages to the Bahá'í World 1950-1957. Wilmette, Ill., Bahá'í Publishing Trust., p. 41.
[166] Ibid., p. 134.
[167] Effendi, S. (1981). The Unfolding Destiny of the British Bahá'í Community: The Messages from the Guardian of the Bahá'í Faith to the Bahá'ís of the British Isles. London, Bahá'í Publishing Trust., p. 290.

> achieved heroic band Bahá'í pioneers laboring diverse widely-scattered African territories, particularly Uganda, heart continent, reminiscent alike episodes related Book Acts, rapid dramatic propagation Faith instrumentality Dawn-Breakers Heroic Age Bahá'í Dispensation. Marvellous accomplishments signalizing rise establishment administrative order Latin America eclipsed. Exploits immortalising recently launched crusade European continent surpassed. Goal seven month plan initiated Kampala Assembly, aiming doubling twelve enrolled believers outstripped.
>
> Number Africans converted course last fifteen months, residing Kampala outlying districts, Protestant, Catholic, Pagan backgrounds, lettered, unlettered, both sexes, representative no less sixteen tribes, passed two hundred mark...

I was particularly looking forward to welcoming Ḥasan Balyúzí and John and Dorothy Ferraby as representatives of the British National Spiritual Assembly.

'Alí and Rex were very involved in arranging the buses to collect the Africans, attending as the guests of the beloved Guardian.

I was to conduct a visit to Jinja on the sightseeing tour and arrange a demonstration of African singing and dancing by a Busoga women's club. This was organised by the mother of a new Jinja Bahá'í – Patrick Menya – who, with Patrick's sister, also accepted the Faith.

On 6 January 1953 we placed an advertisement in a local paper – the *Uganda Argus*, giving the principles of the Faith.

I was in close touch with the Persian Africa Committee with whose secretary, Jalál Sahihi, I began a correspondence that lasted many years. The big problem was going to be one of visas and of accommodation for the Persian friends, but we finally were assured that enough places would be available. Bed spaces were booked with mattresses for the African visitors at the Mengo Social Centre; accommodation in various hotels on the outskirts of Kampala was booked for our Persian friends and other overseas visitors. A local African 'cook' was hired to provide morning and evening meals in the grounds of the Bahá'í Centre on Kagera Road.

In the meantime, we had shared with the Africa Committee some of our concerns relating to:[168]

> The name to be given to the African huts we were being given for Bahá'í use – 'centres', 'Ḥaẓíratu'l-Quds', etc.
>
> The question of polygamists enrolling in the Faith for instance: 'If a man had three wives and after he became a Bahá'í one died or 'ran

[168] Unpublished letter (personal archives).

away', could he replace her?'

As the newly enrolled believers had no administrative experience nor had any background of any administration, committee work or consultation, what could we do in the many places where there would be more than nine believers at Ridván? It would not be possible for all areas to have a pioneer visit them during the 24 hours of the 20 – 21 April. Should we set up machinery to have a local gathering wherever there were more than nine believers, or only form assemblies where some supervision could be exercised by members of the Uganda Teaching Committee and new Bahá'ís with sufficient knowledge?

These problems were shared by the British Africa Committee with the Guardian. In their letter to him of 27 January 1953[169] they were able to advise him that through our efforts with the authorities and with support from the Colonial Office, one big problem had been solved. The Principal Immigration Officer had agreed to grant all visas necessary and had advised the East Africa Office in London and British Consuls in places where intending visitors lived, authorising them to issue visas on the basis of the names we were able to submit to him.

THE KAMPALA CONFERENCE AND AFTER 'LIGHT OVER AFRICA' 12 – 18 FEBRUARY, 1953

It was a great relief when the marquee arrived. Poles had to be made to measure and a gang of helpers was needed to erect it. We were very fortunate that Alan Elston, an engineer, was available to supervise this work. The British National Spiritual Assembly had printed a very dignified programme which contained a cable from the Guardian dated 30 November 1951; a message of welcome from Hand of the Cause Músá Banání; photographs of the Master, the Temple in Wilmette, the Shrine of The Báb, the Ḥaẓíratu'l-Quds, Kampala, Louis Gregory and Ḥájí Mírzá Ḥaydar-'Alí; a statement on the conference itself; a list of some of the outstanding events in the Bahá'í history of Africa up to 11 June 1952; and quotations from the Writings, in English, Swahili, Luganda and Hausa.

All the Hands as well as Ḥasan Balyúzí, Elsie Austin and Sami Doktoroglu of Istanbul signed my copy.

There was great excitement when the Africans from Teso, Mbale, and

[169] Unpublished letter (personal archives).

Palissa arrived – most had never been to Kampala, and some had never left their tribal areas before. As might have been expected, it took some time to arrange meals. Richard St Barbe Baker, who had recently arrived from his trip around the Sahara desert, helped with this.

Two of the visiting Bahá'ís, Nabil Mustapha and Hussein Gollestani, were doctors and they were amazed with some of the ulcers and other ailments found among the Bahá'ís. They set up a regular 'sick parade' every morning and did sterling work. Assisting them just as assiduously was a young Bahá'í who had had some medical training – Yedison Esubere of Ngora.

Altogether there were about 230 participants representing 19 countries, which included 10 Hands of the Cause (Músá Banání, Leroy Ioas, Dorothy Baker, Horace Holley, Dhikru'lláh Khádem, Ṭaráẓu'lláh Samandarí, 'Alí-Akbar Furútan, Valíyu'lláh Varqá, Shu'á'u'lláh 'Alá'í and Mason Remey) over 40 Persian Bahá'ís and more than 120 Africans.

It was decided to seat the participants in groups spaced as widely apart as possible in the tent. The largest group were English-speakers, then those who spoke only Ateso, and smaller groups of Persian, Swahili and Luganda speakers. It was quite an experience – when the speaker was using English, immediately he or she paused the translation was loudly made in the four other languages; if it was in Ateso, it then had to be repeated in English and then simultaneously translated into Persian, Luganda and Swahili. Some likened it to bedlam, others to Babel, and Horace Holley opened one of his talks by saying that he had spoken in great halls each with a difficult echo to contend with, but that this was the first time he had experienced the echo coming back to him in four different languages!

It was a moving experience, particularly to witness the joy and surprise on the faces of the Africans who were greeted with embraces from all the Persians and from Leroy Ioas, on behalf of the Guardian, following his expressed wish. It was also, for many, something of a culture shock to find many of the women unconcernedly nursing their babies while they sat in the tent or walked around the garden, or to see many of the Africans getting up and walking out at all times, which was most unusual for many of the visitors.

This was also the first time that I had any experience of working with Persians en masse. Albert Joseph of Manchester, Ḥasan Balyúzí and Asher Nazar were adults who had lived in England for many years; I had had brief administrative encounters with Lotfu'lláh Hakím as well as quite a number of younger Persians, such as Adíb and Zarin Taherzadeh, Mehdi Samandarí, Habib Hazari and Iraj Pooshti, who had come to England to study and pioneer, and twenty months with the Bananís and Nakhjavánís.

I had come to realise how different in so many ways was our approach to various aspects of life, but the degree of difference did not become apparent until I had to try to organise a day out in Jinja with Bahá'ís who had had no prior experience of 'Western' organisation. To get them onto the buses on time, to get them back on the buses after the stopovers, to try to explain that not everyone they met was a Bahá'í to be hugged, and to make myself heard above the continual conversation necessitated my raising my naturally loud voice. It was not surprising that from that time and for many years at subsequent international gatherings, I was regarded as 'the sergeant major'!

What was a revelation to many of us from the West was the way in which the African villagers responded to the portrait of the Báb. They showed a tremendous reverence and some of them prostrated themselves before it. The whole viewing was carried out with great dignity and feeling.

There were two public meetings. One for mainly European and Indian visitors was held in the Hall of Makerere University College, with Ḥasan Balyúzí and Horace Holley as speakers; the other, mainly for African visitors, was held in the tent and was addressed by Dorothy Baker and Mathew Bullock.

After the conference, Mr Banání and Mr Khadem were taken on visits to various centres around Uganda while a group of visitors, including a member of the Africa Committee, spent a couple of days travelling around Teso from Tilling. Other visitors dispersed to visit Nairobi, Dar-es-Salaam, Ethiopia, and Egypt.

The returning Africans gave a tremendous boost to the teaching work, not only by the enthusiastic reports of what they had experienced, but because they had returned, as the people left at home had been convinced that the 'white people' who had collected them would never let them come back. Some were convinced even then, in 1953, that their relatives had been taken away as slaves or would be eaten!

In his message to the conference, the Guardian used the most moving phrase, 'I welcome with open arms the unexpectedly large number of representatives of the pure-hearted and spiritually receptive Negro race, so dearly loved by 'Abdu'l-Bahá'. [170] He went on to pay tribute to the several national communities who were involved in the Africa Campaign and the 'small band of Persian, British and American pioneers' and announced no fewer than 12 objectives to be achieved 'circumstances permitting' during the following decade.

[170] Effendi, S. (1971). Messages to the Bahá'í World 1950-1957. Wilmette, Ill., Bahá'í Publishing Trust., p. 135.

A letter dated 18 February 1953 was sent to the Guardian from the Kampala Conference:[171]

Our dearly loved Guardian,

With reverence we humbly extend to you our heart-felt gratitude and thanks for your dedicated spirit and love which made it possible for us to be your guests at the first Bahá'í Intercontinental Conference held in Kampala. We have never had such a privilege in our life – a privilege of being guests of the revered and loved Guardian of the Bahá'í World; participating in a world Conference consisting of many people from different countries, diverse races and social background; and seeing with our eyes a real portrait of His Holiness the Báb, the Martyr Prophet of God's Faith. Truly, the uncovering of this sacred portrait has brought us – Negro believers of Africa – and others present at the Conference, we believe, closer in spirit to His Holiness the Báb, the co-Founder of our Faith. May our lives be a sacrifice to Him!

We also thank you for sending to us your special representative, Mr Leroy Ioas, who, with much eloquence, expounded your wonderful and most exciting cable regarding the carrying of Bahá'u'lláh's Message to remote islands and countries which had not been privileged to hear it, and for enabling many Hands of the Cause of God to be present at the memorable sessions of this historic Inter-Continental Conference, dedicated to further the Cause of Bahá'u'lláh. These dear and pure souls deserve our thanks for making this Conference a success and for sharing with us the same sentiments evoked by the atmosphere instigated by the results of the deliberations concerning matters of vital importance as set forth in your cable. Our joy and happiness, indeed, know no bounds.

Finally we are ready and prepared to keep the brilliant light of God's conquering Faith going, carry out the latest, most glorious crusade begun during the entire eleven decades of Bahá'í history, and keep the precious name of the beloved Faith of Bahá'u'lláh stainless while constantly turning our faces to you from time to time humbly beseeching you for prayers and blessings.

We are your most humble servants,

In the Service of Bahá'u'lláh, African believers attending the Bahá'í Inter-continental Conference in Kampala.

At the beginning of April 1953, we had to give some thought to the election of the local Assemblies. I had to attend my own in Jinja and then

[171] Unpublished letter (personal archives).

dash off to help Tito Wanantuzi in Bugisu, while 'Alí had to arrange meetings with different Bahá'ís in different areas who would collect the believers together for the voting between sunset on 20 and 21 April. Although there were only Kampala, Jinja and 10 others 'up-country' to organise, it was an exciting and colossal job. However, this was simplicity itself when compared with the problems that later developed.

It was about this time that, quite 'out of the blue' I received a letter from Dorothy Baker. She wrote on 18 March telling me of an 'ardent Bahá'í' girl in Rome who was in need of some encouragement and felt I may be able to help and said, 'way down in my heart I suppose I do have a thought that you two might be the answer for one another'. She continued:[172]

> I have thought of you again and again since leaving Kampala, and pray for your continued success and joy. Surely so valiant a spirit will be rewarded in this world and the next, beyond our present imagination. You are surely one of those characterised as 'Men of the unseen' who will 'rush forth from their habitations and enter the cities'. I love your strong spirit and shall be waiting breathlessly to hear every detail of your unfolding service.
>
> *Warmest love, Dorothy.*

I had spent Easter in Teso and on my return had written to the Guardian on 9 April, telling him of some gifts for him that I had collected from the dear friend Esubere who had helped with the 'sick people' at the conference. Violette was to collect these from me as she passed through Jinja. This letter and his reply of 26 April follow:[173]

> 9 April 1953, Jinja.
>
> *Dearly beloved Guardian,*
>
> Taking advantage of the Easter holiday, I spent the 3rd to the 6th April in Teso, spending one night in Ocakai and two in Ngora. Arriving back to Ngora late at night from Ocakai, I found Esubere and his wife laboriously trying to write a message to their dearly loved Guardian – it was very moving. A small mud hut, a rough wood table, a smoking lantern, pages from an old exercise book, using stubs of a crayon pencil, 10 p.m. – when most Africans have been long in bed, and these two dear souls were trying to put a few words together to accompany some gifts as they had heard that 'Mrs Violette' was to visit Haifa. Immediately I arrived, all was put on one side, the food prepared hours before for me was brought, and

[172] Unpublished letter (personal archives).
[173] Ibid.

the bed prepared. The following day saw so much Bahá'í activity that there was no time for writing, and as I was to bring the scribbled notes in Ateso for translation to Kampala so that a nice typewritten letter would be put together by Olinga, there was some consternation that these notes were not ready. It was therefore suggested that they tell me in English, and I write to you on their behalf, handing the letter and presents to Violette as she passes through Jinja.

First I must say a word about Esubere. He sent a letter to you some weeks ago, addressed, I believe, to the 'Guardian of the Bahá'í World, Haifa'. He is a very new Bahá'í and remained firm in the Faith in spite of a severe test even before his declaration was accepted. He was of tremendous help during the Conference with the very large daily sick parade, as he has had some medical training. He was then invited to attend a special course we had in Kampala, where he helped with the translating. He was determined to see a community develop in Ngora, for as this is the centre and main township for the district where most of the Teso work is, he felt it should have an assembly, and round about his house too.

It is interesting to note that Ngora, and Kobwin in particular, where there are to be six local Spiritual Assemblies, was the district which first took to Christianity, and there is strong feeling between the people of Ngora and the remainder of Teso because Ngora always claims to be in the lead. The headquarters of the CMS for the diocese of the Upper Nile is at Ngora, and is actually on land usurped from Esubere's father. 400 yards from his present house is the Girls' School, where a girl of 18 is studying – she being the first of the Acholi tribe to accept the Faith, she has already taught many of the pupils about the Faith (dangerous work in a Mission School) and she recorded the Acholi translation of the prayer for Unity when Mrs Sears visited Teso after the Conference; this school is actually on the site of the house where Esubere was born.

The senior cleric is Archdeacon Calcroft – when I met him during the Christmas holidays he was astonished by a remarkable series of events. He had just returned from home leave; he heard of the Faith for the first time when he was in England; he came back to Teso after a long absence though it was really his 'parish' and found the Faith well established; then at Christmas time who should turn up but one of his old choir boys whom he had not seen from the time he left his first parish in England 25 years ago; and this same choir boy was in Teso teaching the Bahá'í Faith!! When I told him that it was in that same church where I was in the choir that I heard the name Bahá'í first of all, he nearly collapsed. Saying that he ought to know more about this new thing in his district, he requested literature. When, later, he was called upon to give some written support to an ex-teacher of his who had accepted the Faith, he was not unhelpful and showed a fine spirit indeed.

Now Esubere has a wife, Ruth Lucy, who has accepted the Faith, and another wife somewhere, also Lucy, whom we have not seen, and two children – very young: this letter is to contain the greetings and love from these. One of the gifts, a head stool, is very old – perhaps 150 years and is carried on the shoulder and placed under the head when the owner is resting. It is of a kind much used by their forefathers, now its use is confined to the sister tribe – the Karamojong – who live in areas yet untouched by any civilisation. I think that this stool represents Esubere's most treasured possession. His wife, Ruth, sends the drinking calabash – this is considered by them to be of great beauty; in fact the two gifts carry a deep abiding love for their Guardian. I am to say that when you receive them, you will meet Esubere and his wife. They both praise God that He selected you to be the guide for all mankind. You must be assured that the hearts of Esubere and his wife are on fire, they are burning with the Faith. They beg your prayers for the Assembly which will be formed on 21 April – they do not doubt its formation. I am to convey their greetings for the Baha'i New Year and again express the deep thanks which Esubere put in his earlier letter, for the Conference, and for the Africans' attendance. They are eagerly awaiting a 'message of God' from you if you can spare the time.

By the time the substance of this was given to me, the Acholi girl – Rebecca Abitimo, had arrived from the school to help in the teaching, and Esubere asked that her love and greetings, and the greetings of his old mother, be added.

We then went to a nearby partly built, almost complete hut, much larger than his own house, which he is building for his Bahá'í Centre, and held a meeting attended by about 30 enquirers. As a few Bahá'ís arrived from Kobwin, we left them to carry on with the new contacts, whilst he, Rebecca and a very devoted soul from Acissa, who had cycled more than twelve miles to see me, helped me to interview some thirteen new declarations from among Esubere's friends. There should be about fifteen Bahá'ís there in this important place by 20 April – almost entirely the unaided work of Esubere.

In all there will be about fifty declarations in Teso between the Conference and Ridván, and ten new assemblies in Uganda.

Your letters dated 6 February did not reach here until the day I left for Teso – 3 April – 8 weeks. As a letter can get through in four or five days I am enclosing the envelope in case you wish to check on the delay – the Kampala letter was similarly delayed.

May I please add my own expression of devotion, and beg your particular prayers that I may become more dedicated and overcome the weaknesses which from time to time do so much harm. I have no ambition beyond being a good Bahá'í, but it is dreadfully hard at times.

Philip

He replied to me on 26 April 1953:[174]

Dear Bahá'í Brother,

Your letters dated July 7th, August 26th, November 21st, 1952 and January 23rd (2), and April 9th, 1953 have been received by the beloved Guardian, and he has instructed me to answer you on his behalf. He has not written to you before, because he was very busy, and also because he felt he would be able to offer you most hearty congratulations if he delayed! Now, after the formation of not only the Jinja Assembly, but also eleven others throughout Uganda, he compliments you on the wonderful work you have achieved there, in collaboration with the other believers. It has brought great joy to his heart, and indeed to the hearts of all the Bahá'ís.

He hopes that, during this coming year, you and 'Alí Nakhjavání will devote yourselves as much as you can to consolidating the new assemblies, and assisting the new believers to gradually understand better the Administration, and its application in Bahá'í Community Life. Tact, love and patience will no doubt be needed, and one cannot expect these new believers to do everything in the same way that the old and tried Communities do. Indeed individuality of expression, within the framework of the Administrative Order, is preferable to too great a uniformity.

The Guardian feels sure that your dear mother and father, who shared in and were part of the sacrifice you made in going to Africa, rejoice from on high at that which has been accomplished. He assures you of his loving prayers.

With warm Bahá'í greetings, R Rabbání

[174] Unpublished letter (personal archives).

In the Guardian's own handwriting:

May the Almighty bless your splendid services to His Faith, guide and sustain you always, and enable you to extend continually the range of your historic and deeply valued accomplishments.
Your true and grateful brother, Shoghi

JINJA 1953

When I first arrived in Jinja, I felt obliged to associate with some of my fellow Europeans until I became known, and would go to play Canasta or Scrabble with a Mr Peter Theale, and became quite friendly with him. His wife, Dreda Theale, eventually became a Bahá'í. I also associated with several of the scientists working with the East Africa Fisheries Department. From them I learned that they would be interested in any crocodile eggs and any snakes my men found when I was carrying out malaria control measures along the lakeside, which they kept for visiting scientists from Regent's Park Zoo. Any unusual fish from the swamps were also appreciated. Humphrey Greenwood was one such friend. One day I had the idea of draining a swamp on the outskirts of Jinja by sinking a well near the stream that supplied it and running a channel from the swamp to the stream to the well. This was filled with broken tiles, glass, and sand so that the water would be filtered by the time it reached the well.

This worked so effectively that people came from miles around to collect water, much to the annoyance of the Public Works Department, which had installed a 'stand pipe' half a mile away and made a small charge for the township water thus supplied. Before long, however, the people who got their water free from my well liked the taste better and actually drank the swamp dry!

A large number of snakes lived in the trees in the swamp and, as it became possible to get into the swamp to cut down the trees and reclaim the land, there would occasionally be a terrific outburst of African cries and shouts as my labourers would discover a snake and proceed to beat it to death. They were very frightened of snakes, not only from the fear of snakebite, but due to them being taboo for some tribes. One day when I was inspecting the area the cry was made: 'nyoka!' – snake! and I rushed to see it. It was a large, thick specimen with a beautiful skin and I thought it would be a lovely specimen for the zoo. I therefore pinned its head to the ground with a stick and picked it up with my thumb on its head and my index finger of my right hand below. All the Africans ran away. As I was carrying it to my car, wondering how to drive with it in my right hand, but not gripping it too tightly as I did not wish to kill it, its lower jaw retracted and it sank its fangs from its upper jaw into my index finger. I dropped it and some porters ran forward and chopped off its head.

I put on a firm tourniquet and rushed off to hospital. When I went into the surgery of the District Medical Officer (DMO) surgery, I found him syringing out the ear of the Provincial Medical Officer. He looked up in annoyance, asked me what I wanted and carried on while I told him that I had had a serious snake bite and then he just said I was to wait until he had finished.

Believing time to be of the essence I went to another office and rang the Fisheries. On receiving a description of the snake, Dr Greenwood said he would be right around with some antidote and was there within five minutes. He gave me the injection and then released the tourniquet as my finger was swollen and turning blue. Eventually the DMO came in to see 'what all the fuss was about' and was amazed to learn that from my description Dr Greenwood had recognised that a Gabon viper whose poison could kill within 15 minutes had bitten me.

The DMO therefore dressed the wound, gave me an injection of penicillin and put me to bed. Humphrey Greenwood had gone to the swamp to pick up the dead viper and reported that when he had lifted it up by its tail, three partially digested rats emerged. The first was quite well decomposed, the second showed some signs of digestion, while the third was only just showing signs of being killed.

Apparently, the last had not been long swallowed and my life was said to have been saved by the following: that the recently swallowed rat had absorbed the venom and there had not been time for the viper to build up another lethal dose; that I had immediately put on a tourniquet; and that I had had the rapid anti-venom injection before the tourniquet was released.

I never felt any concern that day though I will bear the scar of the snakebite and a slightly damaged nerve on that index finger until I die. On the next day, however, I was covered from head to foot with a rash – apparently I was allergic to the penicillin injection. My finger was swollen, sore and painful for a few days, so I spent about three days in the hospital and was then given 10 days leave to recuperate. I went to Kitale in the Kenya Highlands accompanied by Munyambibi, his wife Maria and a well-educated African whose name I cannot remember, who was then studying the Faith. There I was able to meet Enos Epyeru who had responded to the local pioneer call and was in Eldoret.

I was warmly welcomed back to the Fisheries on my return by the officers who took the credit for 'saving my life'. I continued to supply snakes and fish for the remainder of my time in Jinja.

There is an interesting sequel to this: when I moved to London in 1974 as Secretary of the UK National Spiritual Assembly, I found myself only a few minutes' walk from the Natural History Museum and promised myself a visit there one day. Early in 1975, there was some news about 'an object' being located by sonar in Loch Ness and, interested in whether it might be possible for there to be a 'monster' living in the depths, they interviewed an expert from the Natural History Museum. He was a Dr H Greenwood.

I thought I would surprise him so I went round and asked to see him saying it was just 'a friend'. I could only speak with him on the internal telephone but as soon as I spoke he came rushing down from his laboratory to see me. He first wanted to know about my snakebite and then we chatted all the way up to his laboratory. He stated that it was the most amazing coincidence that I should have contacted him that morning. He had become a world authority on a certain genus of fish of the species Haplochromis; he had already published two volumes on them and was working on a third. He was still working on samples stored in bottles dating back more than 20 years. That very day he had come across one which was somewhat different from any other and he had named it 'Haplochromis – var. Hainsworthi' because on the slip in the bottle it listed my name and the date and place I had bottled it for him! Another interesting sequel to the swamp episode was that prior to being drained, the neighbouring plot could be purchased very cheaply by an African, so it was bought by a local resident who had accepted the Faith as the site of a future Bahá'í Centre for Jinja. With the clearing of the swamp it became quite valuable and eventually a Bahá'í centre was built there.

TEN YEAR PLAN LAUNCHED

The specific sections of the British Global Crusade that affected Uganda were studied at the conference and were firmly etched in our minds. The Guardian had referred to 'magnificent victories achieved African Continent exceeding highest hopes'! We did not immediately feel directly involved in those parts of the message that referred to the British Cameroons, British Togoland, Madeira and South West Africa, but we were concerned about 'consolidation Kenya, Tanganyika, Uganda', particularly in the light of the Guardian's letter to me of 26 April. We were also aware that we would later be involved in goals 3, 4, 6, 7 and 9 – referring respectively to the establishment of a Regional National Spiritual Assembly for Central and East Africa, the purchase of land for a Temple, the conversion of the Kampala local Ḥaẓíratu'l-Quds into a national institution, the National

Spiritual Assembly's incorporation and the purchase of national endowments.

Our relative complacency was shattered by a cable from the Guardian to the British National Spiritual Assembly dated 13 May 1953:[175]

> Urge full fledged Bahá'í Assemblies British territories Uganda Tanganyika Kenya now regarded most powerful pillars swiftly emerging steadily consolidating highly promising African Bahá'í community set glorious example through prompt measures initiation extension work through despatch surplus members local communities including Africans neighbouring territories French Somaliland Ruanda-Urundi Madagascar French Belgian Congo Comoro Islands even Algeria Morocco accelerating thereby process forming local assemblies establishment National Assembly Central East Africa adding fresh laurels Crown already won pioneering field African continent.

Before this arrived, the Africa Committee had raised with the Guardian one of the ideas emerging from the conference, that a Bahá'í school for Africans be started. Over £1,000 had been contributed for this project and interviews with the Assistant Chief Secretary and the Deputy Director of Education indicated that the government attitude to the Bahá'ís might be more favourable. The committee was reluctant to initiate the extensive investigations which would be necessary if this proposal was accepted without the Guardian's approval.

The committee also passed on a suggestion that the Kampala Bahá'ís concentrate on building up a large and impressive community rather than diverting resources elsewhere. The cable of 13 May partially answered the latter point and the Guardian's letter of 25 June added some detail, saying that the school idea was 'premature'.

Another question raised by the Africa Committee related to the drinking of alcohol. Drunkenness from native-made beer, whether it was made from bananas or from fermented grain, was very common and it was considered natural for men and women to partake of this 'waragi'. An immediate ban was not only doomed to failure, but also unless the diet was changed would deprive many of their main source of vitamin B. The Guardian restated the need to ensure that we should not put so many obstacles in the way of new believers that they feel it impossible to accept the Faith. However, once accepted, it should gradually be brought home to

[175] Effendi, S. (1981). The Unfolding Destiny of the British Bahá'í Community: The Messages from the Guardian of the Bahá'í Faith to the Bahá'ís of the British Isles. London, Bahá'í Publishing Trust., p. 299.

new Bahá'ís that they are expected to live according to the laws of Bahá'u'lláh.

It was not long after this that an unusual case was brought to us for decision. One Teso believer had three wives, each with her own hut. One day a young girl about 15 years old came to his home with her few belongings in a bundle on her head saying that she was his wife and had now come to join him. Not only had he become a Bahá'í and was aware of the law but, he said, he just could not afford to build another hut and feed another mouth. On looking into this we found that the man's father had been drinking and gambling many years before; the local tribe being notorious for their addiction to gambling. He had been gambling with a man who had lost everything to him and finally had won the baby daughter for his son who was now a Bahá'í. All her life the girl had been brought up to know that although she lived at home she was the wife of our friend. When she was old enough she just packed up and walked to her 'husband's' home, expecting to be welcomed with open arms. We decided that as she had been properly 'married' according to local custom this had to be obeyed and our friend had to honour the pledges of the two fathers, make the fourth wife welcome and try to treat all his wives with equity.

Following the 13 May cable to London, the Guardian cabled the Bahá'í world on 28 May calling for an immediate world wide response to the call for pioneers, announcing at the same time the establishment of a 'Roll of Honour'. Two paragraphs from that cable, coming so shortly after the cable of the 13 May, presented a real challenge to all the pioneers in Uganda:[176]

> Once again I appeal to members of all communities to arise and enlist, ere the present opportunity is irretrievably lost, in the army of Bahá'u'lláh's crusaders. The hour is ripe to disencumber themselves of worldly vanities, to mount the steed of steadfastness, unfurl the banner of renunciation, don the armour of utter consecration to God's Cause, gird themselves with the girdle of a chaste and holy life, unsheathe the sword of Bahá'u'lláh's utterance, buckle on the shield of His love, carry as sole provision implicit trust in His promise, leave their homelands, and scatter far and wide to capture the unsurrendered territories of the entire plant.
>
> Would to God that Bahá'í warriors, six score and ten, the number required to fill the gaps in the still unconquered territories of the globe, will promptly arise and enrol themselves to achieve the gaps ere the conclusion of the opening year of the decade-long, greatest

[176] Effendi, S. (1971). Messages to the Bahá'í World 1950-1957. Wilmette, Ill., Bahá'í Publishing Trust., p. 49

> collective enterprise since the memorable episodes associated with the Dawn-Breakers of the Heroic Age.

On 5 June, Leroy Ioas wrote on behalf of the Guardian to the British National Spiritual Assembly and his letter included the following:[177]

> The settlement of these virgin areas is of such an emergency nature, that he feels pioneering in one of them takes precedence over every other type of Bahá'í service – whether it be in the teaching or administrative fields of the Faith. So important is it that the National Assembly may delay initiation of steps to fulfil other phases of the Plan, until all these areas are conquered for the Faith. Nothing, absolutely nothing, must be allowed to interfere with the placing of pioneers in each of the 131 goal countries....'
>
> The Guardian has cabled you, and at his direction I have written the Friends in Uganda, Kenya and Tanganyika of the importance of their spreading out, and if possible sending pioneers into the surrounding areas in Africa, such as Belgian Congo, Ruanda-Urundi, Somaliland, and even South West Africa. He wishes you to follow up this matter closely. The Guardian attached great importance to the Ashanti Protectorate, and if any of the Friends can go there, particularly any Persians you may be assisting in getting located, he will appreciate it.
>
> As the Guardian's dramatic cable indicates, an illuminated 'Roll of Honour' on which will be inscribed the names of the 'Knights of Bahá'u'lláh' who first enter these 131 virgin areas, will be placed inside the entrance door of the Inner Sanctuary of the Tomb of Bahá'u'lláh. From time to time, the Guardian will announce to the Bahá'í World the names of those Holy Souls who rise under the conditions outlined in his message, and settle these areas and conquer them for Bahá'u'lláh.

In his letters to the three East Africa Territories, Mr Ioas had emphasised the need to spread into neighbouring countries, to follow closely the advice of the British National Spiritual Assembly and to send monthly reports to the secretary-general of the International Bahá'í Council. The combination of all these messages started a period of intensive activity in Kampala.

[177] Effendi, S. (1981). The Unfolding Destiny of the British Bahá'í Community: The Messages from the Guardian of the Bahá'í Faith to the Bahá'ís of the British Isles. London, Bahá'í Publishing Trust., p. 303.

CALLED TO BE A KNIGHT OF BAHÁ'U'LLÁH

This activity did not immediately affect me, as I was firmly under contract with the government. I had earned some six months' leave to be taken later in the year and was very involved with the deepening work of the new communities as Secretary of the Uganda Teaching Committee. In addition, the Guardian had indicated in 1952 that it was good for the Cause for me to remain in government employment.

All this was shattered by a cable I received in Jinja on 29 June 1953:[178]

> Advise pioneer British Togoland or Cameroons – loving prayers surrounding you.
>
> *Shoghi.*

When I first recorded this in 1993 I wondered, and still do, what prompted the Guardian to send me that cable. Had I at some stage earlier offered to go anywhere in the world – I have no record of any such statement but I distinctly remember the shock of receiving that cable. I immediately went to the Senior Health Inspector and advised him that I was putting in my resignation, asking how long it would take to extricate myself from my contract commitments. To be considered were the number of weeks notice I had to give, the calculation of whatever leave I had earned, how much I needed to repay on my car loan, and what would need to be done about a replacement officer. The government reaction was unexpected – they just did not want me to go and were not prepared to let me go before the end of my contract in February 1954. This I explained to the Africa Committee and to the Guardian – I received a cable from him on 22 July:[179] Advise defer until contract completed. *Love Shoghi.*

I therefore began to plan for release in early 1954. My personal records do not cover this crucial period but while I remember the sequence of events I do not know what was put in writing to the Guardian at the time. I have been able to put together a rough picture from copies of letters from the Africa Committee to the Guardian, which only came to light in July 1993. The story is as follows!

The senior entomologist in Kampala had long been planning to set up for the Uganda Medical Service a new unit to be called the 'Vector Control Division'. This would handle the control of all diseases transmitted by some vector, except sleeping sickness, which had an independent East African control organisation. This 'control' included malaria, onchocerciasis, plague, bilharzia and sleeping sickness in areas outside

[178] Unpublished cable (personal archives).
[179] Ibid.

those demarcated as being under the control of the East Africa Unit. For this new 'division' he would need special premises, additional staff and transport, and a field officer who was not a professionally trained entomologist. For this he had already applied for me to be transferred from the Health Office in Jinja and to be stationed in Kampala. This meant that the new post would come into effect at the end of my contract and would be permanent. I would be taken on as an employed member of the British Government Overseas Civil Service rather than locally employed by the Uganda Protectorate, and the post would carry a substantial increase in salary with pension rights. My alternatives were therefore: I could:

- Complete my contract and go straight to West Africa
- Complete my contract, go to West Africa for six months' leave and return to the new job in Uganda
- Complete my contract, go on leave to England and then return to the new job in Kampala

The idea of a six months' leave every three years was based on the medical view that officers in the Colonial Service in tropical climates should have a substantial break in their own countries. This was strongly emphasised for those in Uganda which is on the equator and mostly between 5,500 and 6,500 feet above sea level. If I were to return to the new job in Uganda it would be necessary for me to visit London to complete all the documentation and have medicals, etc., at the Colonial Office.

A cable from the Guardian dated 4 October 1953 presumably refers to this: 'Approve Hainsworth six months leave.'[180] What I did not know at the time was that on 23 September the Africa Committee had put in a report about me to the Guardian and suggested that I adopt alternative (b), the suggestion of the senior entomologist, that I should go by car to British Togoland, taking with me an African Bahá'í who would pioneer there. The committee continued:[181]

> Our Committee is very much inclined to favour this scheme. It seems to us that Philip ought in four months to be able, with his experience of teaching in Africa, to get teaching satisfactorily started and even perhaps leave some new believers when he returns. We have felt very concerned at the possible loss of the only white British Bahá'í in Uganda and moreover Philip's services are invaluable in administering the new communities there, and organising the teaching and consolidation. A great deal depends on

[180] Unpublished cable (personal archives).
[181] Unpublished report (personal archives).

him as secretary of the Uganda Teaching Committee. The Africans are learning, but are not ready, we feel, to take full charge.

Philip put the scheme to us without expressing any personal reference, except the fear that it might seem as if he was trying to back out of his pioneer project, which we feel certain is not the case. We have to give Philip an answer in time for him to inform his boss by the 1st of November. Therefore, since you gave Philip his instruction to pioneer, we should be very grateful for cabled guidance as to whether we are right in wishing him to accept this scheme, or whether he should pull up his roots and prepare to settle in West Africa.

Had I been aware of this letter I would have pointed out the need to go to London for the Colonial Office documentation. As it was, I have no record of how the final decision was conveyed to me but the Guardian must have approved alternative c) as that is the one I eventually adopted. One of the factors which must have been taken into account was referred to in a letter to the Guardian from the Africa Committee, also dated 13 August, relating to the situation in Nairobi, which incidentally resulted in several pioneers actually becoming Knights of Bahá'u'lláh. In this letter, the Africa Committee stated that Ted Cardell would go to South West Africa; Ursula Samandarí should join her husband wherever he was able to settle; Tahirih Vatanparast would go to a South African territory; and asked permission for Azíz and Soraya Yazdí, Irene Bennett and Clare Gung to remain in Nairobi. The Yazdís had just obtained, after a year's negotiation, residence permits to stay in Kenya and it would not be received favourably if they then left and may have had a negative effect on any future similar applications by Bahá'ís. Regarding Irene and Clare, they wrote:[182]

We wished to retain Irene Bennett and Claire Gung, British believers, until the negotiations regarding the recognition of the Faith by the Registrar of Societies in Kenya have been completed, because of the impression on the authorities. When two of our members were in Kampala they met with the Uganda Principal Immigration Officer, who told them that one of the reasons the Uganda government was suspicious of the Faith was the fact that only one of the pioneers there was British. In Kenya the attitude is, we believe, even more pro-British and pro-white race than in Uganda.

[182] Unpublished letter (personal archives).

The Guardian cabled on 31 August:[183]

> Approve retain Yazdís, Bennett, Gung.

Not only did Ted Cardell become a Knight of Bahá'u'lláh for South West Africa, but the American pioneers in Nairobi, Mr and Mrs Fred Laws, became Knights for Basutoland. Ursula Samandarí joined her husband Mehdi and both became Knights of Bahá'u'lláh for Italian Somaliland and later, in October, Clare moved to Southern Rhodesia as one of the Knights for that territory.

I have sometimes pondered the significance of these actions – what might have happened in my life had I unreservedly responded without conditions to the probably unprecedented invitation by the Guardian to be a Knight of Bahá'u'lláh for either Togoland or Cameroon, which was later filled by Enoch Olinga? Would the Yazdís and Irene have become Knights of Bahá'u'lláh?

UGANDA KNIGHTS OF BAHÁ'U'LLÁH

For some time in late 1952 Rex and Mary Collison and 'Alí and Violette Nakhjavání had been following up visits to Aggrey Memorial School, a private missionary school in Mengo, Buganda, where several of the students, including the African choirmaster/schoolmaster Frobisher Kagwa, had become Bahá'ís. Students at this school came from many parts of Africa, and the choir had a fine reputation, with some gramophone records to its credit. One of the students with whom the Collisons became very closely associated was Dunduzu Chisiza (from Nyasaland). On receipt of the call for pioneers to virgin areas, the Collisons and Dunduzu decided to go immediately to open up Ruanda-Urundi. They left for Usumbura, as it was then called, and became the second, third and fourth Knights of Bahá'u'lláh. It is interesting to note that Enoch Olinga was in the next list of Knights and Peter Lugayula, from Budo School, was in the third list. Max Kanyerezi was listed for French Equatorial Africa. It later transpired that Peter Lugayula and Peter Kabisa had actually gone not to Ashanti, but to Livingstone College in the Gold Coast.

'Alí and Violette Nakhjavání made an epic journey of over 6,000 miles, driving three African Bahá'ís to new pioneer posts. They left Kampala on 27 August, travelling to Usumbura, Costermansville and Kamma in the Congo, where they left Samson Mungono; to Leopoldville and Brazzaville,

[183] Effendi, S. (1981). The Unfolding Destiny of the British Bahá'í Community: The Messages from the Guardian of the Bahá'í Faith to the Bahá'ís of the British Isles. London, Bahá'í Publishing Trust., p. 321.

where they left Max Kanyerezi; and to the British Cameroons, arriving on 15 October, where they left Enoch Olinga. They arrived back in Kampala on 21 December and their journey was summarised by the Africa Committee in their letter to the Guardian on 31 December 1953.[184]

With that letter was a report of a visit to Uganda of Bill and Marguerite Sears. As this trip was a prelude to their pioneering in South Africa and as I was peripherally involved, comment must be made on it. During the Kampala Conference Marguerite had been the representative of a group of Bahá'ís who, in the United States, were particularly interested in the work in Africa, although at that time there was no USA Africa Committee. She was very happy with the conference, the visit to Jinja and the evening activities we had at the Silver Springs Hotel and it was relatively easy for me to persuade her to go back to the States with every intention of persuading Bill to join her in pioneering to Africa.

When the news came that they were to come on a teaching trip in October 1953, I arranged their itinerary to the major teaching areas before they left for other East African centres. Unfortunately, Bill had had a serious illness, probably a heart attack, which meant that he had to take the journey as easily as possible. For the meeting in my house in Jinja I rigged up a microphone by his bed and he spoke to the 30 or so Africans assembled in my sitting room using my radio loud speaker. He loved the African scene and the Africans and they appreciated his love and humour. A report was written about the visit which I never saw – it must have made most entertaining reading, but a part of it appeared in *The Bahá'í World*, vol. XII, in an article titled 'Black Sunlight'.

At the first Teso Conference in Tilling there were 150 Teso believers and contacts, and we started literacy classes, particularly for the women. There had been a great response to the call for 'local' pioneers: Enos Epyeru had gone to Eldoret, Kenya; Anthony Mukhobe to Kapsabet, Kenya; Tito Wanantsusi to Mwanza, Tanganyika; and Peter Mutabazi to Bukoba, Tanganyika. Local Bahá'ís had gone to teach, and sometimes to settle, in Masaka, Gulu, Lira, Pallisa, Tororo and Arua. Mrs Aggrippina Olei, ex-wife of Nathan, had gone as the first African woman to pioneer on her own.

As part of our extension teaching work I had invited some of the new Bahá'ís from over the border in Kenya, men of the Luhya tribal group, to spend a few days at my home in Jinja to deepen in the Faith. These Awaluhya were part of a large tribal group that lived around the foothills of Mount Elgon (Masaba). In Uganda they were known as the Bagisu, but in

[184] Unpublished letter (personal archives).

Kenya there were several groups, including the Kabrasi, Maragoli and others who, though the dialects were different, their basic language structure was the same. It is of interest to note that their greeting, unlike that of many other Bantu languages that related to 'news', was 'mulembe' ('peace'). Three of those who visited my house on this occasion became real stalwarts of the Faith in Kenya.

When, after six months' employment, I had been 'confirmed' in my post as sanitary overseer, I sought to obtain recognition for Bahá'í Holy Days. I had listed the nine days when work is forbidden and obtained permission to take time off for any two of these. Any dates which did not fall on a statutory holiday or weekend could be taken but would come out of the 16 days per year I was allowed for 'local leave'.

To make this official, it had to be published in the *Uganda Gazette,* and this meant that from that time on it was applicable to all government employees. By April 1958, we had the National Spiritual Assembly incorporated in Uganda as well as the Kampala Local Assembly.

1954

The Uganda Teaching Committee was meeting as frequently as possible between the weekends when we were out teaching, mostly in the Eastern Province (Tororo, Mbale, Palissa, Teso and Lango) and I wrote to the Guardian, as the committee secretary, on 15 June, 15 October and 25 November 1953, and sent a personal letter to him on 28 January 1954. The letters explained the developments in my job, gave the date I would be going on leave to England and asked permission to go on pilgrimage. In January, we were devastated to learn of the death in an aeroplane crash of Hand of the Cause Dorothy Baker, remembered with such affection from the Kampala Conference. It was not until more than 30 years later that I learned of Dorothy's rousing call to the United States nation at Convention of April/May 1953 when, at the Guardian's instructions, she called for a more dynamic approach to the pioneer calls for service in special areas. This resulted in the formation of the USA African and the Indian Committees. In her address, she cried:[185]

> 'Alí Nakhjavání and Philip Hainsworth lived with the Teso people; they ate the food of the Teso people; they slept on straw mats or leaves, or whatever it is that you sleep on among the Teso people. The rain falls on your head and salamanders drop in your tea, if there is tea. And they stayed! They stayed! Is there an 'Alí

[185] Unpublished report (personal archives).

> Nakhjavání in America? Is there a Philip Hainsworth? Up to the present, no!

On 29 January, the Guardian cabled:[186]

> Regret postponement pilgrimage necessary. *Love. Shoghi.*

During this time there was a great deal of activity in Kampala which did not affect me directly, as I was busy with the Group in Jinja and did not go as frequently to Kampala as in 1953. This was mainly concerned with the purchase of a piece of land for the future Mashriqu'l-Adhkár. According to a detailed report to the Guardian from the British Africa Committee dated 23 February, land could only be bought:[187]

- By non-Africans if it was Crown Land, and the government had to be convinced that it was in the best interests of the people. There was, however, none of this for sale.
- By Africans who were natives of Uganda and usually, in Buganda (the country) if they were Baganda (i.e. born in Buganda)

It was therefore recommended by a lawyer and accepted by the Africa Committee, that two Baganda Bahá'ís could buy a plot to be held in Trust for the future National Spiritual Assembly. Eventually, on 20 April, Joseph Mbogo and Erisha Kiwanuka purchased a piece of land not too far from the Ismaili Mosque on one of the hills overlooking Kampala (Kibulizira Hill). It was a six-acre plot some two-and-a-half miles south of Kampala.

GUARDIAN'S TESTIMONIAL

In February 1954 I received a thrilling letter from Jean Campbell, a Bahá'í from Oxford, writing from her pilgrimage. She wrote that the days were so:[188]

> ...full and pass too quickly. Rúḥíyyih Khánum suggested I should write to you from here since the Guardian had been speaking in praise of you and the wonderful service you and 'Alí Nakhjavání have rendered in Africa. He was singing the praises of the British Bahá'ís and went on to speak of you. He repeated his description of you as the Livingstone of the Faith in Africa and said that *you* had thought of work there *before* he did. So, Philip, whenever you may feel things are not going as you wish just recall this wonderful testimonial.

In January, February and March the Africa Committee sent several

[186] Unpublished cable (personal archives).
[187] Unpublished report (personal archives).
[188] Unpublished letter (personal archives).

letters[189] about various difficulties and questions from different African territories and these were still being pursued when we had to plan for the formation of a large number of new local assemblies. Azíz Yazdí came for a month from Nairobi to help us in April.

On 5 April 1954, the Guardian cabled me, care of Mr Banání:[190]

> Overjoyed deepest loving appreciation, *Shoghi.*

On 6 May, the Guardian wrote through his Assistant Secretary, Leroy Ioas, to all National Assemblies, urging them to write to all pioneers, saying:[191]

> He attaches the utmost importance to the services which they are rendering; in fact, he feels there is no service in the entire Bahá'í world as important as their pioneering work in the virgin areas. They have achieved a great station of service… They can and should become the spiritual conquerors of these new lands

On 11 May 1954, he wrote to the Uganda Teaching Committee:[192]

> *Dear Bahá'í Friends,*
>
> Your letters of June 15, October 15 and November 25 1953, with enclosures, have been received by the beloved Guardian, and he has instructed me to answer you on his behalf.
>
> He is also, in order to save himself the extra effort of yet another letter, replying to the personal one from Mr Hainsworth, dated January 28 1954. As he has answered him through a letter written by me, and has also cabled him, I will not go into detail in this letter. The Guardian hopes that, at a future date, it will be possible for him to make the pilgrimage. During the coming months it is out of the question.
>
> The news which your Committee has conveyed to him has greatly rejoiced his heart. Indeed he feels that, of all the countries in the Bahá'í World, Uganda has made the most progress since the inception of the Faith there a few years back and indeed during this year. He is immensely proud of the achievements of both the pioneers there and the African converts to the Faith. They have set a very high standard, and shown forth most exemplary devotion. The spirit of the African believers is very touching, very noble, and indeed presents a challenge to their fellow Bahá'ís all over the

[189] Unpublished letters (personal archives).
[190] Unpublished cable (personal archives).
[191] Effendi, S. (1965). Messages to Canada (1923-1957). Toronto, Ont., National Spiritual Assembly of the Bahá'ís of Canada., p. 43.
[192] Unpublished letter (personal archives).

world. It seems that God has endowed these races, living in the so-called 'dark' continent, with great spiritual faculties, and also with mental faculties which, as they mature in the Faith, will contribute immensely to the whole, throughout the Bahá'í World.

The power of Bahá'u'lláh is being witnessed during the opening years of the Ten-Year Crusade, we might almost say, as never before. Certainly in the teaching field, there has been the most extraordinary leap forward – in one year, one hundred countries!

He will remember all of you also in his prayers in the Holy Shrines, and he compliments you on the wonderful work which you have done during the past year. All the Bahá'ís, including the Guardian himself, are very proud of Uganda.

In the Guardian's handwriting:

Assuring you of my personal prayers for the success of every of every effort you exert for the promotion of our beloved Faith, and the realisation of every hope you cherish in the service. Your true brother, Shoghi

On 4 June 1954, the Guardian wrote to the British Africa Committee and referred to our work in a very positive way: [193]

Of all the places in the world where the Bahá'í Faith exists and is spreading, the Guardian is definitely most pleased with Africa, and most proud of Uganda. He feels that the spirit shown by white and negro pioneers alike in that continent, presents a challenge to the Bahá'ís everywhere in the world, and that old and staid communities may well learn from, and emulate the example of, the believers of Africa, many of them scarcely a year old in the Cause of God!

Two days later the Guardian drew the attention of the British National Spiritual Assembly to the need to open Cambridge to the Faith saying, 'He feels the time has now arrived for the opening of that city and the expansion of the teaching work there.'[194] This letter was to assume great significance to me in a few months' time.

It was about this time that Bill Sears was on pilgrimage – he may or may not have known at this time that he had been appointed by Hand of the Cause Músá Banání as one of his first Auxiliary Board members.

[193] Effendi, S. (1981). The Unfolding Destiny of the British Bahá'í Community: The Messages from the Guardian of the Bahá'í Faith to the Bahá'ís of the British Isles. London, Bahá'í Publishing Trust., p 328.
[194] Ibid., p. 331.

From Bill's pilgrim notes we read:[195]

> Find out what they did in Uganda and emulate it. You will find that it was small things that have touched the hearts. Not speeches, but love. South Africa will be more difficult, but the principle of approach is the same. South Africa is most difficult. The difficult countries have been given to the United States. Find out what was done in Uganda and follow this example....
>
> Uganda is the spiritual heart of the continent. It has been the centre of activity. It is because of the love and lack of prejudice of any kind that the work has progressed so rapidly there. The concentration was on the native African. This is the emphasis that must be followed in South Africa....
>
> The Guardian spoke several times in praise of the work in Uganda. It is important, he said, to understand that the real reason for the tremendous accomplishments of Uganda was that there was a Hand of the Cause there. The Hand, he told us, was the spiritual heart of the teaching work, just as Uganda was the spiritual heart of the continent. The Hand of the Cause in Africa, he said, was absolutely without prejudice and possessed a truly pure heart.... We must emulate Uganda. It will be more difficult, but the principle will be the same.... Establishing a Ḥaẓíratu'l-Quds is important. It was the rallying centre for all the work in Uganda. Soon it will be the centre for the Central and East African work, a national regional centre....
>
> We have been thinking too much about the white race and not enough about mankind in general, he said. Now is our chance to contribute our share to the conversion of these races.
>
> We must work in order to have the majority of believers belong to these races. Only love can do this. Complete elimination of our own wishes and supplanting these with service to the African. This is the keynote to be sounded....

On re-reading these notes in June 1999, I was once again impressed with the prescience of the beloved Guardian. On 27 June 1954, the Africa Committee wrote to the Guardian regarding a report that they had received from Mr Banání. It should be remembered that Mr Banání was not able to read or write and 'Alí Nakhjavání had to handle all his English correspondence while Mrs Banání and his daughter, Violette Nakhjavání, helped with his Persian letters. These four, Alan and Mary Elston and myself, were the seven 'experienced Bahá'ís' referred to, as the Collisons

[195] Unpublished notes (personal archives).

were the Knights of Bahá'u'lláh in Usumbura. I quote several passages from that letter:[196]

> The committee wishes to bring to your attention the difficulty of the situation in Uganda, about which Mr Banání has written us. As you know, there are now twenty-four local assemblies there and nearly 700 believers, scattered over about eighty localities, using five different languages for teaching, and some of the believers not yet literate in any of them. All of them, in spite of their wonderful devotion, are very new believers, and although some of them are learning very quickly, they need a good deal of guidance and teaching still. To cope with all this there are seven experienced Bahá'ís, pioneers, of whom Philip Hainsworth is about to go on leave.
>
> Mr and Mrs Elston can keep Kampala going but perhaps not much more, Mr Banání has all the work of his Board and 'Alí Nakhjavání must give a great deal of his time to helping him. Mr Banání asked us to consider how we could help to find a way 'that will strengthen and consolidate the victories won – leave alone the scoring of other fresh victories'.
>
> The urgent need seems to be more believers of experience and knowledge and we are taking some steps to try and get some more pioneers to Uganda, though none of our projects is at all certain of success, all are yet somewhat nebulous. We have heard that Mr and Mrs Sabrí had considered settlement in Uganda and that he has the possibility of a job there, and that they are on your advice at the moment trying to settle in Northern Rhodesia or Nyasaland. Is it at all possible that the scope of their settlement could be widened to include Uganda, in view of the above situation? If this were so, we should be most grateful for cable advice, which we could pass on to them.

The Guardian approved the request regarding Hassan and Isobel Sabrí[197] and in the December 1954 issue of the *Bahá'í Journal* it was reported that they had settled in Kampala.

MIDSUMMER LEAVE 1954 AND AFTER

I flew to England for six months' leave during which time I had three major objectives – to be of service to the National Spiritual Assembly, to sign my new contract in London and to try to find a wife. My first task, therefore, was to consult the National Assembly and I was asked to pioneer

[196] Unpublished letter (personal archives).
[197] Unpublished (personal archives).

to Cambridge to 'open' it in accordance with the Guardian's wishes. I took a train to Cambridge, found a place to live from an accommodation bureau, and bought myself an old 3.5 litre Jaguar. I moved in with Mr and Mrs Flack, 98 Newmarket Road, and it was there that I had my first firesides. Jack Flack was a Gypsy horse-dealer who had settled into 'city' life by marrying a 'gringo' (non-Gypsy) and drove a large van to fairs and markets around East Anglia selling general goods. Neither of the Flacks became Bahá'ís but they were sympathetic, and Gladys Flack introduced the Faith to their friends, two of whom, Elaine and Shirley Rogers, eventually became the first Bahá'ís in nearby Newmarket.

When I learned that Hand of the Cause Hermann Grossmann was to visit London, I went to meet him and he took me to the British Museum to show me the statue of an Egyptian Pharoe who, he claimed, was in fact the Jew, Joseph. Hermann was an Egyptologist and his theory was that Joseph, after becoming the Governor of Egypt, eventually became a pharaoh. It was astonishing to look at the statue from one angle and see the characteristics of the dreamer and philosopher as Joseph and from another angle look at the statue of an aristocratic administrator and ruler as was the pharaoh. If his theory were ever proven to be correct, it would revolutionise the Egyptian dating of their ancient kings.

I later took Dr Grossmann to the summer school in Exeter. We were talking on the way down of the need, and opportunity, as George Townshend was a Hand of the Cause, to make overtures to the clergy of the Christian Church. We found the Exeter school and as we swung into a car park in the precincts of the Cathedral, a gentleman in clerical garb scurried across in front of us and I nearly pinned him against the wall. Hermann and I laughed loudly when we later related our story of how we made contact with the clergy!

During these six months, I made many contacts in Cambridge and addressed meetings at the Spiritualist and Unitarian Churches, gave some firesides in Newmarket, visited many Bahá'í communities around the British Isles and eventually arranged for my niece, Kathy Hainsworth, who had accepted the Faith at the age of 15, to take over my rooms in Cambridge as the pioneer – much to the distress of my brother, Kathy's father, who was still unsympathetic to the Faith, although his wife, Annice, had become a Bahá'í.

On one occasion, Kathy invited her boyfriend, Sydney (Sandy) Ackroyd, who was serving in the Royal Air Force (RAF) not far from Cambridge, to visit us. We had such a good time together that he really saw a different side of the Faith. Not long after my return to Uganda, I heard that he had accepted the Faith in Cambridge.

During my visits to Oxford, I had become quite close to a young musician who was a Rhodes Scholar and had accepted the Faith there – Daniel Jordan. We attended a seminar in Belfast where Dan met a new Bahá'í, Nancy Blair, whom he later married, and I met Lizbeth Greaves. It was during this leave that I met up again with John Firman, on leave between contracts, in England, who then formally registered as a Bahá'í in early 1955.

VISITS TO GERMANY

In August, I went to Germany, where I spoke on a number of subjects with Anneliese Bopp as my simultaneous translator. It was my first experience with such a translator, as all translation in Africa had to be made in short passages with a long wait for the translation, as invariably the translator would take much longer to put a passage into an African language than the English I used.

On one occasion when Anneliese was not available, I was trying to converse without success with a number of elderly ladies. It transpired that one lady had been a nurse during the German occupation of Tanganyika in the First World War, so I chatted with her in Swahili and she translated into German.

At the summer school near Esslingen I met Gerhard Bender's parents. Gerhard had been the German POW in Nottingham[198] and I was really feted by them in gratitude for helping Gerhard. It was not until I met Dr Udo Schaefer in North Wales in October 1993 that I learned that in fact he had attended that school as a newly enrolled Bahá'í and remembered some of my talks. After the School, I spoke in Stuttgart and Bonn and then returned to Cambridge.

From there I asked the Guardian if I might go on pilgrimage, possibly on my way back to Uganda, and I wrote to Enoch Olinga who, after one year, was getting well settled in the Cameroons.

The Guardian replied by cable on 22 October:[199]

> Concentrate work Cambridge more meritorious than pilgrimage. *Love, Shoghi.*

On 19 October, Enoch wrote and his letter reached me on 26 October, being sent on to Leicester where I was conducting a Seminar for the Group

[198] This meeting was described on p. 62.
[199] Unpublished cable (personal archives).

there. From Enoch's letter it will be seen how special was our relationship – here are some extracts:[200]

> Your most wonderful letter of October 5 has come to hand, and the kind thoughts contained therein have given me great joy and delight indeed. I am very sorry that you are experiencing backache, and I do ardently pray for quick recovery, that Bahá'u'lláh may remove every complaint you may have so that you may exert more efforts to helping with the teaching in Europe. The friends there will do well to learn from you the methods and techniques applied by pioneers in Africa. In fact they will have first hand or first class information.
>
> Yes, you often talk of those most thrilling days we all spent together as brothers, co-workers, etc. I would assure you that, although the hours have long since passed away, but the fragrance of those days remains with me always. Dorothy tells me of the fine work you are doing there. Surely it will bring much joy and delight to the blessed heart of our Well-Beloved.
>
> Every time I recall the past happenings, especially the enviable company I used to enjoy with you, Philip, I pause in praise of the Lord in thanksgiving for His bounties, a number of times indeed. It is true that you have not been writing; it is true that my physical eyes are bereft of your radiant and inspiring face; but my spirit is always communing with you. You remember our first Assembly picture which we took in 1952, I have it here with me, and every time I feel terribly homesick I look at it. Your effulgent smile is truly animating indeed. I like the picture.
>
> By the way, Philip, so you still love snakes? (laugh). I understand they trained you and you did not like the training! Probably it is equally true to say that the 'thanks' of snakes is a bite!...
>
> Another problem which I am experiencing and trying to combat is money. I must tell you this for you are well conversant with the nature of the African people. As you may know, 95% seem dependent on friends. Here I am almost everything, and as the 'family' is getting large and large, the allowance I am getting from London is as nothing. Of course the London friends are trying their very best to keep me happy and to safeguard the interests of the beloved Faith in this territory. Dorothy is wonderful. 'The number of your 'spiritual grandchildren' is increasing rapidly. You will soon have thousands of them here. We are anticipating a solid mass

[200] Unpublished letter (personal archives).

declaration, the Teso type, from three very big villages. It is the question of financing the project. Our fund is low. In Uganda I used to contribute to the fund very irregularly, but now I have come to a fuller realisation of the significance of Bahá'í funds.

A year ago two days ago I arrived in Victoria. Thanks to Bahá'u'lláh for His tender mercy and grace.

On 16 October 1954, George Townshend wrote to me, and although I have no record of what I wrote to him and what was the 'Kampala pamphlet' to which he refers, his answers are of interest. The letter was written from his home in Dundrum, Co. Dublin:[201]

My Dear Philip,

I loved hearing from you and we should love to renew our friendship here, but alas our little house is already overcrowded, and Adíb and Zarin [Taherzadeh] are moving house and have no furniture at all!

The enclosed 'Kampala' pamphlet is very precious and I only send it you because of my very warm regard for you. Only one pamphlet now remains to me and I don't know how to get another!

I have time enough to answer your questions but my strength and my health is not too good and I am in my 79th year.

Acts 1 v 11 [? his writing is difficult to decipher here] is not to be taken literally: it means that if you have *faith*, God will send you the power to recognise it when He returns, much in the same way He enabled Mary Magdalene to see Christ's spirit rise when His body lay dead.

The Guardian in 'Haifa Notes' says definitely Jesus *did* say on the cross – 'Why hast thou forsaken me?' The Aramaic won't bear the other interpretation anyway.

Jesus' prophecy of the lightning from East to West refers to Bahá'u'lláh , as did Muhammad's 'the Sun shall rise in the West' and refers to the prominent part played by the West in this Dispensation.

Study the Kampala Pamphlet carefully, it is full of small points which are of great teaching value.

My second article on 'Christian Contacts' contains new stuff of great significance.

The prophecies of Isaiah 53 fit BH even better than Christ: e.g. BH *was* in prison and Jesus was not!

[201] Unpublished letter (personal archives).

No more now, alas. I wish we could see you somehow but it does not seem possible. Later, my health will improve and I will see you then somehow.

Meantime, give my love to my revered and very dear friend Banani and his family: don't forget.

With love and greetings and all best wishes from the whole family, from Nancy, Brian, Una and especially from myself, I am,

Your fellow servant in the Great Cause, George Townshend

Just before returning to Uganda on 4 January 1955 I was able to attend the first meeting to be held in the newly acquired centre at 27 Rutland Gate, though it was not dedicated officially until 15 January, when 150 souls packed the public rooms for the largest ever Bahá'í meeting in the British Isles.

RETURN TO KAMPALA

When I returned to Kampala I found that Isobel and Hassan Sabrí had settled in Uganda from Dar-es-Salaam and were very welcome indeed as the teaching work was snow-balling. Shortly after arrival, I learned that my close colleague and one-time flat-mate, Dick Backwell, and Vida had left to pioneer in Guyana and Ian Semple had been elected on to the British National Spiritual Assembly to replace him.

Reporting to my new office in Kampala – the Vector Control Division, Uganda Medical Service – I found I had a fascinating load of work and could see it would take me to all parts of Uganda. Living in government 'bachelor' quarters not too far from the Kampala Ḥaẓíratu'l-Quds and the home of the Banánís and Na<u>kh</u>javánís enabled me to give much of my free time to the work in Kampala and the Uganda Teaching Committee as well as the extension teaching going on all around Kampala.

Part of my work was in onchocerciasis control. It was during one exercise – surveying the rivers, measuring the flow downstream on the dosing days, and placing the equipment on the selected sites upstream and meeting large gatherings of the local inhabitants – that I received in the West Nile District a cable from Violette in early July 1955, to say that the Guardian was contemplating the building of the African Temple in Kampala and would I co-operate with Mr Banání to obtain government permission to go ahead with the construction?

PLANNING THE TEMPLE

The third Mas͟hriqu'l-Ad͟hkár in the world had been scheduled to be built in the vicinity of Tehran and a site had already been purchased, but in 1955, persecution of the Bahá'ís in Írán had considerably increased and it became clear that the Guardian considered it unwise to proceed with building there.

The actual decision to go ahead could not have been taken until the Guardian had marshalled all the facts about the possibility of building in Uganda. Unfortunately, I have no record of the cables sent to Mr Banání or me nor of that call to the British National Spiritual Assembly to make a start on the Kampala Mas͟hriqu'l-Ad͟hkár. Neither is anything recorded in *Unfolding Destiny* to indicate this decision between the Guardian's letter of 5 August[202] and the one written on his behalf by Leroy Ioas on 22 August.[203]

All I have is a copy of a letter that I wrote to the Guardian on 12 July.[204] It became clear, however, that this Temple of Africa was to be 'compensation' to the Íránian believers for their sufferings and their inability to go ahead with the building of their own Mas͟hriqu'l-Ad͟hkár. In his cable to all National Spiritual Assemblies via the US National Assembly, the Guardian wrote on August 23 about the persecution of the Bahá'ís in Írán and said:[205]

> Historic decision arrived at raise Mother Temple Africa City Kampala, situated its heart constituting supreme consolation masses oppressed, valiant brethren Cradle Faith.

On receipt of Violette's cable, I had to write my views to the Guardian and from this letter of 12 July, it is clear that:[206]

- I made suggestions to Violette on how to answer the Guardian's cable;
- As Mr Banání and 'Alí were in Egypt, I could not immediately consult with them;
- I was over 400 miles from Kampala and would be on a project there until mid-September. If, when Mr Banání and 'Alí returned, they felt that my presence was essential, I could take a couple of days off and fly to Entebbe and back.

[202] Effendi, S. (1981). The Unfolding Destiny of the British Bahá'í Community: The Messages from the Guardian of the Bahá'í Faith to the Bahá'ís of the British Isles. London, Bahá'í Publishing Trust., 348.
[203] Ibid., p. 356.
[204] Unpublished letter (personal archives).
[205] Rabbani, R. (1988). The Guardian of the Bahá'í Faith. London, Bahá'í Publishing Trust., p. 225.
[206] Unpublished letter (personal archives).

- I was unaware of the terms of the purchase of the land, as it had all been handled in my absence. However, my enquiries led me to believe that if the land which was owned by the Bahá'ís was outside the actual township limits, the owners would be absolutely free to erect any kind of building on it. If the land had been within the township of Kampala, it would have been necessary, according to the law, to have provided an assurance to develop some kind of a building within two years from purchase. As I knew of no such undertaking being given, I was confident it was outside the Kampala municipal boundary. This information had been previously given to me while in Jinja by the district commissioner, who had himself suggested we obtain a piece of land outside the gazetted boundary of Jinja and then build a Centre in bricks, or mud, or any material we wished. I had heard, however, that a comment had been made to the Land Office when the trust was set up for its purchase and it was registered in the names of the trustees, that it was eventually for use as a Bahá'í Temple.

In response to my letter, the Guardian wrote on 13 August 1955:[207]

> *Dear Bahá'í Brother,*
>
> Your letter of July 12th has been received by the beloved Guardian, and he has instructed me to answer you on his behalf.
>
> He appreciates the difficulties with which you are faced, in trying to give your ideas to him from such an isolated point.
>
> You should write your views to Mr Banání. If he finds the officials are proving difficult or hesitant, then the Guardian would urge that you make a special trip to Kampala, so that you can go with Mr Banání, and do your utmost to arrange for this permission.
>
> The Guardian attaches great importance to this project. Any service you can perform in connection with it will be deeply valued by him.
>
> *With warm Bahá'í greetings, R. Rabbání*

In the Guardian's handwriting:

> *May the Almighty bless, guide and sustain you always, aid you to extend the range of your meritorious services, and win great victories in the days to come.*
>
> *Your true brother, Shoghi.*

A survey of the site revealed serious defects as a future Temple site: because of the contours of the hill, the building would not be seen from anywhere within Kampala and there were difficulties of access and water

[207] Ibid.

supply. This was reported to the Guardian with the suggestion that a search be made for an alternative site.

On 4 November the Guardian cabled, 'Disapprove change Temple site'.[208]

When we learned the requirements for a Bahá'í House of Worship from the letter written on behalf of the Guardian to the National Spiritual Assembly by Mr Ioas, 22 August,[209] we made contact with the best-known architects in Kampala, Messrs Cobb, Powell and Freeman, and got to know Mr Freeman very well. He advised us that as we had invited several architects if they wished to submit designs embodying these requirements, they were bound by their rules to the effect that if more than one architect was to submit designs for any one building, a competition should be held. The British National Spiritual Assembly decided not to hold such a competition as the Guardian had asked for designs and estimates within two months, but commissioned a well-known British architect with African experience to submit a design. When we received the rough sketches of the proposed building, we were unanimous in our feeling that this was not the right design for our Temple and so advised the National Assembly. They appeared to favour it, however, and it was a tremendous relief when we learned that on 28 October the National Spiritual Assembly had sent the designs to the Guardian, and he had rejected them.

On 18 November, to our great relief, the Guardian wrote to the National Spiritual Assembly that he 'was very discouraged by these drawings'; that the 'style is wholly unsuitable for a Bahá'í Temple' and he told them until they heard again from him they should take no further steps.[210]

Apparently the National Assembly responded that perhaps the design could be modified rather than rejected outright but on 13 December Mr Ioas wrote that the Guardian's decision was final as the design was 'too extreme for any modification to render it possible as a temple'.[211]

In the meantime, the Guardian had been pressing for the purchase of land for an endowment as a goal of the Plan, preferably in Uganda, but if not possible, in some other part of East Africa.

On 16 December he wrote through Leroy Ioas that the National Spiritual Assembly should buy a small plot of land in Uganda at a cost of approximately $1,000, which had been donated by Hand of the Cause

[208] Effendi, S. (1981). The Unfolding Destiny of the British Bahá'í Community: The Messages from the Guardian of the Bahá'í Faith to the Bahá'ís of the British Isles. London, Bahá'í Publishing Trust., p. 358
[209] Ibid., p. 356.
[210] Ibid., p. 358.
[211] Ibid., p. 359.

Amelia Collins, and a piece was purchased through Paul Mukasa, brother of Max Kanyerezi, on Kikaya Hill.[212]

On 11 July 1956 the Guardian wrote a lengthy letter to the British National Spiritual Assembly in which he informed them that Charles Mason Remey had completed a design for the Kampala Temple which met with his approval.[213]

1956

This was to be a most fateful year, but we entered it very quietly, gradually preparing the believers for the election in April of the first Regional National Spiritual Assembly of Central and East Africa. On 20 September 1955,[214] the Guardian had written to the British National Spiritual Assembly that it would have 76 delegates apportioned amongst the local Spiritual Assemblies formed in 1955 within the countries which would be represented by the new National Spiritual Assembly: 53 for Uganda, 11 for Kenya, 5 for Tanganyika, 2 each for Ruanda-Urundi and Zanzibar, and one each for the Belgian Congo, French Equatorial Africa and Seychelles. Plans were made to allocate the delegates to the local Spiritual Assemblies of Uganda, to have the delegates elected and arrange for their transport to and accommodation in Kampala.

FIRST NATIONAL ASSEMBLY IN AFRICA SOUTH OF THE SAHARA ELECTED

The second Convention ever to be held in Africa south of the Sahara was that called to elect the Regional National Spiritual Assembly of the Bahá'ís of Central and East Africa on 23 April 1956. It was opened in the Budonian Club, Mengo and continued in the tent at the Ḥaẓíratu'l-Quds, Kampala for three days (24 – 27 April), convened by the National Spiritual Assembly of the British Isles and opened by their Chairman, Ḥasan Balyúzí, at the express instruction of the Guardian. Sixty-one of the 76 delegates and 30 visitors were present. 'Alí Nakhjavání was elected chairman and I was elected secretary. Mr Banání, as the only Hand of the Cause for Africa, was present for the opening of the Convention and the election of the National

[212] Ibid., p. 361.
[213] Ibid., p. 367.
[214] Effendi, S. (1981). The Unfolding Destiny of the British Bahá'í Community: The Messages from the Guardian of the Bahá'í Faith to the Bahá'ís of the British Isles. London, Bahá'í Publishing Trust., p. 357.

Spiritual Assembly, and then had to fly with 'Alí to a similar Convention being conducted in Cairo for North-East Africa on 24, 25 and 26 April.

There was also a Convention held in Tunis for the election of the Regional National Assembly of North and North-West Africa held from 30 April to 2 May.

It was an indication of the supreme dedication of Mr Banání that although he had been in England with Mrs Banání for medical treatment on the advice of the Guardian, he had flown straight from London to attend the Convention in Johannesburg held on 21 April for the National Spiritual Assembly of South and West Africa, he then without rest to Kampala, Cairo and Tunis before coming back to Kampala.

As soon as 'Alí returned, the officers were elected as follows: 'Alí Nakhjavání (chairman), Azíz Yazdí (vice-chairman), Philip Hainsworth (secretary), Hassan Sabrí (treasurer), Jalál Nakhjavání, Sylvester Okurut, Max Kanyerezi, Oloro Epyeru and Tito Wanantsusi. The four African members were all from Uganda.

The large contingent of Ugandan members no doubt reflected the large number of delegates from that country. Details of the election and a photograph of eight members (as Tito Wanantsusi was not present at the time the photograph was taken) were sent to the Guardian on 26 May[215] and the reply was received on 10 June:[216]

> *Dear Bahá'í Friends,*
>
> Your loving letter of 26 May was presented to the beloved Guardian, and he has directed me to respond on his behalf.
>
> He is greatly pleased, and values most highly, the establishment of the National Spiritual Assembly of the Bahá'ís of Central and East Africa. This is an historic act, and one that augurs well for the future of the Faith in that promising land. Surely this new pillar of the House of Justice will win many victories for the Cause of God, and spread the Faith rapidly throughout the vast areas coming under their jurisdiction.
>
> The Guardian will pray for the Assembly, the members, and the success of its work.
>
> When your statistics are amplified, the Guardian will appreciate early advices.
>
> The Guardian was happy to receive the photo of the nine friends, eight of the Assembly and Hand of the Cause Músá Banání. When a

[215] Unpublished letter (personal archives).
[216] Unpublished letter (personal archives).

photo is ready of all nine of the Assembly, he will appreciate having it for placement in the Mansion of Bahá'u'lláh.

The Guardian sends you all his loving Greetings.

Leroy Ioas

In 1956, the government was encouraging the expatriate officers in the Overseas Civil Service in Uganda to take a short tour which gave three months overseas leave after 15 months' service, instead of six months after two-and-a-half years. This meant that I was to go immediately after the National Spiritual Assembly election, but in order to attend a special course at Mytchett, Surrey, in spraying equipment, I was granted an additional short period for this purpose.

At the first meeting of the National Spiritual Assembly it was agreed that as I would be away for only three months, I could be released from secretarial duties for this period and no vacancy would need to be recognised.

HOME LEAVE

During this much shorter home leave, I had to attend to the production of a film of the work with onchocerciasis control, the equipment course, meet with the British National Spiritual Assembly and spend some time in Cambridge to see how the work was progressing; I seemed to have very little time to get around the community.

When I met with the National Spiritual Assembly in England I was not only able to report on the African Convention, but also on two significant developments.

The first concerned Muhammedi Luganda – a Ugandan Muslim who had accepted the Faith and, after some deepening, become a stalwart teacher. One evening on returning home, he found his wife in bed with another man and in the heat of his anger had killed the man. Muhammedi had then reported to the Police and said, 'I am a Bahá'í and I must now forfeit my own life as a recompense'. The African judge, when the case came before him took the view that it had all happened suddenly when Muhammedi was emotionally very disturbed and under great provocation and gave him a long prison sentence. He began this at the Kitalya Prison Farm. Muhammedi was an ideal prisoner and obtained permission for Bahá'ís to visit him and take books to the prison library. Rex and Mary Collison, now back from Usumbura, and Isobel Sabrí visited the prison, collected six confirmed 'declarations' which were followed by 11 others and soon there was a record of 60 prisoners attending the meetings when the pioneers visited them. A series of regular meetings was planned and then the prisoners eventually wrote to the Guardian.

The second development was that one of the Bagisu living in Bubulo on the outskirts of Mbale had been pressing for a Bahá'í school. Javan Gutosi was very enterprising and had been one of the early Bagisu (after Tito Wanantsuzi) to accept the Faith. He had obtained the use of some semi-derelict buildings belonging to the coffee producers for whom he worked, and had started a school with a teacher, all financed by levying a small school fee for each student and by a substantial contribution from himself. He had by this time a total of 47 children as pupils. Gutosi's vision was that this would grow into a fully-fledged Bahá'í school under the auspices of the new National Spiritual Assembly.

In the course of my holiday, during a visit 'up North', I spent a day or two with William and Madeline Hellaby in Lancashire. Bill was coming very close to the Faith but had very seriously to consider the effects of his possible resignation from the Unitarian Church in which he was an ordained minister. I promised Madeline that I would write to the Guardian about him and ask for his prayers. I wrote as promised on 29 August. I had also sent a report of my travels to the National Teaching Committee and almost immediately, Marion Hofman, again its secretary, replied on 28 August 1956:

> Your splendid and thrilling report has just come in, and I am sending it off to Ernest Gregory to read. The news of the Hellabys is simply wonderful. I shall certainly write them and also send a line to Ian Semple, who knows them well. This could be of great importance for the work in future.
>
> It is really quite impossible to thank you for all of this in words. It seems to me that a brass band and banners would be more appropriate. I assure you the Committee has the deepest appreciation of your efforts, and we are all aware what an important part your travels have played in the developments this summer. No doubt, it was all part of a providential plan for our Home Front. God succoureth whom He will, with the hosts of heaven and of the earth – an approximate quote – and I'm sure you are one of those sent, just as you were during the Six Year Plan when you came out of the Army. May Bahá'u'lláh bless all your needs, dear, and give you as much happiness as you have given us help!

While in Mytchett I attended a public meeting at 27 Rutland Gate and was so distressed with the interruptions during that meeting that I wrote to the local Spiritual Assembly on 3 September, expressing my unease and making a few suggestions to which they responded appreciatively on 13 September.

When I met with the British National Spiritual Assembly I was asked to attend a 19 Day Feast shortly before I was due to leave for Kampala and to speak on pioneer needs for East Africa. The Feast was on Friday, 8 September.

On reaching 27 Rutland Gate, I was stopped at the door with a demand for my registration card or some other form of credential. Not having any, I was not being allowed entry but because of my vehement protests, I was told I could meet the London local Assembly, then in session upstairs. I was fuming when I went in and looked around – they were all Bahá'ís from overseas except one who was apparently the recording secretary – I recognised her as Kathleen Hyett, the sister of Stan Lowe at whose Bahá'í wedding I had officiated in Blackpool some years previously. I looked around then and commented that I thought they were carrying their security measures too rigidly – here was I, a pioneer from the British Isles before most of them had come to the country; I was the secretary of the newly elected Regional National Spiritual Assembly of Central and East Africa; the National Spiritual Assembly of the British Isles had invited me to this Feast to speak to the friends; I had been on the National Spiritual Assembly of the British Isles and secretary of the National Teaching Committee during the winning of the Six Year Plan; and the only British Bahá'í on the London Assembly there was a lady who had become a Bahá'í as a result of my teaching – and they were not prepared to let me in!

John Long, chairman of the National Spiritual Assembly, who was in the centre, then came upstairs with a temporary credential that he had typed out for me. Subsequently, I went into the Feast, which had just begun, and I was guided to a seat on the back row.

I MEET LOIS FOR THE FIRST TIME

During the consultation, it began to be clear that the atmosphere had changed considerably from the time at the end of my last leave when I attended the first meeting in that building and I voiced my concern and stressed the need to extend a warm welcome to strangers.

At this time, I noticed a young lady I had not previously met and had a strong urge to get to know her. I asked who she was and was told she was a new Bahá'í and a very capable secretary who had just been appointed to the new National Public Relations Committee. This really whetted my appetite. I subsequently learnt that she had been asking who was that rude stranger who had had the gall to criticise the local Assembly!

When I was called upon to deliver my speech I mentioned, among other things, that the first African Bahá'í from Uganda to come to study in England was due to arrive at the airport the next day, Sunday – it would be good if a number could join me in welcoming him. Only three Bahá'ís accepted this suggestion.

It seemed natural then that, when the usual cup of tea was served after the Feast, this group should meet together – imagine my surprise when I found that one of the three was the young lady I had noticed. When I was introduced to her as 'Philip Hainsworth' she said, 'Oh, you are the person I would like to meet my mother', and she told me why. After consulting my diary I told her that it would not be possible this trip.

The other two Bahá'ís were Ralph and Rosemary Crates and it was arranged that the four of us would travel to the airport in Ralph Crates' car. The new Bahá'í offered to serve coffee and biscuits afterwards in her flat, which was very near the Ḥaẓíratu'l-Quds, for those who could not come to the airport.

I was quite excited, as I not only recognised a kindred soul, but everything I was hearing about her I liked more and more.

Sunday came and we went to the air terminal, waited and waited until all the passengers of the appropriate flight had passed through – no Ugandan! I finally checked the passenger list and found he had not caught the plane. As our little group broke up, the young lady told me she had planned to go to the Albert Hall to hear the Vienna Boys' Choir that evening and I said I would like to go with her. First we had to telephone a London Bahá'í to ask him to tell those who were expected at her flat that the party was off. We went to the telephone booth, typical of that time, with doors that folded inwards in two sections. We both got into the box although there was not a great deal of space, closed the doors and she made the call. But, how to get out! There was a great deal of pushing and squeezing to get the doors open – we became very closely associated! That was how my relationship with Lois Houchin really began!

The concert was wonderful!

OUR MARRIAGE: LOIS AND PHILIP

I had to go back to Mytchett to my machinery course and suggested to her that she come down to Cambridge to a talk I was chairing there the following week. It was arranged that she would come down by train on the Friday evening and would stay in the same guesthouse (overlooking Parkers' Piece) as Dr Moayad, the Persian pioneer then living there.

However, my mind was full of my new experience and I could not wait to see her again, so I decided that I would go to London on the Thursday evening to the public meeting and persuaded Ted Cardell to drive me there. I was quite annoyed to learn that she had made other arrangements for that evening and I did not have a chance to speak with her!

The meeting on the Friday night in Cambridge was in a hotel with Richard St Barbe Baker as speaker with me as Chairman. I met Lois at the railway station; we had dinner together and went to the meeting. I was so happy that the whole evening passed all too quickly. We walked back afterwards and, reluctant to break off our conversation, we sat on a bench on Parkers' Piece, talking about Lois' singing, her present job with J Arthur Rank as PA to a producer/director. I told her about life in Uganda and my new job as secretary of the National Spiritual Assembly and finally, at 3.00 a.m., asked her if she would come back with me to Uganda! She accepted and that was how we decided to marry.

This meant my getting a couple of weeks' extra leave and arranging a registrar marriage by special licence. She had to be released from her work and break off her engagement to another young man, as well as obtain permission to marry from her mother, who was the only living parent.

Lois' notes of these events were substantially the same as mine, and she later summarised them in a letter she wrote to 'Amatu'l-Bahá Rúḥíyyih Khánum.

On Saturday afternoon, Lois had a meeting with the National Assembly as a member of the PR Committee, but not having spoken with her mother, said nothing of our proposed engagement. On Sunday morning, we travelled to meet her mother and I formally told her mother that we wished to marry. She was most surprised that she had been asked and found it difficult to understand that she had the power to prevent our marriage. She eventually agreed and we took her out to lunch. Afterwards we went back to London where I had to meet with the National Assembly. I then told them that, as they had not seen fit to allow me to recruit a stenographer to pioneer to Kampala, I intended to marry one! Lois then came to meet with the National Spiritual Assembly.

Lois' mother had said that she would want to provide the wedding cake. As I knew that the traditional way to make a rich wedding cake was to use beer for the mixture, I told her she should not put in any beer, and reluctantly she agreed.

Ḥasan Balyúzí had agreed to conduct the marriage and David Hofman would say a few words.

On 17 September, I wrote to Bobbie Kamming, of the London local Spiritual Assembly:[217] '

Dear Bobbie,

Will you please ask the LSA to arrange for the wedding of Miss Lois Houchin and myself on Saturday 29 September at 3.30 p.m.

We are both Bahá'ís and are, as yet, in good standing. Lois' mother is the only living parent and has given her consent. She will be present at the wedding.

We are deeply grateful to Ḥasan Balyúzí who has accepted to conduct the marriage and to Mrs Backwell and Mrs Leedham who are attending to the catering. Mrs Houchin will provide a wedding cake and meet all reception expenses.

I believe some twelve or fourteen Bahá'ís from outside London will be present and about 14 non-Bahá'ís, so please be so kind as to plan accordingly, as you are in a better position to know how many London Bahá'ís will be present. (As a member of the London Community, Lois was anxious that anyone who wished to come should be able to do so).

You may care to announce it at the Feast.

Thank you so much for everything.

With deepest Bahá'í love,

Philip.

On the same date, I cabled the Guardian: '

Lois Houchin, new devoted London Bahá'í and myself marrying 29 September prior return Uganda. Pledge joint service beloved Guardian beg prayers confirmation. Deepest love, Philip Lois.

On 19 September the Guardian cabled:[218]

Lois Philip Hainsworth Heartfelt congratulations assure loving fervent prayers success. *Shoghi.*

The arrangements were complex but went without a hitch. Lois' mother's consent was obtained; the marriage was arranged at the Registry Office, Kensington; George Barnley was cabled and responded that the marriage extension of leave had been granted; Bobbie Leedham, Gladys Backwell and Jeannette Battrick offered to collaborate to organise the Bahá'í reception; 27 Rutland Gate was booked for Saturday 29 September, three weeks to the day after we had met and the London local Spiritual Assembly agreed to witness the marriage.

[217] Unpublished letter (personal archives).
[218] Unpublished cable (personal archives).

About this time, I re-established contact with Ernest Hartley, the man with whom I had shared a room on being called into the Armed Forces in January 1940 and whom I had left in Helen's Bay, N. Ireland when I went into hospital in Londonderry. Apparently, he too had applied for a commission in 1943 but had to return to the Leeds Tribunal, withdraw his 'objections' and agree to accept a commission in any arm of service. Due to his pre-war experience in movement control he had gone into an arm of the service which utilised this experience and had reached the rank of major.

On his release, he had become a pharmaceutical representative, had married, and was living in a flat off Kensington Church Street – within walking distance of Lois' flat. On the evening before I had to visit the Kensington Registry Office to arrange for a special licence, Lois and I went for a meal with Ernest and his wife, Christine, and he agreed to go with me to the Registrar's Office. This turned out to be quite hilarious. The Registrar had to ask me many questions, and for very few of those relating to Lois did I know the answer!

'What was her mother's address?' I was astonished when Ernest said, 'I can tell you that', and looked it up in a little book he had. 'What was her date of birth?' Again, Ernest produced the answer. 'What are her home and work telephone numbers?' Yet again, Ernest knew the answers. The registrar, in amazement, asked, 'Which of you is actually marrying this young lady?' I knew Ernest had only met Lois the previous evening but it came to light that at the Hartley's flat she had used the telephone and had left her notebook by the telephone: Ernest had brought it to give to me for her. All the answers he had from this little book! The Registry Office wedding was extremely simple, held in a very dignified room in the Kensington Registry Office, as Lois had a flat in Kensington and my temporary address was that of the Backwells in Barnes. Lois' mother and brother – Anne and Michael Houchin – Ernest and Christine Hartley, Lois and I were the only ones participating. Mrs Houchin then took us all to lunch at Veeraswamy's in Regent Street after which Michael took Lois to her flat to change into her wedding dress.

I went with her mother to 27 Rutland Gate. Due to the dense traffic Lois was half-an-hour late at Rutland Gate – very traditional! I remembered little of the morning's events but much of the Bahá'í function is very clear. The room was full, Ted Cardell was taking photographs, a cine film was being taken, Bobbie, Jeannette, and Gladys had excelled themselves and everything went without a hitch. Lois was radiant and I was just bursting with happiness and could not believe it was real. David was his usual eloquent self and raised a particularly loud laugh when he said that he 'had known Philip for eighteen years and had worked closely with him on committees and the National Spiritual Assembly and this was the first time Philip had done something with which he was in full agreement!'

Our wedding certificate was signed by Ḥasan Balyúzí and John Ferraby, then chairman and secretary both of the London local Assembly and of the National Spiritual Assembly, neither of whom had been present at the meeting which would not at first let me into the Feast of the 8 September. This was some 13 months prior to their appointment as Hands of the Cause in the Guardian's last letter to the Bahá'í world.

While the refreshments were being enjoyed and compliments being given to Lois' mother for her wedding cake, I noticed her having a good laugh with another non-Bahá'í friend who had accompanied her (Mrs Witham) so I said, 'You did not put any beer in the cake, did you?' She said, 'No, but I laced it with brandy!' We kept this a secret.

I found that I was so excited with the whole day's activities that I developed a twitch in my eye and it seemed to Lois that I had a permanent wink!

Ralph and Rosemary Crates, Ralph an old friend of Hassan Sabrí's and Rosemary who had accepted the Faith as I danced with her at the Exeter summer school in 1954, lent us their car for our very brief honeymoon. Our wedding night was to be spent at the Compleat Angler, Marlow, but when we arrived we found that there had been some mix-up and no room was available. The apologetic receptionist arranged for us to have a room in a nearby hotel, but we had dinner at the Angler. It was a dinner dance and we both went on to the floor to dance, wondering if the other could dance! We were both happily surprised with each other's prowess and the joy of dancing together soon overcame the annoyance of the mixed-up booking plans.

Tickets had to be booked for the plane to get us as quickly as possible to Uganda, so we had a mad rush parcelling up Lois' books and music. Just before we had married I had spent an evening at her flat and two things stood out in our minds from that occasion – Lois was absolutely astonished that I ate a whole pound of sausages, and I was enraptured by her singing. She sang 'Voi che sapete' from the 'Marriage of Figaro' among other selections from opera. I just could not believe that so talented a girl – a highly qualified secretary, a cultured theatregoer and frequenter of art galleries, and a trained opera singer – could be interested in me. Later I used to say jokingly 'I married my culture', but it was true, and later I had cause to reflect upon the strangeness of the girlfriends in my life prior to meeting Lois. My first girlfriend was my dancing partner, which lasted about six years but died off when I became a Bahá'í as she was a most vehement atheist. She, Winifrid, married a dentist who did not dance. Ursula Frener, whose professed reason for not becoming engaged was that I was not interested in opera and here I was, marrying an opera singer.

The response to my letter to the Guardian of 29 August was actually written the day before our wedding and was dated 28 September 1956:[219]

> *Dear Bahá'í Brother,*
>
> Your letter of August 29 has been received by the beloved Guardian, and he has instructed me to answer you on his behalf.
>
> He will be happy to hear from the Rev. W Hellaby; and he feels, when he leaves the church, he should courageously give the Faith as his reason for doing so.
>
> The Guardian says you, yourself, should not be discouraged. You have already accomplished much, and will no doubt render even greater services in the days to come.
>
> He assures you of his loving prayers for those whose names you have mentioned, as well as for your constant strength and guidance in your labours.
>
> *With warmest Bahá'í greetings,*
>
> *R Rabbání*

In her own handwriting:

> *Dear Philip,*
>
> The beloved Guardian was most happy to hear of your marriage and hopes your union will be blessed and enable you to achieve even greater victories for our Faith with the help of your wife.

In the beloved Guardian's handwriting:

> *May the Almighty bless your union, reward you abundantly for your past labours, that are indeed truly historic, and enable you, together with your wife, to render memorable services to his Faith and its nascent institutions, in that promising continent.*
>
> *Your true brother, Shoghi*

We arrived in Entebbe on 8 October and went straight to a wonderful reception at 4 Kagera Road. Lois was radiant and captured everyone's heart, particularly when she sang 'The Holy City'. I was absolutely bursting with pride. We had a quiet laugh together when we saw how much a few members of the community, for whom we had brought small boxes of wedding cake, enjoyed it.

We spent our first night in Kampala at a hotel, then moved for a few

[219] Unpublished letter (personal archives).

days to the Ḥaẓíratu'l-Quds until we moved into the nearby Government Hostel and then to our first home in Queens Road, quite close to my office at the Vector Control Division.

Immediately Lois became involved in the work of the community, typing my correspondence and minutes for the National Spiritual Assembly, visiting extension teaching goals with Violette Nakhjavání and others, and in the affairs of the Kampala local Assembly. She was also appointed to the Temple Committee and was elected its secretary.

On 11 October we wrote to the London local Spiritual Assembly:[220]

> *Dear Bahá'í Friends,*
>
> Lois and I are very sorry indeed that life has been so hectic since our marriage, that we have not been able to write to your Assembly to express the deep, the very deep gratitude we feel for the wonderful arrangements which were made for the wedding and for the loving care and planning which contributed so much to the success which it undoubtedly was.
>
> We have written to Mrs Backwell and personally thanked Bobbie Leedham for their fine work and we hope to write soon to Bobbie Kamming and Jeannette Battrick, for all that they did, and we hope your Assembly will convey our gratitude and pleasure to the friends at the next Feast.
>
> Needless to say we had a royal welcome here and a very moving meeting with the Kampala community and all in all we are completely happy and deeply grateful to Bahá'u'lláh for His bounty and blessings.
>
> We have also received a wonderful letter from our beloved Guardian with special personal notes from him and from his wife
>
> *With warmest love to you all, Lois and Philip.*

On 12 November Lois wrote a long letter to Rúḥíyyih Khánum giving her a full description of how she became a Bahá'í and how we had met and decided to marry. The following quotations illustrate the general tone of this letter:[221]

> The letter which you and the beloved Guardian wrote to us here so completely delighted us that we were swept off our feet – Philip was so happy that he almost wept. We received it at the end of a most wonderful day – the Kampala friends had given us a most moving welcoming party and we had had an altogether thrilling day. Philip tells me that he feels sure you would like to know about

[220] Unpublished letter (personal archives).
[221] Unpublished letter (Lois' personal archives).

> how we met, and our wedding, and perhaps a little bit about me, so here we go!

There then followed a description of the already mentioned visit to London airport:

> So we went to a concert together – to hear the Mozart Requiem and a Beethoven Mass, beautifully performed by the Vienna Philharmonic Orchestra, the Wiener Sängerknaben and some of the Vienna Opera Chorus – it was a wonderful concert, and we both thoroughly enjoyed it and began to know each other. Then we went for a long walk, and later had coffee, talking all the time. By the time Philip left, I think we both knew that 'this was it' although neither of us had actually said anything. He asked me if I would go down to Cambridge to see him the next weekend and I agreed. He completely surprised me by coming up to a public meeting on the following Thursday, but we hardly had a chance to speak together. The following day I shot off to Cambridge, where we had dinner together before his meeting and talked until 2 am afterwards. It was then that we decided that we would marry and arranged to go to London the next day to meet my mother and ask her permission.... He completely captivated her and we obtained her approval (she is our only living parent) and the next day we met the National Assembly and arranged the wedding for two weeks later. The thing at which we still don't cease to wonder is the fact that all this seemed to go so smoothly, almost as if it had always been meant to be.... Everything went right for us – little things which seemed to be out of place suddenly went right – like Philip's trying to get the civil ceremony arranged for the same day, the registrar saying it was impossible and that there was not likely to be a cancellation, Philip's arranging it for the following Monday (two days after the Bahá'í Wedding) and then, out of the blue, the registrar telephoning me to say that there HAD been a cancellation. We were so pleased, because it meant that we could after all comply with the Guardian's instruction. The other thing which struck us forcibly was my passage over here working out so well. BOAC had told Philip quite categorically that it was unlikely that there would be a cancellation for his same day, let alone the same flight, and there *was* one. Oh, all sorts of little things seemed to happen to help us.
>
> Our wedding was a beautiful one – Bahá'ís came from all over England to see Philip married, and everyone was so happy. Ḥasan Balyúzí conducted the ceremony most beautifully, and even the non-Bahá'ís present enjoyed it immensely.

We are both very, very happy, dear Rúḥíyyih Khánum, and that is principally what this long, long rigmarole is to tell you. Mama Banání told me that you would be happy to hear this, because you know that our dear Philip has been trying to settle down for so long now. I am proud and deeply happy that he chose me to be his partner, and I hope that I shall be able to help him in his work here, or wherever it may take him.

The pioneers here are the most wonderful people and they have been so kind to me – right from the very first moment when they met us at the airport at Entebbe they extended their love to me, a stranger, in a way which I had never met before. Since then they have made me feel as if I have come home, and have drawn me into their activities. I want to say again how happy we were to have your letter to us – and I would like to try and tell you how very much it meant to Philip – both that and the telegram you sent for the wedding – because he loves you both so very, very much. So much, that although I have never met you both, he has imparted some of that love to me.

1957

On March 28, 1957 Rúḥíyyih Khánum replied to Lois:[222]

Dear Lois,

Your letter arrived and I set it aside to read it when I could go over it and enjoy it.

Shortly after the letter, Lo and behold! Bobby Leedham turned up with a picture of you and Philip which she gave me, a very lovely photograph taken in the country, so the letter and the photograph went very well together.

You sound to me like the right person for Philip. We are all very glad to get him off our hands! If we can now succeed in getting Ted Cardell married, a large number of Bahá'ís will sigh with relief! It's really awful to have had two such nice pioneers on the shelf for so long.

I think you are lucky to get Philip and he to get you. You will have your ups and downs I presume like the rest of the human race, but the Cause helps wonderfully in this relationship as in others. How nice that your mother should have liked him and given her consent.

[222] Unpublished letter (Lois' personal archives).

> I'm afraid that you will not only have to consider yourself permanently 'on the water wagon', but your cuisine on the water wagon too. This question has been asked many times of the Guardian – whether wine, etc may be used in cooking, and he says no. Owen Battrick who was here a short time ago with his wife, with a very wry face informed me that he had spent a long time becoming an expert on lager and wines. All that thrown down the drain!
>
> I can well imagine you are happy with the Banánís and other Bahá'ís there. They are unusually fine people, and so easy to get along with. I miss not seeing them.
>
> It would certainly be lovely if you could come here with Philip on pilgrimage- I hope the time is not too far off when you will. That may have been the wisdom in Philip's not being able to come the last time he asked.
>
> Give Philip my love, and tell him that presumably he's at last found something to repress him a little. My love to you too, Lois, and I look forward to knowing you personally at a future date.
>
> *Rúḥíyyih*

In April 1957, Isobel Sabrí went on pilgrimage and wrote to us from there. In her letter she wrote:[223]

> I think you, Philip dear, would like to know what the beloved Guardian asked me to tell you and especially the NSA. He said:
>
>> It is very important for the NSA to establish good relations with the Government of Uganda. The NSA must be *very* watchful, and if it sees the slightest sign of misunderstanding by the Government, the NSA should take immediate steps to correct the situation. There must always be an harmonious relationship between the Faith and the Government. Philip Hainsworth should act as liaison between the NSA and the Government. It is 'providential' that Philip is in the service of the Government. His is a very important and great responsibility. The missionaries are watching you (the NSA) and when they see the Temple begin to rise they may try to persuade the Government to make the Bahá'ís stop building the Temple. When this happens your relations with the Government must be firm and harmonious. They must respect us. The NSA must instruct Philip what to do and say on their behalf, and then he must carry

[223] Unpublished letter (personal archives).

> out their instructions. It is a most important responsibility which is now Philip's.

> This is, Philip, to the best of my ability to remember, what the beloved Guardian said. He spoke most seriously. The previous evenings he had spoken of the four activities within the Faith today – he said they are important in this order (1) Interpretation, (2) Protection, (3) Propagation, (4) Administration. I understood him to imply that this new responsibility of yours is under No 2 – protection. So you can see its importance. The beloved Guardian has such a love for Leroy for one reason – because he has helped to cause the Faith in Israel to be very greatly respected by the officials of the Government. This no one told me – it was as evident as the morning sun.

> I told the beloved Guardian of what a wonderful and active person Lois is and of how diligently you both serve. He seemed pleased. He asked me to send you both his love. Please, forgive me this short note – more will follow. I spoke of you both several times to Rúḥíyyih Khánum – she said that Philip is blessed to have found such a fine wife – Lois to find such an active and devoted Bahá'í. I am sure that the beloved Guardian is well pleased with you both. I have prayed for you both.

I had said that 1956 was to be a fateful year – it was indeed. I met and married Lois; I was elected Secretary of the first Regional National Spiritual Assembly of Central and East Africa; I had been involved in the formation of many local assemblies in Teso and Bugisu; I had made a significant contribution to the teaching work in England during my leave, and the National Spiritual Assembly of the British Isles had welcomed several new Bahá'ís who were to make their marks in subsequent Bahá'í history – John and Rose Wade; Charles and Yvonne McDonald; Vera and John Long; David Lewis and, of course, Lois.

During 1956 Enoch Olinga went on pilgrimage – the first African Bahá'í to do so – and when he returned to Victoria he sent a report to a number of his friends. From this, one paragraph was of particular significance to us in Kampala:[224]

> UGANDA – HEART OF AFRICA: The beloved Guardian said that the Cause is spreading rapidly in Uganda. Uganda is the spiritual heart of Africa, said he: 'You should be proud of this, for you are a member of the Uganda Community. The Guardian said there were 1,800 believers and over 125 centres in Uganda. The Mother

[224] Unpublished report (personal archives).

Temple of Africa will be built in Uganda, your home, he said. Have you seen the design of the Temple? I will show it to you. I have already sent one to the National Spiritual Assembly of Central-East Africa. They are now consulting local engineers about it, the Guardian said to me. Soon the excavating of the foundation will be started.... The Guardian praises the devotion of Mr Banání, Mr 'Alí Nakhjavání and Mr Philip Hainsworth. The work has spread in Africa due to Mr Banání, 'Alí and Mr Philip Hainsworth. For they do not only bring people into the Faith, but create in them the spirit of dedication to the service of the Faith. In fact, Persian pioneers are doing a lot in Africa he said. The Guardian also mentioned many names of the American pioneers in Africa, particularly those in South Africa. He was happy about the services of the Collisons and the Elstons. Bill Sears do know him? is a wonderful Bahá'í. He has much love for the African people. You know of his farm in Johannesburg. The first National Convention of South-West Africa was held in his farm. The white and Negro Bahá'ís met in his farm. There is much colour prejudice in South Africa, he said. John Robarts is also a wonderful Bahá'í. You know him don't you, the Guardian asked me, after that he mentioned several other names of the American pioneers in Africa.

TEMPLE PLANNING AND CONSTRUCTION

When Mason Remey's design for the Temple had been received in August 1956, the National Spiritual Assembly took it along to Mr Freeman and he accepted on behalf of the firm, Messrs Cobb, Powell and Freeman of Kampala, to be the site architects. He had several comments to make:[225]

- To do the building justice it would require more than twice the budget allocated by the Guardian
- That the depth of the steps and the overall height should be altered to cut down costs
- That the open-sided design was not appropriate for the Kampala area (See below)

That while the Guardian had turned down the appeal of the British National Spiritual Assembly to change the Temple site from Kabulizira Hill, it would be almost impossible to build it on that site. Since the British National Spiritual Assembly had put the case to the Guardian, the situation with regard to an access road had deteriorated as the owner of the land

[225] Unpublished notes (personal archives).

would not give right of way; there was doubt about getting an adequate water supply; a new housing development project was planned which would ultimately encircle the site; tenants still on the site would require costly crop compensation and, finally, the land survey had determined that the actual site was 250ft down from the crest of the hill and that even if the Temple were built there, it would not be seen from Kampala.

Our National Assembly, at one of its early meetings, had decided to place all these facts before the Guardian with the strong recommendation that the Temple be built on the 13 acres bought in the Kikaya area in the names of Erisha Kiwanuka and Joseph Mbogo, and the Kibulizira land be designated the Endowment Land.

The Guardian agreed and this news was given to me when we landed at Entebbe Airport.

To the advantages of this exchange was added the news that five additional acres actually on the crest of Kikaya Hill could be exchanged for three acres of the Kibulizira site and an extra half-acre could be purchased.

Once this exchange was agreed, it became obvious that the original design of Mason Remey was impracticable. His experience had been largely in Hawaii, where rain, when it fell, came straight down, but such was the configuration of the hills around Kampala that, during the rainy season, the winds drove water at all angles, sometimes almost horizontally across the top of the hills. This would be disastrous for a building such as that designed by Remey without any doors – only pillars to hold up the roof and with louvres in the walls.

The Guardian agreed to the inclusion of a honeycomb design of concrete with glass that had been suggested by Mr Freeman, and agreed to the modification of the steps, providing the overall proportions were maintained.

The next and most important problem was how to scale down the initial estimates of Mr Freeman of some £110,000 to the Guardian's requirement of £42,000. It was agreed after many hours of consultation that the main design should be kept as given by the Guardian and all economies should be made on the finish, particularly on the mosaics suggested by Mr Freeman on the internal pillars.

It was found that there would be a very narrow margin of land between the Temple building itself and the property boundary, so three additional acres were obtained which would allow for the building of a small caretakers' cottage. Paul Mukasa, one of Max Kanyerezi's brothers, exchanged two acres of his very valuable land near Makerere University for the two required at the Temple site and donated one of them as a gift. Max and Erisha were the Trustees for the additional land. This raised the total to an irregular-shaped plot of 21 and a half acres, with the top of the hill and the full slope facing Kampala. Lois and I, as secretary and chairman of the Temple Committee, were constantly engaged in the different aspects of this work.

A preliminary survey by a government geologist revealed that the configuration of the land was such that the sinking of a bore hole was unlikely to yield water, but it was considered absolutely essential to have a permanent source of fresh water for the construction as well as for the gardens surrounding the building if we were to keep our costs down. We heard of an itinerant bore-hole engineer who had had a great deal of success working for Mowlem Construction, and he visited the site and pointed out where he would be prepared to sink the well. An estimate was given for the drilling, for the lining of the well, the installation of an electric pump and the construction of a hut over the well and pump. Arrangements were made for access to the site and for the Electricity Board to install mains electricity. An African caretaker, Músá Ngabe, was appointed, a timetable of six months to complete all blue prints and the first tenders to be sent out and a completion date two years hence were all decided upon.

Whilst it had been agreed to economise on the finish of the interior, it become obvious that the exterior should be well made with self-cleansing finishes so that the rains would wash off the red dust of the underlying red ironstone (murram) which was the basis of all the Ugandan roads and which blew around during the dry periods of the year.

In February 1957, the Guardian had cabled:[226]

> Ensure no delay commencement excavations.

On 1 April, the lowest tender for the levelling of the site at the top of the hill and the making of the access road was accepted. By August, the Guardian had sent us a message to expedite the work and it was agreed to sign the first contract for the foundations stage, in advance of the completion of the drawings, to enable the actual foundations to be laid out with one of the nine doors facing 'Akká to be marked.

In the meantime, some quite significant events had taken place.

One day as some of us were walking over the rough land at the crown of the hill, a most interesting find was made by Rex Collison. As a soil chemist, a geologist and a keen archaeologist, Rex was turning over some loose 'stones' with his feet and picked up some pieces with evident excitement. 'These are man-chipped flints and at least one stone hand axe', he exclaimed. 'This must have been the site of some very ancient prehistoric tribe, and we are about to build a new-age House of Worship

[226] Unpublished cable (personal archives).

here.' Subsequently the artefacts were sent to the Nairobi museum, Rex's identification was confirmed and they were dated at about 30,000 years old.

Before relating the story of the next event, it is worth noting that Lois, while fitting in wonderfully with the Bahá'í life in Kampala, was obviously missing her cultural environment of London and her music. In addition, we knew that when the Temple, upon which both of us were working so hard, was to be dedicated, we would need choral music and we had been wondering how we could find a choir. At this time, after our return from Bugisu, Lois started work as personal assistant to the Director of Information, and he put her in touch with a lecturer at Makerere University who was also a musician. This led to Lois being invited to sing the soprano solos of choral works – I went along as chauffeur and was inducted into the male chorus! Another member of the chorus, Alice Calder, was also a fine accompanist who later did a great deal of work with Lois with her concerts and broadcasts. One day, when driving rather distractedly from the dentist at Nakasero Hospital, I went too fast across a crossroad and smashed into another car. Neither driver was hurt, but both cars were too badly damaged to be repaired. Alice Calder was the driver of the other car.

I found that for my job and for service to the Faith it would be better to get a good new four-wheel drive, long wheel-based Land Rover. One was not available in Kampala at short notice, but there was one at the importer's garage in Dar-es-Salaam. I went to pick it up and 'ran it in' driving back to Kampala.

The access to the Temple site was, before the final road was completed, very rough and bouncy, and on the day that the bore-hole digger was due to start we visited him and on several subsequent occasions before he struck water. Pictures of this occasion show Lois very pregnant at this time and it was thought that perhaps the jolting would precipitate our child's birth. The baby was however very stubborn and refused to be born. The news at the bore hole was good, however. The man had struck a good supply of water at 50ft, but had decided to carry on at least to 150ft as his contract specified that depth. He struck again at 130ft that ensured a good, permanent supply of clean water. He fitted the pumps and pipes and the electricity was connected.

After considering all the tenders for the foundations contract, it had been decided not to accept the cheapest or the dearest but, on account of the reputation for his work, the firm owned by Amar Singh Nandhra was selected. On anniversary of the Birth of the Báb, 20 October 1957, the contracts for the foundation and for the drilling were signed and it was our great joy to be able to cable loving Birthday greetings to the Guardian, giving him the news of the contracts and that the work on the foundations would begin within a week. This was, as we learnt later, the last message to reach him in London and he cabled his last words to the Bahá'ís of our Region on 31 October 1957:

Delighted contract Temple. *Loving Appreciation. Shoghi.*[227]

GUARDIAN'S LAST MESSAGE TO THE BAHÁ'Í WORLD – OCTOBER 1957[228]

Not only was this message to assume the greatest significance as being the last circular message he wrote but it contained much information of vital importance to us. It gave us details of the Hands of the Cause who would attend the Intercontinental Conferences on his behalf and what they would bring for display and to be buried in the foundations of the Temple. It also carried the news of the appointment of Enoch Olinga, William Sears, and John Robarts as Hands of the Cause for Africa. This was very disturbing news for me as I had known Enoch quite well before his pioneering to West Africa, had been closely involved in his acceptance of the Faith and the troubles he had had at the place of his work, the reputation he had there and the kind of life he had lived before becoming a Bahá'í. I just could not see in him what the Guardian saw and it worried me. Lois, who worked for the Director in the Ministry of Information from which Enoch had been dismissed in 1953 was equally unhappy. I did not for a moment question the Guardian's decision but I could not understand it.

I cannot remember how it was worded but in some way Lois and I advised Rúḥíyyih Khánum on 17 October that we were facing serious tests, to which she responded in her amazing letter of 6 November.

It should be noted here that plans had been going apace for the 1958 Intercontinental Conference called for by the Guardian in his October 1957 Message, to be held in Kampala with representatives of the British, American, Persian, N.E. African, Indian and Iraqi National Spiritual Assemblies, and with the particular blessing of 'Amatu'l-Bahá Rúḥíyyih Khánum's presence as the Guardian's own representative.

Lois and I were so excited at the chance to welcome Rúḥíyyih Khánum that Lois wrote personally to her on 17 October.[229] Among several matters in this letter, Lois also referred to tests we were both facing with regard to

[227] Unpublished cable (personal archives).
[228] Effendi, S. (1971). Messages to the Bahá'í World 1950-1957. Wilmette, Ill., Bahá'í Publishing Trust., pp. 124ff.
[229] Unpublished letter (Lois' personal archives).

one of the Hands of the Cause and about which I had written personally to her. She must have received this just as she left Haifa with the Guardian or had had it sent on to her, as she replied post-dated and sent her letter back to Haifa for mailing to us from there, as it was actually dated 6/11/57, two days after the passing of the Guardian and the contents clearly indicated she had had no premonition of this tragedy. In the light of all that followed, it is a most illuminating letter:[230]

> *Dear Philip and Lois*
>
> Just a note to you both as I am tired and in a hurry. So much to do these days!
>
> Don't either of you worry. We all have tests and the very meaning of the word is, to me at least, a thing that suddenly bites you unawares on the heel as if you had stepped on an adder! It strikes you all of a heap-if it did not would it be a test? The main thing is to survive them – they always look so small in retrospect! I'm afraid I don't take tests very seriously any more. Life is so full of them, big and little. By now you are probably both beginning to wonder what it was all about. For take it in stride I know you did!
>
> As to the 'party'! We will have to wait until I get there and see how much strength and time I have. I still can barely take in the fact that I am actually *going* there. It is almost too good to be true! And how I am looking forward to seeing all my friends (which certainly includes you both!) and meeting the African Bahá'ís.
>
> *Until then, much love, Rúḥíyyih*

The first address we used in Kampala was 'Banání Private Bag', but then we obtained our National Spiritual Assembly box – PO Box 2662 (which is still in use nearly 50 years later) and we had 'BAHÁ'Í FAITH KAMPALA' as our cable address. When Lois and I moved to Queens Road, cables were delivered there.

SHOCK – THE PASSING OF THE GUARDIAN

On the evening of 4 November, a cable was received from Haifa saying:[231]

> Beloved Guardian desperately ill Asiatic flu inform believers supplicate prayers divine protection Faith.

Mr Banání had received a like message and immediately I had contacted 'Alí and Hassan and we had a meeting at our house. I had a

[230] Unpublished letter (personal archives).
[231] Rabbani, R. (1969). The Priceless Pearl. London, Bahá'í Publishing Trust., p. 449.

strong feeling that the Guardian had passed away but Hassan was very angry with me for even expressing such a thought. We agreed to keep closely in touch after advising all available National Spiritual Assembly members. On the following day, the cable was received advising us of the Guardian's passing[232] and some people heard it on the BBC news. This was followed by a cable advising all National Spiritual Assemblies that the funeral would be held in London on Saturday, 9 November.[233] Lois was in the bath when I took it in to her, weeping unashamedly. She said immediately, 'You must go', although she thought that this would be her last bath before going to Nakasero Hospital to have our first baby.

Arrangements were rapidly made and Mr Banání, 'Alí, Hassan, Azíz Yazdí (who joined us from Nairobi) Jalál Nakhjavání (from Dar-es-Salaam) and I flew to London on 6 November to attend the funeral. Lois and the other ladies who had driven to Entebbe to see us off returned to Kampala, Lois to await the arrival of our first baby, due that day! In fact, the baby, Richard, waited until the day of my return from the funeral – 14 November 1957.

The memory of the journey to London, what happened on our arrival, where we stayed, our visit to the Ḥaẓíratu'l-Quds to get the details of the funeral, was virtually obliterated from my mind with the sense of loss and with the grief that we found in all the hundreds who came together during those bleak, wet November days. I know that at some stage I stayed with Lois' mother in Twickenham, but I can remember nothing about the journey back afterwards.

Vivid in my mind is the memory of car after car after car leaving 27 Rutland Gate following the hearse, the cortege was a mile long, police had to hold up the traffic for ages to let us all pass, but I cannot remember with whom I travelled nor where exactly I sat in the chapel – it was, I know, somewhere near the front, with Rúḥíyyih Khánum and the Hands of the Cause sitting behind the coffin and the readers and chanters at the front. Some 300 believers left Rutland Gate and others in cars joined in the line. I remember seeing, at the start of the Edgeware Road, a couple of young people running and waving – they were Dan and Nancy Jordan, just arrived from Dan's station in the Army in Germany. I was able to lean out of the car and tell them to get into one of the cars following ours.

The article written by Madeline Hellaby about the funeral that so poignantly describes the occasion and was published, unknown to her, in

[232] Hands of the Cause of God, l. (1992). The Ministry of the Custodians 1957-1963 - An Account of the Stewardship of the Hands of the Cause - With an Introduction by the Hand of the Cause Amatu'l-Bahá Rúhíyyih Khánum. Haifa, Israel, Bahá'í World Centre., p. 7.
[233] Ibid.

the commemorative issue of the *Bahá'í Journal* of January 1958, which included some remarkable passages: '

> And what shall I say of Saturday? Has London ever witnessed such a funeral? Surely the most highly-respected leader, the best-loved king of all time, mourned by all his countrymen, cannot have united so many hearts in such love and grief. What other international gathering could have been so utterly devoid of barriers or caused so much amazement? Passers-by stopped and stared. They did not merely look – they stared. Their wonderment was plain: Who can this be? Such a long procession, so many nationalities represented, and all mingling together without segregation, and yet we know not who it is they mourn. He is obviously important – why do we not know who it is? O wondering bystanders! You will not find it in your newspapers. The time is not ripe.
>
> O coffin-bearers! You who witnessed all, were not your hearts moved to tears and wonderment by what you saw? Have you ever assisted at a funeral like this one? What were your feelings as our Beloved received the last expressions of grief and devotion from nigh on four hundred people from both East and West? You who are used to tears, were not even you moved, to see men weep like this? Did you notice how, after a warm and sunny morning, at the very moment when the first believer collapsed in tears at the head of his coffin, the heavens also wept? Did you notice how cold it went suddenly? – and did you notice how, at the moment of the coffin being lowered into the grave the heavens wept again? And did you not marvel at what was sprinkled over the grave? – not dismal earth, but perfume. O heavenly fragrance! Small wonder that you have found your way so often into the writings of Bahá'u'lláh. May the fragrance of our lives be wafted through the world as you, O attar-of-rose, were borne upon the winds of heaven from that blessed spot!

At the graveside the prayer of Shoghi Effendi 'Dar in layliyi layla' was chanted in Persian and Bahá'u'lláh's prayer 'Glory be to Thee, O God, for Thy manifestation of love to mankind' was read in English and the grief-stricken widow paid her respects to the one she had worshipped and served with such devotion and passion.

I cannot remember how long it took for all the believers to file past the coffin before it was lowered into the grave. One's own grief was heightened by the sight of the heroic figure of 'Amatu'l-Bahá Rúḥíyyih Khánum, knowing how much she must be suffering as she watched each tearful face bend over to kiss the edge of the coffin and listen to the sobbing which arose from each shaking believer. Eventually the last one had passed, the coffin was lowered, the rose petals scattered over that precious box, and the hushed crowd began to disperse. As we moved away, word was passed around that Rúḥíyyih Khánum wished the Hands and some of the National Spiritual Assembly members to return before the grave was filled in. I was one of those asked to remain and was standing there at the SE corner of the grave. I listened as different members of that small band of his servants read or chanted prayers in different languages. Then she called across to me, 'Philip, the Guardian loved the Africans so much and was so proud of the work in Africa; will you say a prayer in Swahili?' I was stupefied. I had no Swahili prayers and even if I had, I would have had difficulty in reading one, but I had to respond. From my prayer book, I looked up the Unity Prayer and gave an impromptu, very poor, but seemingly understandable translation. 'Alí, Hassan, and Azíz later expressed their appreciation, but I alone knew how inadequate a translation it was.

The following morning I went back and took masses of photographs of the vast number of wreaths from all corners of the earth that were piled high over and around the actual grave. A display of these photographs was made for the January conference where many orders were given for sets of those photographs, developed, and produced in the dark room in Kampala to which I had free access.

I caught a plane back to Entebbe, arrived there on 14 November and rushed to Nakasero Hospital where I found that Lois had just given birth to our first child, Richard Nabil, and I was able to see them as she was giving him his first feed.

The following few weeks flew by with amazing rapidity, but nothing seemed to assuage the tremendous sense of loss and emptiness left by the passing of the Guardian. The joy of having a son and making all the necessary adjustments in my approach to life thus involved, which, at the age of 38, were not inconsiderable; the increasing tempo of work for the forthcoming conference and all the initial problems associated with the work at the Temple site and the finalising of the designs and contracts, partially filled the gap.

However, the news that there was no Will left much room for speculation and rumours spread around... There was a child but for his protection he had been brought up in secret! There could be another Aghṣán who had remained faithful and might be a Guardian! These were always followed by news that they were just baseless rumours.

On 19 November the five Hands of the Cause who were members of the International Bahá'í Council, with four others chosen by Rúḥíyyih

Khánum, broke open the seals which had been put in place on the Guardian's apartment. They examined his desk and safe and, after a thorough search, signed a document saying that Shoghi Effendi had executed no Will or Testament of any nature whatsoever.

The Hands assembled in Bahjí and on 25 November issued a "Unanimous Proclamation of the 27 Hands of the Cause of God" to the Bahá'í world.[234]

Hand of the Cause John Robarts, on his way home to South Africa, called in Nairobi and then to Kampala to share with us the proclamation and Lois and I immediately wrote a letter to Rúḥíyyih Khánum which reflected our feelings at that time:[235]

> It was our great privilege to meet with the revered Hand of the Cause John Robarts, who came especially from Nairobi to convey to us the news from Haifa before he returned to South Africa. The pioneers in Kampala were able to hear the Proclamation and to make a copy of it, and later in the day a number of the dear African friends gathered to hear the news. As the official Proclamation from Haifa has not yet been received and the full National Assembly is meeting on this coming weekend, the National Spiritual Assembly Executive decided to take no action on the Proclamation beyond calling on the Territorial Teaching Committees to arrange for large gatherings throughout their areas to enable the believers to hear the news personally as planned at the forthcoming National Assembly meeting.
>
> Lois and I felt, however, that we would like to write immediately to assure you and the revered Hands in Haifa, of our joyous acceptance of the decision of the Hands at Bahjí and our unqualified loyalty to their plans.
>
> Your personal letter was received a few days ago and it gave us great comfort at this time, though we realise that it must have been written very shortly before the passing of our beloved Guardian.
>
> It seems impossible to realise that our beloved one has left us and there comes to my mind the thoughts that we shared with each other after the passing of your father and of my mother, and of the beloved Guardian's consoling words about both my father and mother. All of these, however, pale into insignificance in comparison with the blow we are now suffering and which must

[234] The proclamation is reproduced in full on p. 28 of *The Ministry Of The Custodians 1957-1963: An Account of the Stewardship of the Hands of the Cause*, Haifa: Bahá'í World Centre Publications, 1992.
[235] Unpublished letter (personal archives).

have meant so much more to you personally than to the thousands of his loved ones the world over. In spite of this, Lois and I feel that you will not misunderstand us if we try, perhaps clumsily, to express the deep feeling of relief and even of joy that has grown in us since the Proclamation of the Hands caused us once again to turn to the Will and Testament and the Dispensation and read them with new understanding. Like the tests which you referred to in your letter to us which when overcome make us wonder why we allowed them to cause us concern, the confusion and uncertainty into which we were thrown are now replaced by a new feeling of strength and dedication which made us wonder why we had never before read the Will with understanding. In fact, when we look back on these recent events and hear of the beloved Guardian's tiredness and the brutal assaults of the Covenant breakers and his own relatives, we must feel grateful to Bahá'u'lláh for having called him to reap his reward in the Abhá Kingdom, from which we feel certain he will continue to assist us, free from the limitations imposed by a worn-out human frame.

These reflections, beloved Rúḥíyyih Khánum, can never ameliorate the deep personal loss of the love and companionship which has been yours for the past twenty years. We do feel, though, that if the friends the world over can realise the bounty of these days when they are being called upon to grow up, when the world Order of Bahá'u'lláh is about to be born, when the Institutions of the Cause are going to come into their own, and when the labours of the friends will determine when mankind can next be assured of infallible guidance through the election of the Universal House of Justice, then the Beloved's sacrifice will not have been in vain.

Dearly loved Rúḥíyyih Khánum, please do not worry about acknowledging this letter – we know how overburdened you will be, but do please convey on our behalf, to the Hands in Haifa, the personal assurances not only of our own loyalty and dedication, but of determination to do all we can to rouse the friends to their new responsibilities, guided by the beloved Guardian through the Custodians in the Holy Land.

In humble love and devotion, Philip and Lois

One of my reactions was to draft an article expressing how I felt we should face up to the new crisis in our Faith. As I write this I cannot recall anything about the content of either the article or a letter we sent to the Hands of the Cause from our National Spiritual Assembly, but the reaction to the draft of my article from David and Marion Hofman to whom it had been sent is of interest.

David wrote on 9 December:[236]

> Marion showed me your summary of the position which arrived this morning, and I want to write to you at once. I know how you feel … how we all feel. We have the inestimable privilege here of being able to visit the grave, to meditate in privacy by it. We have also had the wonderful advantage of hearing Ḥasan, directly back from Haifa, read us the proclamation and tell us our duties. My heart goes out to all the Bahá'ís in distant lands … bearing responsibility now such as they have never had before. I don't mean only the Hands … their distress and agony must be beyond description … but all of us who have been the body of the Cause for years now, and whose feet must now be 'brass like' and souls like granite.
>
> The chief thing about your notes which I want to write about is the apparent assumption that the Guardianship is finished. How can this ever be? How can anyone dare to think such a thing. God is not mocked, and Bahá'u'lláh, the Master, and the Chief-Builder of the World Order are not betrayed. I refer you specifically to *The Dispensation* (the Guardian's spiritual testament) and the Master's Will. The passage about the Administrative Order, where he deals with the Guardianship and the Universal House of Justice. 'Divorced from the institution of the Guardianship the World Order of Bahá'u'lláh would be permanently mutilated … etc. He speaks of future Guardians … and shows how the WOB[237] cannot function without its twin pillars. Furthermore if there were to be no Guardian, the institution of the Hands would die out, for only the Guardian can appoint them. I think you are right on one point of fact when you say that the Will provides for another appointment in the event of Shoghi Effendi's firstborn not being suitable. Do read meticulously every passage referring to Shoghi Effendi and the succession.
>
> It seems to me that the situation is that we have suffered a dreadful blow. 'O Thou Who slayest the lovers.' We are to be without a Guardian for some time but God doeth whatsoever He willeth, and no-one can tell me that the Brightest emanation of His mind, the Child of Bahá'u'lláh and the Master, the Kingdom of God is to be permanently mutilated; that the Holy Ones of the Cause were lacking in foresight.

[236] Unpublished letter (personal archives).
[237] World Order of Bahá'lláh

We've had it 'easy' up to now; from now on we have to be men and live by faith. How or when another Guardian will be given to us, is God's business. We can only follow the Hands and supplicate.

Share these ideas with whomever you like; the Covenant is clear and firm, and don't let anyone tell you that God has changed His mind. He doeth whatsoever He willeth.

You must lead the way with the first Conference; how I wish I could be with you all.

Much love, old son, and to Lois and your heir. David

Marion followed this with a letter dated 12 December:[238]

Dearest Philip,

I was very grateful to receive your draft article. You ask my views and if I had time I would write at length – but I fear this won't happen. We need a night's talk together.

Personally I take my stand on two things:

1. The future is being held from us for the time being.
2. We have the revealed Word of Bahá'u'lláh, the Writings of the Master and the explanations and messages of the Guardian. I am studying these like mad – seeking for fresh understanding, and also for assurance. I do not intend to depart one word from these, and I place upon *each word* the same importance I always have. You will get an idea of what I mean if you read the extract from the Maxwell notes on p 4 of the enclosed.

I accept wholeheartedly the Proclamation. I think it is all that could have been said in the circumstances, and I think it covers any eventuality. It is very carefully worded and, as Ḥasan showed, has no innovation in it.

I do not accept various *interpretations* of the Proclamation which I have heard, or interpretations which go beyond the Will and the Dispensation. In other words, I still place my entire trust, as I have grown up doing, in the words of the beloved Guardian – and I stake my soul's future on them. I find it constitutionally impossible to go beyond them. They and they alone repeatedly confirm and assure me. I want no other theories but shall just wait to see what God has in mind. We know it is something and I personally believe that there is wonderful meaning in all this for the evolution of the World Order.

PS. Am thrilled about Richard. Please give Lois my dearest love

[238] Unpublished letter (personal archives).

and congratulations. I *love* the photo she sent me some months ago and mean to frame it. *Marion*

THE INTERCONTINENTAL CONFERENCE, KAMPALA – JANUARY 1958

On 1 January 'Amatu'l-Bahá Rúḥíyyih Khánum wrote a joint letter to the three National Spiritual Assembly officers resident in Kampala – 'Alí, Hassan and myself – regarding the programme for the conference. The following extracts are of interest:[239]

> In a meeting with the Hands of the Holy Land, the programme for the Kampala Conference was discussed, and I am enclosing for your information a revised programme which we feel would be more suitable; please note: The showing of the Portrait of Bahá'u'lláh cannot come at the end; the beloved Guardian himself, as I remember, was the one who fixed the time for its showing at the Chicago Convention, and it came the first day. Before the friends pass by this sacred picture I will anoint them with Attar of Rose which belonged to the beloved Guardian. I think very careful arrangements should be made to befittingly display the Portrait: it should be on a table, placed on the right as you face it, and next to it on the left the Holy Dust from Bahá'u'lláh's Tomb and next to this the fragment of the plaster from Máh-Kú. Flowers should be placed on either side of the table (if the table were very large there could be in vases on it, but I think this a little dangerous as they might get knocked over). You think about the plan for this and when I arrive we can still discuss details before the actual showing.
>
> I will not be able to present the Hands' Message the first day; I fear both I and the believers may be too overcome with feeling to give proper attention to this important message; we have therefore put it off for the following day.
>
> We all feel that as the purpose of this Conference, the very first one of the five the beloved Guardian convened, was to stimulate, reward and inspire the African believers – there are not enough of them represented on the programme; naturally, you have to choose people who are capable, but haven't you got them?
>
> I suppose that in arranging for the devotional session out at the Temple site you have allowed plenty of time before it gets dark? The actual ceremony of placing the Holy Dust (which will be in a

[239] Unpublished letter (personal archives).

small box and will not take up more than 6 or 8 square inches) and the plaster from Máh-Kú by me and Mr Banání respectively in the small vault to the right of the door facing the Qiblih, should not take long at all. Presumably you will have someone there on hand to seal this vault carefully and solidly with cement while we stand by. Any other plans you have for this occasion I am sure will be excellent, such as readings, etc.

Unfortunately I shall not be able to attend the Unity Feast on the night of January 22nd, as my plane gets in at Entebbe from Nairobi at 18.40 and I will be very tired. I know that someone will be on hand to meet us; however I would appreciate it if nobody tries to see me when I pass through Nairobi on the trip to Kampala. Believe me dear friends it is only in order to fulfil the wishes of our beloved Guardian that I am going to Kampala. I am quite heartbroken and utterly exhausted. My only hope is that God will give me the strength to do as He wishes me to. If on my way back from Kampala I am feeling strong enough, then it might be possible if the friends care to, for some of them to see me as I go through Nairobi, but on the way out I must have as much rest as I can to prepare myself for the conference. On the evening I arrive in Kampala I would however like very much to consult with those responsible for the success of the Conference regarding exact plans for the next day. We must all exert every effort to have this important conference perfect and as our beloved Guardian would wish it to be.

Within the limits of my strength I shall try to be present with the friends as much as possible, as my only joy can come from being with the dear friends – old and new!

The Hands of the Cause here join me in sending you their loving greetings. They feel confident the Conference will be an outstanding success and mark the opening of a new epoch in the unfoldment of the Faith in Africa – just as our Guardian wished it to be.

Officially accompanied, on the Guardian's instructions, by Dr Lotfu'lláh Hakím, Rúḥíyyih Khánum was also escorted by her cousin, Mrs Challoner Chute and arrived as planned by plane from Nairobi.

We had gained much in experience from the 1953 conference and for several weeks we had been making block bookings in hotels, social centres, clubs, etc., with the hire of mattresses and washing utensils for low cost accommodation for the Persian and African believers who had limited resources. Weeks and weeks of preparation were needed to plan all the allocations, the transport for the African friends, the reception of the five aircraft at the airport with special buses for the many Persian friends who were expected, and contingency arrangements to be made for those who were expected to arrive without visas and proper inoculations.

In all, more than 300 Persians arrived, mostly very late at night or in the early hours of the morning and each plane had to be met; there were some 450 African believers with a grand total of 950 from 38 countries. In addition to Rúḥíyyih Khánum there were Hands of the Cause Ṭaráẓu'lláh Samandarí, Músá Banání, Enoch Olinga, John Robarts and Bill Sears, 16 Board members and representatives of 11 National Spiritual Assemblies.

For me, the highest point of the conference was the moment when Rúḥíyyih Khánum arrived at the packed cinema and walked the length of the auditorium to the stage – the whole audience rose and sang 'Alláh'u'Abhá'. Those of us who realised the effect it was having upon her, at her first public appearance after the funeral of the Guardian, wept unashamedly as she walked onto the platform with such grace and dignity and, obviously, herself deeply moved. The tangible emotion in that hall is impossible to describe – the love that went out to Rúḥíyyih Khánum from every heart expressed in an audible sigh.

'Alí Nakhjavání greeted her '...The central light of our conference and its glorious crown; the beloved gift of our dearly cherished Guardian and his precious trust among us...' in a voice trembling with tears.

Her first few words came, 'I don't know with what voice to address this conference – it is so hard to speak – it seems so unbelievable that I should ever have to stand here, and the Guardian not be in Haifa!' Then for a moment she could not speak, her voice caught in her throat. But then she gathered strength and spoke of the love the Guardian felt for the African friends and his achievements during the last 36 years.

On a scorching hot Sunday afternoon – 26 January – the friends gathered on the concrete foundations of the Mother Temple of Africa, awaiting the arrival of Rúḥíyyih Khánum. A very few chairs had been brought to the hill for her and the Hands, everyone else sat on the concrete. A special small vault had been left to the right of the doorway which was to face the Qiblih and into this Rúḥíyyih Khánum and Músá Banání placed two silver boxes, wrapped in silk scarves, one containing dust from the Shrine of Bahá'u'lláh and the other a piece of plaster from the ceiling of the room in Máh-Kú in which the Báb had revealed the Bayán. Full details of the conference are too voluminous to be used here.

Following the conference, Lois and I had Rúḥíyyih Khánum to a meal at our house and then I drove her and Violette Nakhjavání on a tour of Pallisa and Teso. On the way to Kolonerio Oule's village in Pallisa, we had to pass over a wide swampy river on a ferry flat-bottomed boat that took a large number of foot passengers, and one or two motor vehicles.

As we were starting off, the steersman swung the ferry around and it got stuck. I was so furious at the thought of Khánum being stuck there in the heat that I got a number of the locals to go into the water with me and manhandled the boat into the clear water. I had some good photographs of the occasion that I sent to her but as I was taking them, when I was not in the water, I did not feature on them. I believe Violette took one of me in the water that I have seen but of which I cannot find a copy.

1958 – 1963

Following the conference both Lois and I were very heavily committed. Lois with our young baby Richard, the typing that came from my National Spiritual Assembly work and the Temple Committee work that, as secretary, fell largely on her shoulders and which necessitated frequent visits to the site. We also took many meetings with the architect, structural engineer and building contractor, as well as continuing the teaching work in Kampala and around Buganda.

The territories that formed part of the Central and East African National Spiritual Assembly and therefore fell within my ambit as its secretary were Uganda, Kenya, Tanganyika, Ruanda-Urundi, Zanzibar, Belgian Congo, French Equatorial Africa, and Seychelles.

My work in the Uganda Medical Service as a field officer with the Vector Control Division enabled me to visit all the Uganda Townships to carry out malarial control investigations, recommend actions to be taken and in several places obtain funding to carry out major drainage works. This, in addition to my work with the other areas of Vector Control such as onchocerciasis and bilharzia surveys, some tsetse control work with the senior entomologist and the tsetse control Officer, Jack Hinchcliffe, and even some plague surveys in the West Nile area, enabled me to travel widely throughout Uganda. This in turn gave me an opportunity to follow up teaching work in Arua, Gulu, Moroto, Lango, Mbale, Tororo in the north and east and in Mbarara, Fort Portal, Bundibugyo (among the pygmies or Batwa) and Kabale in the West.

When dealing with Ruanda-Urundi, the Belgian Congo, and French Equatorial Africa, Lois' knowledge of French was invaluable, and she acted as an interpreter when working for the Uganda Department of Labour.

In all, during 1958 I was on the Temple, Uganda Teaching, Bahá'í School, *Bahá'í Gazette*, *Bahá'í News* and Music Committees and Lois was on the Temple, *Bahá'í Gazette*, French-speaking Territories and Music Committees.

On 14 May 1958, we received a lovely letter from Rúḥíyyih Khánum:[240]

> *My Dear Philip and Lois,*
>
> I was so happy to receive your letters, and would have answered before , but I wish you could see my desk! On the other hand, I was longing to hear from you both.
>
> Nobody knows how much I missed you all when I left Kampala. It was with the greatest reluctance that I ever left Teso, and Kampala was another wrench. Every time I think of you there – the Hainsworths, Banánís, Sabrís, Nakhjavánís and the other friends, it just seems unbearable that I should not be there. What precious days we had together; in the midst of so much fire and suffering we still found moments of great joy. Such is the mystery of the Cause and such are the bounties of Bahá'u'lláh.
>
> Philip, thank you for the photographs. I thought they were very nice, especially the ones from Teso and on the boat, but you are not on it. Where is your picture? Why did you not send it to me? What a voyage that was! If I ever saw death in anyone's eye, it was in yours when you looked at that steersman, or when you tried not to look at him!
>
> I wished so much that I could have spent more time with you. There was so much to talk about after these many years; but when you both make the pilgrimage that will be a joy. Your baby is adorable, and I hope will grow up to even surpass his parents in service to the Faith, which is certainly saying a lot.
>
> Speaking of pilgrimage, you know you must ask early as your name will go on the list. The beloved Guardian had a long waiting list and we will naturally honor those who requested from him permission to come. As I remember, those who have permission if they all come would fill up a good eight months' period, so you had better put in your request soon, so you can always come at a later date, but if you are not even on the list you will have to wait a longer time.
>
> Do keep in touch with me so that I won't miss Kampala and Africa too much, and please give my love to all the friends there.
>
> *With warmest Bahá'í love to you both, Rúḥíyyih*

[240] Unpublished letter (personal archives).

LEGAL STATUS OBTAINED FOR SEYCHELLES ASSEMBLY

In the National Spiritual Assembly's annual report of 1958, it was noted that in the Seychelles Islands there was one local Assembly, with 8 opened localities and 42 believers.[241] These has developed after the Knight of Bahá'u'lláh, Abdu'l Rahman, had settled there in 1954 from Iraq and several others had followed him. The Assembly was in Victoria, Mahe – the principal island and seat of government.

It had become essential for the growing community to obtain legal recognition and to purchase a Ḥaẓíratu'l-Quds in its name. The building had been purchased through the generous donation of Munír Wakil and his family, also of Iraq, and a Bill was being presented to the Legislative Council. At the second reading of the Bill however, on 10 September 1958, an impassioned speech was made by Dr (Mrs) S Delhomme, wife of the French Consul and a member of the Legislative Council, against the bill. She had three objections – to the presence of strangers in the colony, the establishment of the Bahá'ís in the Seychelles and to their owning land in Seychelles. She particularly referred to the settlement of the Iraqis and spoke of 'false doctrines' and those 'Who have sold their souls to Mammon'. Well known for her staunch Roman Catholic views, she not only voiced her opposition to the bill but asked the government 'to ask those Iraqis to quit this Colony as soon as possible'. The bill failed as the voting was five for and five against and the president did not cast a vote. Dr Delhomme's was the only speech in opposition.

The local Assembly wished to refute Dr Delhomme's statements in a letter to the governor and the press, but on behalf of the National Spiritual Assembly I had to cable them not to do this. We then sent them the wording of a letter to be presented to the governor, if their lawyer would agree, and a detailed letter to the British National Spiritual Assembly asking them to send a supporting letter to the governor through the local Spiritual Assembly.

Following correspondence with the governor, it was learned that the only way forward was by obtaining Royal Assent on a document based on Canadian and Australian law, which was in turn based on French law. Finally the Governor of Seychelles issued his proclamation N°. 13 of 27 April 1959, announcing that Royal Assent had been given to the incorporation of the Bahá'ís of Victoria, Seychelles, (ordinance N°. 12 of 1959) – probably the first time ever that the law of a country has had such

[241] Unpublished report (personal archives).

an addition in order to recognise and give legal status to a Bahá'í local Spiritual Assembly.

CONTINUING WORK ON THE TEMPLE

In order to safeguard the Temple properties a company was established – The Uganda Bahá'í Community (Holdings) Ltd. It was incorporated on 21 October 1959 and only Bahá'ís could be Directors, with Israel Mukasa Kenyerezi and Robert Paul Mukasa (Max and his brother Paul) as the first two Directors. Roger Counihan, a good friend of the Faith was the lawyer who dealt with this incorporation.

The work on the Temple demanded constant examination of the progress to ensure that costs were kept down to the limit imposed by the Guardian. This was particularly so with the final contract, which included the type of wood for the doors, the balance of the coloured tiles for the dome to achieve the right effect when seen from the ground, the type of door 'furniture', the colours of the glass to go into the honeycombed concrete of the walls and the type of wood and the design of the benches.

The builder demanded excellence from his workers and told them, 'This is God's work'. Such was the excellence of the concrete work of the huge interior pillars that we were able to make huge savings in the interior costs by having them well rubbed down and painted, whereas the design showed them to be covered in mosaic tiles. A similar saving was made in the floor treatment. Due to the overall excellence of the building work and the evidence of the builder's desire to keep costs down, it was agreed to award the main contract to the same builder – Amah Singh Nandhra.

It was obvious that plans must be made for gardens around the Temple, and Richard St Barbe Baker suggested the name of a landscape gardener with considerable experience in East Africa, Major Sharp. He visited the site, drew up plans for the paths, the ornamental trees, flower boxes beside the steps and even for the type of grass that would bind the soil, remain green and would not require constant cutting.

MY FAMILY GROWS

By the end of 1958, Lois was aware she was again pregnant and the birth of our second child was due in August 1959. This had to be taken into account when planning and booking our next home leave.

We had written to the Hands of the Cause in the Holy Land on the 14 February and received their reply dated 25 February 1959 which was signed by the seven then resident there:[242]

Dear Bahá'í Friends,

Your letter of the 14 February was received and we note that it will not be possible for you to make the pilgrimage at this time. We hope that at a future date, when your children are older, you will be able to come.

As to where you could render the best service during the period that you will be in Europe: there is a great need in the Scandinavian countries for teachers to assist in the work, and Norway we understand calls for particular attention at this time. If it were possible for you to spend some part of your vacation there, encouraging the friends, uniting them and stimulating the teaching work, we feel that it would be a real service to the attainment of the goals set for that country by our beloved Guardian. However, we suggest that you consult with the Hands of the Cause in Europe, telling them that this is our suggestion and seeing if it meets with their approval, as of course they are au courant with the work there and the needs of the moment.

We hope that your second child will a source of joy to you both, and grow up to be a wonderful Bahá'í .

You may be sure that we will remember you and your family in the holy Shrines and pray for the success of your constant and devoted labours in the Cause of God.

With warmest Bahá'í greetings, In the service of the beloved Guardian,

HANDS OF THE CAUSE IN THE HOLY LAND.

Rúḥíyyih Amelia Collins Mason Remey Leroy Ioas

Paul Haney Jalál Kházeh AQ Faiẓí

In the Annual Report I made to the 1959 Convention I was able to give the following statistics:[243]

In April 1958 there were under our jurisdiction 177 Assemblies and 4,127 believers in 443 centres; six months later 86 new localities had been opened and nearly 600 believers enrolled; by Ridván (although the region was so large that all the figures were not yet available) there were at least 252 Assemblies and 6,437 believers with nearly 400 more declarations awaiting Committee approval,

[242] Unpublished letter (personal archives).
[243] Unpublished report (personal archives).

with a total of 119 tribes and 16 non-African racial groups being represented!

Our National Spiritual Assembly had instituted a *Bahá'í Gazette* which I drafted and Lois edited, and which we had translated and sent out, whenever possible and with some difficulty, in six languages.

RECOGNITION FOR THE FAITH OBTAINED IN CAPITAL OF RUANDA-URUNDI

Lois and I made a long trip to Usumbura, capital of Ruanda-Urundi where, on behalf of the National Spiritual Assembly, contact was made with various government officials, the Head of Native Affairs and the Director of African Housing to obtain permission for the purchase of a Ḥaẓíratu'l-Quds. A letter was drafted and approved by the governor of the territory, recognising the Bahá'í community in Usumbura. The housing director went out of his way to give support in finding a suitable house for the centre.

We had a public meeting, meetings with the community and several consultations with the local assembly. We felt that our visit was particularly blessed. It was followed by a brief visit with Joseph Kebe, a pioneer from Usumbura in Astrida, and we went for a short visit into the Congo.

All this was with Richard in his carrycot in the back of our Land Rover and Lois pregnant with the second baby.

SOCIAL ACTIVITIES IN KAMPALA

Lois' voluntary efforts as Secretary of the Uganda Music Society and mine as 'concert organiser' began to take on a new significance as we developed our musical contacts. She took part in many choral events and we began to think of the composition of a choir of all races to perform at the Temple Dedication. About this time we had met the 'Queen' of Buganda – the Nabagereka – the official wife of the Kabaka. The Kabaka himself was able, according to Kiganda custom, to have many wives but as a Christian he had only one official, legally married one – Damali, the daughter of Christopher Kisosonkali, the ssaza (county) chief of Mukono. Christopher had a beautiful but completely untrained deep bass voice and he was in one of the choirs with which Lois was associated.

We proposed to the Uganda Music Society that Damali should be invited to be 'patron' to the society, and this suggestion was warmly accepted. Lois and I, or Lois alone, would go to the Palace, the official residence of the Kabaka in Mengo, Kampala, to collect her, and take her home after each concert.

Our developing friendships with Charlie Harrison and Bill Buce (whose wife was also a singer) of the *Uganda Argus* meant that Charlie would look favourably at any reports or press releases for the Faith and for the Uganda Music Society. Bill co-operated with us very closely with the printing of thousands of leaflets in the native languages of Uganda, Kenya and Tanganyika.

The Uganda National Theatre was being built about this time and Ted Moon, the musical director of the police band, was to stage the opening concert. Ted asked Lois to sing with the band on this occasion accompanied by the powerful brass. He insisted that she sing 'One Fine Day' from Puccini's 'Madam Butterfly' and she only agreed on condition that she could also sing some Mozart!

UNEXPECTED DEATH OF TEMPLE CONTRACTOR

One of the challenges facing the National Spiritual Assembly came with the sudden death of Amar Singh Nandra. We were not at all impressed with his family, who had taken over the work of the Temple construction. They appeared to have neither the expertise of the old man nor his dedication, so negotiations were completed to continue the work ourselves by employing the Sikh overseer or 'mistry'. He was a good craftsman, had a firm control over his workforce and he did a very good job at a reasonable salary, fully maintaining the high standard initiated by Amar Singh Nandra.

It is interesting to recall that when the work was completed and everything cleared away this Mistry had asked me for a letter of recommendation, which would help him in finding more work. I gave him a good reference.

More than 20 years later, after speaking at a human rights meeting in the Town Hall, Wembley, London, I was approached by a happy effusive gentleman who told me he had been evicted from Uganda by President Idi Amin. He had come to England and on the strength of my letter of recommendation had quickly obtained employment which he kept until retirement – yes, it was the same Mistry of the Uganda Temple!

BY SEA TO LONDON

The expected birth of our second child in August 1959 had to be taken into account when planning and booking our next home leave as we intended to go by sea, buy a car in England, drive it across Europe via Portugal and travel back to Mombasa by ship from Gibraltar and then by road from Mombasa to Kampala.

For Zarin's birth I had planned to leave the Ayah in charge of Richard in our house in Queens Road and to be present at the birth, but the Sister in Nakasero Hospital did not favour the idea. She asked me to leave the bedside for a while to enable the staff 'to carry out an examination' and after a relatively short time she called me in with the words, 'The ladies are waiting for you'. That was on 22 August 1959.

Lois and I had always planned that I should be present at the birth of our babies. I had been airborne on my way back from the funeral of the Guardian when Richard had been born and the hospital sister prevented my being there for Zarin's birth. However, we finally got our wish on 19 July 1968 as I was present when Michael was born.

On the assumption that the new baby's birth would be uncomplicated and would be making normal progress, we had booked a passage for England from Mombasa in September or October 1959, and we left Kampala by train for the two day journey with nappies strung across the carriage. We had a fine voyage to London and the children were magnificent, enabling us to feed them and get them to sleep in time for us to dress for dinner – it was formal dress in those days in first class.

At London docks, we were met by Lois' mother and brother, Michael, and stayed with them for a few days in Twickenham. During this time, I purchased a new Morris station-wagon. We went up to Worksop to spend a little while with Lois' aunt and Lois passed her driving test in Nottingham.

We left for Belgium and stayed with American pioneers – the Baggleys, made some music with Louis Henuzet, visited Liege and left for France, where we stayed in Paris and then on to Orleans, where we stayed with Joel Marangella.

It was in Orleans that Joel was questioning me about a possible will left by Shoghi Effendi and other matters relating to the Guardianship. At that time, I did not detect anything untoward in his questions. We left for Perigueuz and then to St Jean de Luz, in the hills not far from the Spanish border where we stayed with John Carre. Both Joel and John appeared to feel that a way would be found to have a second Guardian. During the night at John's house, it snowed heavily and we left hoping to get well into Spain before the roads were blocked.

We had a most interesting journey – on the road from Biarritz, it took us eight hours to cover 12 miles. A long line of vehicles were in convoy with the drivers moving up to push out the cars which were stuck in the snow and they in turn being pushed by those behind them. The babies had to be fed on liquids made up from snow that had to be melted on a small spirit stove. Instead of reaching Madrid, we spent the night at a hotel in Vittoria to the east of the main highway and reached the home of Charles Ioas in Madrid on the following day.

After leaving Madrid, we dropped down almost to sea level at Seville and Cordoba, where we found it so warm that people were sitting at the outdoor tables of the cafes. Our destination was Portimão in Portugal, where the Hands of the Cause had asked us to spend some time as there were difficulties in the community that needed to be resolved. We stayed with a local family and visited pioneer Jan Coppen (later Jan Mughraby) in Lisbon. After three months in Portimão we drove to Gibraltar arriving on the 1st of April 1960, caught the boat to Mombasa, returned by road to Kampala and back to the abundance of work for the Cause.

In the message from the Custodians (Hands of the Cause in the Holy Land) to the annual Conventions, Ridván 1960, it was reported that 'over 4,000 new declarations have been recorded in Uganda alone since April 1959, nearly 1,200 in Kenya and well over 200 in Tanganyika. In the Belgian Congo, also, the beginnings of mass conversion are becoming evident'. The announcement of 'establishment and registration of the first Bahá'í Publishing Trust in Africa, in Kampala, Uganda' was also reported.[244]

DEFECTION OF CHARLES MASON-REMEY

Almost immediately after our return, the news came that the hints made to us in Orleans and St Jean de Luz about the possibility of there being a new Guardian had taken a dramatic turn. Hand of the Cause Mason Remey had moved to Italy and had made the preposterous claim that he was the second Guardian.

The Hands in the Holy Land announced this on 28 April.[245] We sent a message on 5 May to Haifa: 'National Spiritual Assembly behalf community Central East Africa wholeheartedly repudiate claim Remey

[244] Unpublished letter (personal archives).
[245] Hands of the Cause of God, l. (1992). The Ministry of the Custodians 1957-1963 - An Account of the Stewardship of the Hands of the Cause - With an Introduction by the Hand of the Cause Amatu'l-Bahá Rúhíyyih Khánum. Haifa, Israel, Bahá'í World Centre., p. 196.

assure Chief Stewards loving loyalty.'[246] On July 26 the Hands proclaimed Remey a Covenant-Breaker[247] and on 3 August the handful who accepted his claims were also expelled; these included John Carre and Joel Marangella with whom we had stayed in France![248]

In the midst of all this trauma came the news on 13 July that Hand of the Cause Horace Holley, who had endeared himself to all those present at the 1953 conference, had passed away in the Holy Land.[249]

KAMPALA TEMPLE DEDICATION PREPARATIONS

During the remainder of 1960, we had a great deal of work in preparing for the Temple dedication ceremony. Dan Jordan had provided several choral works, and Lois and I asked George Kakoma to compose a choral piece for us in Luganda in the Kiganda musical idiom. George was a talented musician, the first Ugandan to obtain a degree in music at an English University, who had published a book that presented music in this traditional idiom as well as in the classical mode. He was also commissioned to write the Uganda National Anthem when Uganda became independent.

Most of Dan Jordan's music proved too difficult for the ad hoc choir that we had assembled, as some members could not read music. The final programme for the three musical sections of the Dedication Service were:

> 'O Son of Being' – Dan Jordan
>
> 'The Lord is my shepherd' – 23rd Psalm, arranged by Gordon Jacobs
>
> 'O my Lord, my beloved, my desire! Befriend me in my loneliness' – Dan Jordan, rendered as a solo by Lois
>
> 'O Thou Incomparable God' – George Kakoma
>
> 'God is a Spirit!' Anthem – William Sterndale Bennett
>
> 'O Son of the Wondrous Vision' – Dan Jordan

Our activities in the Uganda Music Society and Lois' theatre work made many friends for us and we were able to recruit for our choir some of the best singers in Kampala – European, African and Asian. Peter Wingard, who had organised many choral activities in the area with his wife Barbara, conducted the choir. Just before this they had put on a performance of

246 Ibid., p. 201.
247 Ibid., pp. 223, 224
248 Ibid.
249 Ibid., p. 217.

Handel's 'Messiah' with a mixed choir of a hundred, bringing in singers from Kenya and Tanganyika as well as from all over Uganda – Lois had sung the soprano solos! Our choir was a small group of 20 but was well trained and balanced. It was interesting to have the final rehearsals in the Temple, as the acoustics were unusual.

Our contact with the *Uganda Argus* was very helpful and a special supplement was planned with as much of the cost as possible being paid for by advertisements, mainly from the businesses which had provided goods and services in the construction work. It was a most impressive eight-page supplement, carrying on the front page a full-page aerial photograph of the Temple. It was published on 14 January and in its inner pages were photographs of the Temple, the initial landscaping, the caretaker's cottage, a close-up of a door and window, an upper window and other features of the building. In addition there were pictures of the Shrine of the Báb, the International Archives building and the Wilmette, Frankfurt and Sydney Temples. There were also articles on the building, on the World Centre and on the Faith itself as well as details of the Conference to be held in Makerere College Hall, the Inaugural Service and the Public Meeting to be held in the National Theatre.

DEDICATION OF THE KAMPALA MASHRIQU'L-ADHKÁR

'Amatu'l-Bahá Rúḥíyyih Khánum and several other Hands, representatives of many National Spiritual Assemblies, and nearly 500 believers from 19 countries were present. David Hofman represented the British National Spiritual Assembly: James Robertson, Lizbeth Greaves and Beatrice Newman represented Scotland, Northern Ireland and Wales respectively.

The events of the 13 – 16 January 1961 included a Unity Feast in Makerere College Main Hall on 13 January. Later that evening there was a 15-minute programme on the Uganda Broadcasting Service about the Faith. The dedication service was held on the morning of 14 January; the African Teaching Conference commenced that afternoon under the chairmanship of Hand of the Cause John Robarts and there was an evening session when Rúḥíyyih Khánum spoke on the Guardian. The Conference continued on Sunday morning under the chairmanship of 'Alí Nakhjavání.

At 3.30 pm that afternoon the public inaugural service was held in the Temple, with every seat taken including many guests of honour and a large throng outside, totalling over one thousand. A beautiful programme was printed with the latest photograph of the Temple 'stuck-in' only a short time before despatch. It included a summary of the Bahá'í Faith, the order of worship of the Saturday's dedication and the Sunday public service, as well as articles on the House of Worship, features of the design and Bahá'í worship, with quotations from Bahá'í Scriptures on the last page.

Among the more than one thousand non-Bahá'í guests at the inaugural service were representatives of the Protectorate and African Governments, senior government officials, the mayor and other leading citizens of Kampala. The governor of Uganda was officially represented by Mr Stone and the Kabaka by Prince Henry Kalamera.

ELECTION OF THE INTERNATIONAL BAHÁ'Í COUNCIL

No sooner had the excitement of the Temple dedication died down than all National Spiritual Assembly members participated in the postal election for the first election for the International Bahá'í Council, appointed in the first instance by the Guardian himself when he said it would be followed by 'its transformation into duly elected body, its efflorescence into Universal House of Justice, and its final fruition through erection of manifold auxiliary institutions constituting the World Administrative Centre destined to arise and function and remain permanently established in close neighbourhood of Twin Holy Shrines.'

The results of the election were announced at Ridván when it was learned that our own chairman, 'Alí Nakhjavání, was the only member from the African continent, and was one of the two Persians on that esteemed body. Of the other seven, six were from the USA and one, Ian Semple (the only European, not to mention a man with whose introduction to the Faith my mother and I had been so closely involved), from England. 'Alí had to go to Haifa and we were informed in July that he would be obliged to stay there. This was a great shock to us, to the members of the Uganda Teaching Committee and all those with whom he had been closely linked in the teaching work but most of all by Mr Banání, for whom 'Alí had not only been his Auxiliary Board member but also his right hand man in his business affairs as well as his functioning as a Hand of the Cause.

I was able to report to the community in the National Spiritual Assembly's annual report to the Convention in 1961 that the total numbers of Bahá'ís were approximately 10,000 in Uganda, 4,000 in Kenya and 1,000 in Tanganyika. In Uganda the Teaching Committee had formed District Teaching Committees (DTC) for Buganda, Bugisu, Bukedi,

Busoga, Lango, Teso and West Nile while the DTCs of Bukedi, Bugisu and Teso had set up 25 area committees.[250]

Two Bahá'í Schools in Uganda were almost completed during the year, one in Tilling, Teso, on land donated by Enoch Olinga which was dedicated by Rúḥíyyih Khánum on 18 January during our visit there. The other was in Dusai, Agule, Pallisa, Bukedi. Both were scheduled to be opened firstly as kindergartens in May – June. Hassan Sabrí and myself formed the Bahá'í Schools Committee for Uganda, with local committees actually to run them.

During the year, Ḥassan, Max Kenyerezi and myself functioned as a legal committee to handle such matters as the recognition of Bahá'í marriage certificates under the then Marriage Ordinance, the incorporation of nine local Spiritual Assemblies, the eviction of a squatter from the Temple land and obtaining exemption for the *Bahá'í Gazette* from the need to pay a newspaper bond. Our good friend, Roger Counihan was our liaison with his firm, Messrs Hunter and Greig.

MY PROMOTION TO SENIOR FIELD OFFICER

In October 1961, through the good offices of the senior entomologist, George R. Barnley, I was put forward for promotion to the post of Senior Field Officer to be effective from 1 July 1962. In his letter of recommendation, Mr Barnley described my duties as:

In charge of all matters of office routine, finance and store-keeping. These duties alone justify the employment of a Senior Field Officer as an administrative officer at the headquarters office of the Tsetse Control Department.

Field Survey and control work, for which duties Mr Hainsworth is competent to work on all vector control problems including mosquito surveys, anti-malarial drainage, larvicidal and residual spraying; Sleeping Sickness inspection; Simulium and Onchocerciasis control; snail and schistosomiasis surveys; propaganda and training of staff; maintenance and repair of apparatus.

I have already mentioned the places in Uganda that I visited in the course of this work as a field officer. Of particular note is the draining of some swampy land in the centre of Gulu, Northern Uganda, which I arranged for the Bahá'ís to obtain while it was of no value. It later became prime land and became the site of their future Bahá'í centre. I also spent some time up Mount Elgon, Bugisu; in the valleys around the 'Mountains

[250] Unpublished report (personal archives).

of the Moon' near Kilembe Mines; in the rivers of West Nile and on a sleeping sickness survey in Madi in the north-western tip of Uganda.

My work involved simulium control. The disease onchocercias – known in other parts of the tropics as 'river blindness' is caused by the simulium fly biting humans around the face and head, the microfilaria which cause the disease affects the eyes and the flies in Uganda also bite humans around the legs and ankles. This work took me into the dense forest of Budongo, near Hoima, Bunyoro, where I had my elephant experience.

On one occasion, entomologist Michael Prentice and I were leading a party on foot through the Budongo Forest as the elephants had destroyed one of the small bridges on the forest path and we did not have the time to rebuild it. A herd of particularly 'kali' (fierce) elephants inhabited the area so we had with us a couple of African game guards with heavy rifles. As we walked along we were discussing the achievement of Roger Bannister in reaching the four-minute mile and Mike was saying that at university he had almost done that himself.

The game guards who were in front came back to say there was a female elephant with a calf and she looked fierce. Normally, an elephant with its large ears can hear people long before they get within sight and will move off: the elephant is somewhat short sighted and relies on its hearing and sense of smell. Consequently the game guard, when seeing elephants in the distance, just shouts 'genda' (hard 'g') which is Luganda for 'go away' and, if they are in a herd, they will begin to move away.

This elephant was alone with her calf and lifted up her trunk and screamed, which indicated she was trying to scare us away, and the party stopped in its tracks. This is usually a bluff but suddenly all the Africans darted away as she lifted her head and charged. Mike and I followed suit and I remember thinking as I ran, 'Yes, I believe he was right and could do the mile in four minutes'. I was very fit and not far behind but was hampered by a rucksack I was carrying on my back. Coming to a bend in the track we found the Africans resting; they said that as we were now out of sight of the elephant she would have given up the chase and we had been saved by some fallen trees between her and the track. I then became the object of amusement when it was remembered that the rucksack that had restricted my speed was full of 'Thunder Flashes' – these were to be used to frighten off elephants and other wild game and the striker to ignite them was strapped to my wrist!

UGANDA'S INDEPENDENCE

During our teaching work in the villages we had often come across government teams trying to teach the Africans the rudiments of British parliamentary democracy, which depended upon having a viable 'opposition'. We were in the same villages explaining Bahá'í administration, which is free from political involvement, electioneering and divisive party policies.

In one case, a young Ugandan political party had a manifesto that aimed at universal state education but we had to advise the believers not to become involved due to its divisive nature.

The efforts of the British government came to fruition with the granting of independence in October 1962; the ceremony was preceded by a dance and fireworks display at Kololo Stadium, Kampala. The Duke and Duchess of Kent attended and during their visit opened the new Mulago Hospital.

I had been one of the many hundreds of people involved in the preparatory work for these two occasions and I learned of an interesting measurement. When planning the seating for the VIPs, we had to measure benches and allow 24″ for visiting 'Royal' bottoms and 18″ for all others!

When the first elected Legislative Council had been formed some time previously, Benedicto Kiwanuka, a Muganda, had been the first Prime Minister. But by the time of the independence celebrations Milton Obote, of the Lango tribe, was the Prime Minister.

ELECTION OF THE UNIVERSAL HOUSE OF JUSTICE

The Guardian had envisaged the holding of the Jubilee conference in Baghdád at the end of the Ten Year Crusade. Due to the unsettled situation in Iraq at the time, the Hands of the Cause in the Holy Land had been obliged to advise the Bahá'í world that this would not be possible, but arrangements had been made to hold these celebrations in the Albert Hall, London. These would follow the election of the first Universal House of Justice, which would take place in Haifa at Ridván, 1963.

We decided to try to make it possible for all members of our National Spiritual Assembly to attend, which meant raising funds for the African members. Those who were on the National Spiritual Assemblies on March 23rd 1963 would attend, and at that time our National Spiritual Assembly members were Ted Cardell and Charles Nalika from Kenya, Oloro Epyeru,

Sosipateri Isimai, Israel Kanyerezi-Mukasa (Max), Kolonario Oule, Hassan and Isobel Sabrí and myself from Uganda.

I had needed a great deal of notice to enable me to make all the necessary plans for my overseas leave and to arrange for my family while I went to Haifa. At that time we had been granted a pilgrimage so it was agreed that Lois would go with Zarin to Haifa then home to England; I would send Richard by plane to join them and then go to Italy, pick up a boat in Venice and travel to Haifa via Constantinople.

We got Richard his first passport dated 8 January 1963, when he was 3′5″ tall!

There is an interesting story connected with Lois' pilgrimage. She met Graham Waterman who helped her with Zarin on the plane home and taught him the Faith on the journey. He became a Bahá'í in London and when he offered to help at the conference, he was asked to be a doorkeeper at the Albert Hall. He was stationed at the stage door to check credentials and initially refused to admit Rúḥíyyih Khánum as she did not have a credential. Shortly afterwards he met and married the daughter of Hand of the Cause Collis Featherstone, and Rúḥíyyih Khánum attended their wedding.

When in Naples I visited pioneer Kathleen, Lady Hornell and while visiting also met two Bahá'ís who were en route to Haifa – Margot Dörnbrack of the German National Spiritual Assembly and Douglas Weeks of New Zealand. Margot was the mother-in-law of the son of my old London friends, Donald and Eaddie Millar; Douglas was one of the sons of Dora Weeks with whom I had stayed in Bristol during the Six Year Plan when he had been just a small child.

I caught the Zim Line boat to Haifa, and discovered that since I had booked the very cheapest berth, I was in steerage; my fellow passengers were Argentinean Jews emigrating to Israel and none could speak a word of English. I had a word with the purser to see if I could pay a little extra and have a cabin and he said I was to see him after the boat sailed. He then told me that he could let me have a bunk in a cabin with one passenger who was leaving at Constantinople and one member of the crew for no extra charge. He warned me that the crew member was the ship's rabbi and he snored very loudly, but he got up every morning to go to the kitchens at 3.30 a.m. This I accepted and found him a most interesting character. He was a Cockney and I was so happy to have someone to talk to in the cabin.

I have no record of the details of the actual occasion of the election of the Universal House of Justice – when I arrived, where I stayed or what I did – but in the official archives it is recorded that the election took place in the House of the Master, 7 Haparsim Street, Haifa, commencing at 9.30 am on 21 April.

The main reception hall of the house had been cleared and the members of each National Spiritual Assembly sat in rows of chairs with their backs to the entrance door with the Hands of the Cause on the left of the hall. The narrow room in which the Guardian had received me was not open. After a welcome by Rúḥíyyih Khánum and appropriate prayers the voting took place in deep silence and as the roll call of members was called the votes were taken up to be placed in the box with the appropriate postal votes being opened and cast. All 56 Assemblies participated, with 288 present, and others offering postal votes. None were able to be present from Arabia, Burma, Cuba, Haiti, Iraq, or Nicaragua, but all nine members attended from the British Isles, Colombia, Central and East Africa, Finland, Írán, Netherlands, South and West Africa, Italy, Switzerland and the United States.

During the years that followed I met some of those Bahá'ís again and again at the five-yearly International Conventions, with fewer and fewer of the first contingent present each time until, at the last I attended in 1993, probably not more than a dozen of that first contingent were present. It was good to see that some of their sons and daughters were then on the National Spiritual Assemblies, including my own son Richard from Russia. Of the 18 Tellers appointed by the Hands, Ernest Gregory of Great Britain was one of the three who made up the 'Supervisory Board', chosen by them to read out the results of the election. Our own Hassan Sabrí was one of the 18 to be elected to the Board.

After all the votes had been placed in the box we realised that our major job was done and that we had participated in one of the most significant developments in the history of mankind, I remarked upon a miracle which had been taking place before my eyes. When the meeting began, all the assembled Hands, without exception, especially those who had been residing in the Holy Land, appeared to be much older than when I had met them on earlier occasions and were carrying evident signs of the strains and responsibilities they had been called upon to bear since the passing of the Guardian, and for which they had been totally unprepared. As the delegates went up to place their voting papers in the box the Hands became visibly brighter, less strained, even younger as they realised what a weight was being lifted from their shoulders.

After lunch all the delegates, the Hands and the families and local believers gathered in Bahjí for the Ridván Feast to commemorate the 100th anniversary of the Declaration of Bahá'u'lláh, followed by a brief visit to His Holy Shrine. This visit was of particular poignancy to me as I remembered my last visit, 17 years previously, when the Guardian had so dramatically bade me farewell.

The Convention sessions began the following morning at Beth Harofe Auditorium, Israeli Medical Headquarters, 2 Wingate Avenue at 10.00 a.m. The opening session was chaired by Rúḥíyyih Khánum and towards the end Ernest Gregory read out the names of the nine elected members of the first Universal House of Justice. Charles Wolcott, who had received the highest number of votes, responded on behalf of the House to the standing ovation.

What was a very moving experience followed when all the Hands, led by Rúḥíyyih Khánum went up on the stage and greeted the members. The rejuvenation of the Hands now continued and was remarked upon by many delegates. Even Músá Banání in his wheelchair and in constant pain appeared years younger and healthier.

Even as I type this, some 36 years later, I can still see them changing and I am reminded of the burden rolling down the hill in the story of Pilgrim's Progress.

It came as no surprise to me that the men of the International Bahá'í Council were all elected – Charles Wolcott, 'Alí Nakhjavání, Lotfu'lláh Hakím, Ian Semple and Borrah Kavelin. Of the others, I assumed that David Hofman was well known through the popularity of his book, *Renewal of Civilisation*, which had gone into many languages and Hushmand Fatheazam for his work as secretary of the Indian National Spiritual Assembly; Hugh Chance and Amoz Gibson of the US National Spiritual Assembly were not personally known to me. It was a sobering thought that on this Supreme Body were my 'spiritual father', a 'spiritual son' and a dearly loved fellow Uganda pioneer! A detailed report of this event may be found in the *Bahá'í Journal* N°. 155 (June 1963).

APPOINTED AS A SPEAKER AT THE ALBERT HALL JUBILEE CELEBRATIONS PUBLIC MEETING

During this time and throughout the remaining two days I was growing more and more apprehensive of the task that the Hands had communicated to me some weeks previously. They had asked me to be one of three speakers at the Public Meeting to be held in the Albert Hall during the Jubilee Celebrations.

On the 2 April 1963, they had written:[251]

Mr William Sears, Mr John Long,

Miss Elsie Austin, Mr Philip Hainsworth

Beloved Friends:

This letter is to inform you more fully of the details of the Public Meeting to be held in the Albert Hall, Tuesday, April 29, at 8pm in which you are to participate.

The overall subject is 'World Peace with Security'. We are asking each speaker to limit his or her time to twenty-five minutes. The chairman will have fifteen minutes, which time should include both his opening and closing remarks, as well as his introductions to the various speakers.

We are asking Mr Hainsworth to open the program as the first speaker, and to deal with the life of Bahá'u'lláh in relation to the significant event we are celebrating, and how the coming of this great Figure has brought the promise of World Peace with Security.

Miss Austin will be the second speaker, and will deal with the Teachings of Bahá'u'lláh, and why they are the foundation for World Peace with Security.

Mr Sears will be the third speaker, and will issue a challenge to the audience to arise and investigate the Bahá'í Faith and to help establish World Peace with Security, and will speak of the prominent part the people of Great Britain have played in the history of the Faith.

The speakers will individually assume the responsibility of supplying the chairman, Mr Long, with the necessary background material, if needed, for their introduction. His opening and closing remarks are left to his own judgement.

There will be an opening and a closing prayer. Both the prayers and the readers will be selected well in advance, and their names and background supplied to the chairman.

With warmest Bahá'í love, In the service of the beloved Guardian,

HANDS OF THE CAUSE IN THE HOLY LAND

Rúḥíyyih A. Furútan Jalál Kházeh John Ferraby

Leroy Ioas Paul Haney William Sears

The four of us had agreed that we would plan the outlines of our presentations and get together in Haifa to finalise them. In Haifa we learned that Elsie (a member of the USA National Spiritual Assembly, then a

[251] Unpublished letter (personal archives).

pioneer to West Africa and the first Negress to become a state attorney) had withdrawn her acceptance to speak and that Bill and I would share the platform. We discussed briefly how we should tackle the subject but Bill had not had time to work on it much and was far from well, so we agreed that we would get together again in London. As it happened, he would use written notes and we met for prayers just before going on the platform. It was the biggest live audience I had ever faced, and it has not been equalled since – some 7,000 – and it was the first time I had had to use a microphone. In my belief that I could project my voice adequately, I did not at first use the microphone but it was made clear as I talked that I should. About halfway through my speech, my mouth dried up so I paused to have a drink and the audience thought I had finished and burst into applause for a few moments. In Haifa, Bill and I had agreed that I would commence with some introduction of what I had experienced in Africa, give some of the history of the Faith and then give the vision of a new society and our confidence that it would be achieved. I still have the notes that I had typed out in the Shulamit Hotel, Haifa, but I do not think I referred to them in my talk nor do I remember how closely I kept to the draft.

I was conscious that David and Marion Hofman were in the front row of the meeting, but I could not distinguish many in the packed audience. It was a great joy to hear from David afterwards that I had given an inspiring and a polished presentation.

Bill gave one of his brilliant talks, though up to the moment he went on the stage he had been quite ill. As far as I can remember he spoke of there being today 'scientific giants but moral pygmies' or some similar expression – he received tremendous applause. In the tapes of the celebrations that I heard when they were later reproduced, there was a great deal of Bill's talk but none of mine!

I subsequently heard about one of the results of this talk: a man from Bermuda was passing the Albert Hall and he was astonished to meet a friend from his hometown who told him he was in London for a religious celebration. As this man himself was searching for truth, he expressed interest and agreed to attend the public meeting. He was so moved by my talk and the way in which I spoke about the work in Uganda that he rushed out of the meeting and phoned his wife saying, 'I have found it'. Before very long both he and his wife became Bahá'ís, were towers of strength in the London area and later pioneered to the Solomon Islands – they were Earl and Audrey Cameron – both of them in the acting profession.

Immediately following the celebrations Lois and Sylvia Schulman (Benatar) gave a concert in the Wigmore Hall which Rúḥíyyih Khánum attended.

I have no recollections of what we did during the remainder of our leave in England, although we did stay for some time with Lois' aunt in Worksop and it is on record (See *Bahá'í Journal* N°. 158, p. 6) that we and the Sabrís attended the Dalston Hall, Carlisle, summer school, 13 – 27 July. This was reported as 'the best Summer School ever!', during which Lois and Sylvia gave a concert. The report said, 'We shall recall the happiness of three declarations; the ebullient and indefatigable Philip Hainsworth, Chairman of the School, rounding up his 'flock' by the clanging of a cow-bell and with vociferous cajoling which ensured a remarkable punctuality on attendance at Sessions!'

According to Lois' old passport we arrived back in Mombasa in August so we must have gone by sea but I do not remember how we moved from place to place – we must have had a car.

UGANDA ANECDOTES 1963 – 67

A few stories of our last few years in Uganda stand out in my mind. Immediately after Ugandan independence, overseas governments began to establish diplomatic relationships with the new government and there was a hectic round of receptions and 'sundowners', to which the Bahá'ís were invited, as we were on the official invitation lists. We in turn would invite groups representing about three governments to visit the Temple and have refreshments in the Collisons' house, which was adjacent to the Temple, and in our own home. We developed particularly good relations with the Israeli embassy where Michael Michaels was ambassador. Some 20 or more years later I was at a function of the Chartered Institute of Journalists in London, of which Lois later became president, when I met one of the younger members of the Israeli embassy I had known in Uganda.

One day I was driving in my Land Rover to Gulu in Northern Uganda when I became aware of a large car coming up after me. At that moment, a wasp came in through the open window and went up my khaki shorts. In my efforts to squash it before it stung me I swerved around the road and when the following car overtook me I saw the irate occupants waving their fists at me. When I reached the Acholi Inn where I was to stay the night I met those travellers and explained my predicament. After a good laugh, we became quite friendly. They were a party from Israel and the leader was a retired army general. He explained that all his life he had been trained in warfare but on his retirement, he had been made Minister of Fauna and

Flora, where he had to preserve and protect and not destroy. He was touring the Uganda Game Parks to study game control. His name was General A Joffe and he invited me to look him up when I next visited Israel. Some time later, I took up his offer and he took me to visit some of the Jewish settlements where the local gazelles were causing trouble and he had to persuade the settlers not to kill them.

At one Convention, when the first group of Pygmies arrived from the Congo, having travelled for very many days to get there, they wore their native dress – what little it was – and carried their bows and arrows.

At this, or another Convention, we were so inspired by the spread of the Faith that had resulted in the total numbers in our region (we were still Central and East Africa) that we resolved to enlarge our numbers by enrolling another 50,000 believers in the year ahead. We closed the Convention singing, 'Fifty, fifty, fifty thousand' (repeated three times), 'Fifty fifty thousand new Bahá'ís this year'.

At yet another Convention, some of the African members of the National Spiritual Assembly were very concerned that there had been some mutterings about getting an all-African National Assembly and not voting for the pioneers. In an emergency session of the National Assembly at night, it was agreed that two of the African members would address the Convention the next morning which they did in a most wonderful way and made the pioneers very proud of them. One of the ringleaders of the divisive movement however, was elected to the Assembly, and the Assembly in session decided to commence an investigation. Subsequently the Assembly received the report while in session, the man was found guilty and his voting rights were removed, with him present, and he had to leave the Assembly!

During this time Lois did some magnificent travel teaching on her own and sometimes with Violette Nakhjavání.

DECISION TO LEAVE UGANDA

It must have been towards the end of 1964 that we wrote to the Universal House of Justice saying that we were seriously considering leaving Uganda as we wished our children to have an English-style education. This was not possible in Uganda and we did not wish to break up the family by sending them to a boarding school in the British Isles. We asked if the House could suggest anywhere in the world where we could settle to achieve this objective and serve the Faith and they replied that our return to the British Isles would be best and we should seek the advice of the National Spiritual Assembly there. This we did, and in their reply the National Spiritual

Assembly suggested that we could best serve the Faith in the Leeds area so we contacted my niece, Kathleen Ackroyd, who lived in Driglington, Yorkshire, to look for a house for us.

Details of a house in Horsforth near Leeds appealed to us and I contacted Robert Jackson, a Bahá'í from Reading who had sold me a Canada Life Assurance policy, to see if he could help. He put me in touch with Bill Higgins of the Leeds Office who negotiated a mortgage with the Halifax Building Society and an appropriate Endowment policy, had the house surveyed and commissioned Les Morris of Walker, Morris and Coles to go ahead and buy it.

I arranged for three months' leave and requested a pilgrimage for Richard and me. We packed up almost all our belongings in a huge crate but left a small amount in store as I had to return to Uganda work out my notice and left on our long journey. Richard and I went on pilgrimage; Lois and Zarin made a teaching trip through Ethiopia, Somalia, Aden, Bahrain and Kuwait thence to Írán.

OUR TIME IN ÍRÁN

Richard and I joined the ladies in Írán where we were all guests of Jalál Sahihi, with whom we had established a warm relationship when he, as secretary of the Persian Africa Committee, had arranged the travel plans for the Persian Bahá'ís to visit Kampala for the Temple Dedication. We had a wonderful visit which included some time in a Tehran branch of Bank Melli, which on one side overlooked the site of the seven martyrs of Tehran, and on the other the ruins above the Síyáh Chál. I was able to climb over the scaffolding, ostensibly to photograph the Golestan palace but really to take a picture of the entrance to the Prison below the waste ground. We also visited the site of Tahiríh's martyrdom, the Home of Bahá'u'lláh, the ruined Ḥaẓíratu'l-Quds, the Temple site, and the home of Mrs Banání. In Jalál's car we went to Isfahan, where we bought some silver, visited the tomb of Keith Ransom-Kehler and stayed the night in the Ḥaẓíratu'l-Quds. We visited the ruins of Persepolis before going to Shíráz, where we paused at the Qur'án Gate, before going to the Ḥaẓíratu'l-Quds. It was there, where we slept in the gardens, that we were 'found' by Iraj Poostchi, who recognised my voice from the days he had spent in Newcastle, England, during the Six Year Plan, and he took us to his home.

In the early hours of one morning, at about 4.00 a.m., we visited the House of the Báb, entering it through a door in a side street and through a tunnel as we had to be very circumspect.

During our stay, we went to the house of the chairman of the local Spiritual Assembly where I gave a talk and we met the chief of police, who was a friend of Iraj.

Later in our visit, we went by train to Bạbu'l-Shah and stayed with a local doctor who took us to Shaykh Tabarsi, but we could not get close to the building as it was also a local shrine and there was a religious commemoration at that time. We also went to Barfarush, where Quddús had been martyred.

During our time in Tehran, we visited the home of Dr Moyahed, whom we had met in Cambridge and who had been the first to be advised of our plans to marry in 1956. His son-in-law was the head of Írán Airlines and he arranged for us to fly to Tabriz (this son was martyred in the 1980s). While in Tabriz we visited the courtyard of Bank Melli, which was where the barracks had been, and stood by the wall of the site where the Báb had actually been shot. We also saw the steps leading up to the room where He had awaited the interviews at which He had been sentenced to death. Our host and guide was the chairman of the local Spiritual Assembly, who was also later martyred.

We also visited Dr Hossein Gollestani and his wife Rizvania (née Éghrahi), both of whom I had known in England during the Six Year Plan. Hossein had been one of the two doctors who had run the 'clinic' at the first Kampala Conference in 1953. When he learned that we were planning to buy a Persian carpet he offered to take us to some merchant friends in the Suk as he was also planning to buy one for someone else. Through his good offices, we got a very good deal and were able to buy one for the price Lois had obtained for her piano before we left Kampala.

We were also well received by Masud Khamsi and family, and met Christine Wade, then married to Dr Changizi, a surgeon who played squash regularly with the Shah.

TURKEY, GERMANY AND HOME TO ENGLAND

After leaving Írán, we went to Istanbul where we were the guests of Sammi Doktoroglu, who had a travel agency, and whom we had met in Kampala and whose daughter I had known in England. The British Ambassador attended a concert arranged for Lois by the British Council. After some time visiting the Saint Sophia Mosque and the mosque near one of the houses where Bahá'u'lláh had lived after His arrival from Baghdád, we followed the route of His journey to Edirne (Adrianople). Here we were received in His House, which had been recently renovated and which had witnessed the rebellion of Mírzá Yahyá. We later drove south to Gallipolli and crossed the Straits to visit Troy en route to the home of the Doktoroglus on the eastern side of the sea.

From Turkey, we went to Germany, where we stayed with Mr and Mrs Rene Steiner. Mrs Steiner I had known as Noura Farridian – the first Persian Bahá'í nurse to come to England (in 1948), where she and Shomais Ala'i (later Afnan) had studied in Northampton. Noura had been Matron in a hospital in Salisbury, Rhodesia, during the Ten Year Crusade. It was while we were visiting the Mashriqu'l-Adhkár in Hofheim, then completed but with the access road unfinished, that I helped to push a small car which was stuck on the side of the road. It was over an open manhole, and I fell into it when the car moved and damaged my knee. Noura bandaged it up and it eventually healed but it began some years later to give trouble and later developed into an arthritic knee from which I suffered for the rest of my life and which did not yield to physiotherapy, heat treatment, ultrasound, acupuncture, herbal remedies, or anything else.

From Germany, we flew to Manchester, where we were met by Kathy and Sandy Ackroyd and taken to our new home in Church Road, Horsforth on the outskirts of Leeds. Early in my stay in Horsforth I went to thank the people in Canada Life for their help in buying the house, met the manager – John Cowen – who offered me work with Canada Life when I came back to England after working out my six months notice in Uganda.

My own plans for employment had been to start up a travel agency for tours to East Africa but John convinced me how precarious it would be to get started, whereas he could guarantee me employment immediately on my return with an income and commission on sales even while learning my new job as a life assurance salesman.

I have little memory of my leave – we were busy settling in, buying needed house furniture and equipment, unpacking the huge crate that arrived with our goods from Uganda, and making it into a Wendy House for the children at the end of the back garden. The house was named 'St Leonard's' but we renamed it 'Sharaf'. The children went to a local primary school and we arranged for Richard to be admitted to Leeds Grammar Prep School.

I left for Uganda in November 1965 and went straight to live in a small flat not very far from my office in Nakasero. Time passed very quickly working out my six month's notice, sorting out my affairs, handing over to my colleague Geoff Ealden in the office, making farewell visits and completing my work as secretary of the National Spiritual Assembly. It was Hassan Sabrí who gave me a letter of credential when I left. I went by train to Mombassa and waited for the boat for England. I was so eager to get home that I left the boat in Naples and travelled by train to London where Lois met me: we stayed the night at the Savoy Hotel before going to Horsforth where her aunt was looking after the children.

I arrived home on 6 May 1966 and commenced a training course for Canada Life in Leeds almost immediately. Lois had gone to the Convention and had gained eight votes, and strangely enough, I had nine votes. Subsequently Lois was appointed secretary of the Assembly Assistance Teaching Committee and was very active; I was put on a Proclamation Committee, which did nothing. By the end of the year I was travel teaching, probably the highlight of which was a new technique I tried out in the first public meeting to be held in Swansea that led to the acceptance of the Faith of Mr and Mrs A. Morse.

BACK ON THE NATIONAL SPIRITUAL ASSEMBLY OF THE BRITISH ISLES

At the Convention of 1967, I was elected onto the National Spiritual Assembly whose other members were John Long, Betty Reed, Joe Jameson, Charles Macdonald, Adib Taherzadeh, Eric Hellicar, Abbas Afnan, and Owen Battrick.

My work with Canada Life enabled me to take on many Bahá'í assignments and fit in all my National Spiritual Assembly commitments; these included attendance at Lyme Park and Dalston Hall schools and regular visits to Lancashire, as well as teaching and committee assignments all over the United Kingdom.

SYNOPSIS

Thus ends my first attempt to put in writing the major events of my life up to the time I re-settled in England after returning from Uganda.

Much of the material that may be of use to future historians when they research the history of the Faith in the British Isles and Uganda has had to omitted.

Personal recollections of such stalwarts of the Faith as George Townshend, Ḥasan Balyúzí, John and Dorothy Ferraby, Dick Backwell, Alma Gregory, Marion and Arthur Norton, Albert and Jeff Joseph, Asher Nazar, Diá'u'lláh Asgharzádih, Evelyn Baxter, Walter Wilkins, Reg Coulson, Hugh McKinley, Ursula Newman and Mehdi Samandarí, Meherangiz and Eruch Munsiff in the United Kingdom; Músá and Samiyyih Banání, Enoch Olinga, Rex and Mary Collison, Alan and Mary Elston, Les Hawthorn and his wife, Ted Cardell, Azíz and Soraya Yazdí, Kolonerio Oule, Oloro Epyeru, Sosipateri Isimai, Claire Gung, Hassan and Isobel Sabrí, Irene Bennett and Max Kenyerezi in East Africa, could have been written as most were alive and very active in 1967.

EPILOGUE

I have been deeply privileged to be involved in many events of great historical significance, to witness the successful conclusion of the Six Year and the Two Year Plans and the British share of the Ten Year Crusade;

I taught the Faith in England, Scotland, Wales, Northern Ireland, the Republic of Ireland, Belgium, France, Spain, Portugal, Germany, Turkey, Írán, Palestine, Egypt, Kenya, Uganda, Tanganyika and Ruanda-Urundi.

I witnessed the opening of Uganda to the Faith and saw it grow to a community of about 100,000 believers; participated in the building and dedication of the Mother Temple of Africa, the election and participation in the Regional National Spiritual Assembly of Central and East Africa; attended the election of the Universal House of Justice and addressed a live audience of over 7,000 during the Most Great Jubilee in the Albert Hall, London.

Above all, I had the unique blessing of spending about fourteen hours in personal discussion with Shoghi Effendi at a time when no pilgrims were allowed to visit Haifa and had been favoured with 15 letters and 16 cables from him.

I have in mind the writing of another book of memoirs to cover the many other significant events with which I have been associated after my return to the National Spiritual Assembly of the British Isles in 1967 but the demand has been so great for the story of these first 48 years of my life that I could not delay any longer.

Philip Hainsworth
September 2000.

POSTSCRIPT

THE FINAL CHAPTER 1967-2001

Philip never completed this autobiography and it was suggested that I write a chapter to summarise his services and cover the key points in his life for his remaining years. It is a totally impossible task to squeeze into one chapter the activities and services of such a man, whose utter selflessness, devotion and dedication it would be difficult to match.

He had sent *Looking Back in Wonder*, the autobiography that you have just read, to be published before he died and had commenced writing a sequel to cover the period covered by this chapter. Only three paragraphs were written before he died and these merely summarised the previous work. From these I quote a few lines that indicate his own feelings about those early years:

> While the thirty years now under review (1967 – 2001) witnessed some unique events, they cannot compare with those mentioned in the first part of my autobiography. The excitement of the first British Six Year Plan and the Africa Two Year Plan could, I am sure, never be rivalled. It was the amazing experiences of my first 25 years as a Bahá'í which really merited the title, "Looking Back in Wonder" and deserved their recording, particularly as most of those great souls with whom I was associated are now rejoicing in the Abhá Kingdom.

During 1966, we had settled in Horsforth, near Leeds: Philip had gone back to Uganda to work out his six months' retirement notice, continuing as a member of the Central and East Africa Regional National Assembly, and then returned to commence work for the Canada Life Assurance Company. There were no Bahá'ís living anywhere near and so we began weekly firesides incorporating an attractive teaching programme.

Philip was much in demand as a speaker at public meetings and summer schools all over the country and at Convention 1967, just a few months after his return to England, he was elected back onto the National Spiritual Assembly. Thus began his last unbroken period on the National Spiritual Assembly of the British Isles, which later became the NSA of the United Kingdom, making a total of 44 years as a National Assembly member. The Proclamation Committee was formed and he became its secretary.

In October 1967, we drove to the Intercontinental Conference in Frankfurt, Germany with Richard and Zarin. Nine months later, our second son, Michael, was born in Leeds and when he was three weeks old, all five of us flew to Palermo. We attended the 1968 Mediterranean conference held in August to mark the centenary of the passage of Bahá'u'lláh from Gallipoli to 'Akká, which was followed by a three day pilgrimage to the Bahá'í World Centre for all Bahá'ís at the conference. Michael, at four weeks old, was the youngest pilgrim and Philip and I carried his cot up the steps of Mount Carmel to the Shrine of the Báb, following the path which the Guardian had told Philip so many years before would eventually be trodden by the kings and rulers of the world.

Richard won a place at Leeds Grammar School and Zarin at Roundhay High School for Girls. Zarin continued to take ballet classes, which she had started as a little girl in Uganda, eventually qualifying as a 'Scholar' at the Royal Academy of Dancing, York section, which involved driving her twice a week to attend classes. Philip continued to travel extensively, speaking on the Faith and doing much public relations work with local dignitaries.

During 1968, we moved to Leeds and the following year we were elected to the local Assembly, Philip as chairman and I as its secretary. For the next few years he spent a great deal of time going through all the letters from the beloved Guardian to the Bahá'ís of the British Isles, resulting in the magnum opus called Unfolding Destiny. This book should be on every British Bahá'í bookshelf, giving as it does tremendous insight into the love and admiration lavished upon the British community by Shoghi Effendi. It was published in 1981 after many years of research: we had expected it to have been completed several years before, but a great many additional letters came to light after the passing of Ḥasan Balyúzí, which involved considerable re-editing.

In addition to this magnum opus he wrote a great many articles and books, which are listed in Appendix 2, but his great pride was in the production of many pamphlets in African languages, commencing with those in Swahili, Chinyanza and Hausa, which he had been encouraged by the beloved Guardian to undertake in 1946. Interestingly, Richard tells the following story:

> I was travel teaching in Africa and sitting in a village waiting to meet its chief. We had some literature to give and I was leafing through the one in the chief's own language. There I found that it had been translated from Bantu and the author was Philip Hainsworth.

His literary output intensified considerably during the years following 1967, and included sections on the Bahá'í Faith in a number of collections. He also collaborated with Hugh Adamson on the impressive Historical Dictionary of the Bahá'í Faith, and with Mary Perkins on a handbook, The Bahá'í Faith, which was translated into five languages, including Russian. This played a considerable part in the development of the Faith in that country in 1989 when there was very little literature available in that language.

In 1974, he was elected secretary of the British National Spiritual Assembly and a period of unprecedented activity started. Philip moved to London to live in the Ḥaẓíratu'l-Quds and it was left to me sadly to sell our beautiful house and garden in Leeds which had been the venue for enormous teaching activity, including a youth school with about 30 participants.

The first few months were very difficult. Philip worked in his office from 7.00 am for 12 hours each day and continued at night in the flat at the top of the Ḥaẓíratu'l-Quds. Richard and Zarin were taking examinations but on most weekends drove with Michael and me to London to be with Philip. At the end of the summer term we moved to Westminster to live in Rutland Gate, leaving Richard to live for a few months in a 'bed-sit' in the home of one of my friends in Leeds. Zarin won a place at Elmhurst Ballet School where she spent three years before deciding to relinquish her hopes of a career in ballet and moving to Greycoat Hospital in Westminster to take A levels, subsequently going to university in Aberystwyth. Michael started to attend Westminster Primary School. Later that year Richard came to London to attend university at Imperial College, Kensington.

During 1974, we made a full pilgrimage as a family that made this a memorable year: we hired a car and visited many other historic sites in the Holy Land, a journey that Philip particularly enjoyed.

Description of life at the Bahá'í centre would need a separate book! Then, as now, Rutland Gate was a pivot with streams of visitors, large numbers of whom were Bahá'ís visiting the grave of the beloved Guardian. The most famous of these was the Maleatoa of Western Samoa, who was escorted by a large party of Bahá'ís to visit the grave. I think that was the only time I was completely alone in the Hazíratu'l-Quds – someone had to stay behind to 'hold the fort'.

Philip began to develop the public relations work, heading a small External Affairs Committee on which I was appointed a member: he made many contacts in government circles and with various organisations, including the United Nations Association, by whose members he was highly respected. His vision and devoted service in this sphere prepared the way for much of the external affairs work that has followed and has borne such fruit.

This was in addition to dealing with all the national secretarial work with only one secretary and some part-time help. At this time, he met Edward Carpenter, then Dean of Westminster Abbey, who was chairman of the UNA Religious Advisory Committee, which held its meetings at the Liberal Club in Whitehall Court. When this facility was no longer available, Philip suggested they hold their meetings at Rutland Gate – they still do, as do other UN-related committees.

1976 was an incredible year: there were continental conferences in Kenya, Ireland and France. Westminster local Spiritual Assembly's Nineteen Day Feast fell just before the Paris conference and a simple Feast for our community suddenly become a huge conference, with large numbers of visiting Bahá'ís joining us. The walls of the Ḥaẓíratu'l-Quds were positively bursting at the seams, and we made panicked visits to the local shops to augment our provisions!

Our family attended all three conferences, with Philip presenting the work done in the United Kingdom. Visits to Nairobi, Dublin and Paris proved to be tremendous learning experiences for Richard, Zarin and Michael. I sometimes wonder if their lives were moulded by their early understanding of the part played by their father – certainly the devotion and service to the Faith of all three of our children gave Philip inestimable joy.

Most poignant of the three conferences was attendance in Nairobi; we were so close to Uganda and wanted very much to visit our friends there, but could not cross the border due to the political situation: this was when Idi Amin was dictator. Only a very few Ugandan Bahá'ís were able to get to the conference, by walking over the border and much of the way. Clare Gung, as a foreigner, was able to attend by travelling an easier route and she told us of the great difficulties being encountered in Uganda at that time, and the shortages of goods there. On one occasion, she opened her large handbag to show me that it was filled to overflowing with boxes of matches. These were unobtainable in Uganda at the time and this good, kind lady had bought a sufficient supply to give to all her friends. This was the last time we saw her.

In 1977, Philip was not re-elected as secretary of the National Assembly and was appointed as public relations officer, in this capacity continuing his successful external relations work. The contacts he made in this field were very helpful when, in 1979, persecution of the Iranian Bahá'ís became much more severe with the new government in Iran. One of the needs which arose in this connection was a visit to the European Parliament in Strasbourg, where he worked effectively among members of the European Parliament to alleviate the situation of the Persian Bahá'ís. Together with Fuad Rizai he did a great deal to ease the difficulties of many of the Persian friends who fled from their country at this time.

Two years, '78 and '86, were special family years, each with a joyous marriage: in 1978, Richard and Corinne (née Kent) were married in Cardiff Castle, and in 1986 Zarin married Soroush Fadaie. Both occasions drew a large number of non-Bahá'ís to attend these weddings, giving tremendous teaching opportunities.

In 1982 Richard and Corinne pioneered to Russia and, here again, stories about these experiences need another book! At that time they were advised to be very careful as Soviet law did not permit the teaching of religion.

Philip was elected as a delegate to Convention every year until his death and attended every International Convention from the first in 1963 until 1993 – seven in all. The International Convention in 1993 was a time of great pride and joy for him, as one of his sons was also a delegate. Richard had been elected to the first National Spiritual Assembly of the Soviet Union in 1991, the only member not born in the Soviet Union, and subsequently on to the Regional Assembly of Russia, Armenia, and Georgia. It was as a member of this body that Richard attended the 1993 International Convention. Subsequently all 15 of the republics of the Soviet Union achieved their own National Spiritual Assembly and Richard now serves on the National Spiritual Assembly of Russia.

Philip made four visits to Moscow: the first, in 1986, was on our way back from the dedication of the Indian Mas͟hriqu'l-Ad͟hkár. In 1990 we participated in a conference called to consider how to administer the rapidly growing Bahá'í community in what was still the Soviet Union, at which he made some excellent suggestions based on experience with the regional work in Central and East Africa. In 1992 we attended the Moscow Satellite Centenary Commemoration of the Passing of Bahá'u'lláh; Zarin and her family attended the satellite in Romania and Michael attended the main conference in New York, so all our family were able to attend one of these historic conferences. In 1996, our Moscow visit was followed by a trip to speak at a Summer School at Gelendjik on the Black Sea and after this we visited Lithuania, Latvia and Estonia.

Also in 1992, we were both among the privileged 19 Bahá'ís chosen by the British community to represent them for the Centenary Commemoration of the Passing of Bahá'u'lláh in the Holy Land. This was a particularly poignant occasion for Philip, as it brought back precious moments spent with the beloved Guardian 46 years before. The Guardian had stood beside him near the Shrine of the Báb and pointed out exactly where the Seat of the Universal House of Justice would be built in years to come.

Nineteen ninety-four was a sad year for him, as he was not elected to the National Assembly at Convention, but he did not become idle although he was already 75 years old.

THE NATIONAL SPIRITUAL ASSEMBLY

Much could be said on the subject of 38 years as the wife of a National Assembly member: he never breached the confidence of the National Spiritual Assembly consultative process, which was often quite difficult for me as sometimes he was obviously worried about this or that problem and would say nothing about it. Thus, of his membership on this institution I can say nothing, except that he threw himself into this work with complete devotion and that a part of him died when he could no longer be involved in it.

One of his National Assembly colleagues, Hugh Adamson, for whom he had great respect, has provided a few paragraphs to indicate his work on this body:

> It is hard to encapsulate the work of this great and noble man in a few paragraphs while yet not under-reporting, or diminishing, his manifold contributions at national and international levels in both the administrative and teaching spheres of Bahá'í activity.
>
> Although lacking the advantages conferred by a formal education, Philip nonetheless was self-educated and beyond question deeply learned in matters relating to the Faith – learning and knowledge he never vaunted at the expense of others. Given his humble beginnings, one could hardly have imagined one less likely than Philip to be so erudite, eloquent and possessed of such a keen, incisive, brilliant and well trained mind – faculties he brought with humility and dedication to the service of the National Assembly.
>
> He was nearly always the first to arrive for Assembly meetings. Without fail he came prepared for the meeting – having read the normally voluminous number of documents and papers circulated between meetings before he arrived; if there were additional interim materials, he would read them conscientiously before consultation began. He took time to read items with care and could always be counted on to understand their context and importance. Having

served so long as a National Assembly member he was able to add historic perspective to most issues.

His consultative style was both direct and constructive; his personality transparent, open and honest. He saw it as his duty in consultation to speak frankly on every issue. He was truthful and candid in his assessments. He was forceful and forthright in the presentation of his position while remaining open to the arguments of others. He could not and would not dissemble. What some saw as gruffness or impatience in Philip, namely his down-to-earth no-nonsense approach, was in reality an indication of the urgency he brought to the work of the Cause. Whenever he felt the consultation was lagging (or "waffling") he would insist that we "get on with the work of the Cause without further delay!" He was at all times acutely conscious of the urgent need to move the affairs of the Faith forward, and never spared himself in that regard. He spoke his mind, cutting to the heart of matters and, at times, expressed a degree of frustration with those of us with less penetrating insight – yet for those who knew him best there was never occasion for offence, because we understood the underlying sweet gentleness of his soul and the loving tenderness of his heart.

He was pragmatic and action-oriented – he looked at what needed to be done, engaged fully in the consultative search for a way forward, and then carried out whatever actions devolved to him with tenacity and perseverance. No task was too small or inconsequential for his attention – he volunteered for chores of all kinds (more often than not those which others were reluctant, unwilling or unable to discharge) and could always be counted on to carry them forward without fail. Many times he was called on (or volunteered) to draft sensitive and/or complex letters or documents. His "drafts" were without fail cogent, eloquent and complete, often requiring no change in either structure or content. He was able to synthesize complex issues and his consultative offerings were concise and addressed the heart of any given matter. Whatever he did not immediately comprehend he would state openly and ask questions until he had the matter or issue within his grasp.

His work as an Assembly member was characterised by unbounded energy, enthusiasm and total commitment. He was someone you could count on to discharge fully and diligently whatever responsibility might be devolved to him. He was capable of single-handed action but worked equally well on co-operative department and/or committee-type work. Over the years he served as a member, or liaison member, of just about every conceivable department and committee ever appointed by the National Spiritual Assembly.

In addition to the spiritual mandates allotted to a National Spiritual Assembly there is, too, a full cross section of the "functions" found in any modern business corporation. Philip was one of those rare individuals capable of dealing with both the spiritual and material dimensions of National Assembly work. He was equally at home dealing with legal issues or teaching, corporate and charity commission fiscal returns or community life, LSA incorporations or social and economic development projects and, importantly, could switch mental gears quickly and effortlessly in order to accommodate such subject changes.

As the National Assembly's External Affairs representative he was fearless and courageous in his promotion and protection of the Faith. Over the years, his work included direct interface with all levels of Government, the media (press, TV and radio), the Charity Commission, Companies House, Interfaith bodies as well as a great many other important non-Bahá'í bodies. Future historians will be amazed at the lasting relationships he established for the Faith.

In the later years of his service on the National Spiritual Assembly the pain of his physical illness was a constant companion, but he was not one to complain or shirk the burdens that fell to him – he never faltered in his devoted services, or in his willingness to shoulder yet more National Spiritual Assembly-related work.

He served as a trusted colleague, co-worker and mentor to me; someone I could turn to for advice, wise council and support in all aspects of my own brief period as National Spiritual Assembly secretary (having himself served with distinction and total dedication as secretary, chairman, vice chairman and member, for nearly half a century).'

BAHÁ'Í ASSOCIATION FOR SOCIAL AND ECONOMIC DEVELOPMENT

Philip also became very much involved in the work of the Bahá'í Association for Social and Economic Development (BASED). Iraj Poostchi has very kindly provided some thoughts, impressions, and reflections of his work with Philip and BASED-UK, which give an insight into this area of activity.

Philip had just returned from the 1992 ISARD (International

Society for Agriculture and Rural Development) meeting at Landegg Academy in Switzerland when he mentioned his thoughts for BASED-UK. In reality, it was his hard work which brought to fruition the idea for a functioning structure for Bahá'í Social and Economic Development work in the United Kingdom.

With his sense of mission and characteristic determination, he followed up his thoughts and eventually founded what we know today as BASED-UK. During the early formative stages I met with him a few times and we discussed how this structure could evolve into something of international status; this was an exchange of ideas and experiences.

Later, as a member of the Board of Trustees, I found a completely different Philip from the easy-going man of previous years. He was very much involved in the day to day work of BASED-UK and with a great sense of determination he had concentrated upon the administration of its different projects.

Although the projects varied in both scope and diversity I found him to be at ease in working on the specific procedures required for the implementation of each project. He was the honorary secretary of BASED-UK and had dedicated himself to monitoring and implementing the decisions of the Board of Trustees and overseeing the work of the Executive Committee. A hallmark of his approach was that he did not sacrifice the immediate gains which a project brought for the long term betterment of its beneficiaries. Nor, for that matter, would he sacrifice the integrity of the Faith to please the international donor agencies. His was the firm belief that if a Bahá'í project is being implemented in the remote rural areas of a developing country, the monitors, supporters, field workers and implementers of the project should be known as Bahá'ís, and their dedicated work should carry the good will and financial support of the Bahá'í community of the United Kingdom.

Several times a number of international projects were presented to the Board of Trustees for approval. When closely examined most were shown to be ill-conceived and had poor management and implementation procedures. It was a hard task, not only for the secretary but also for the Board, to convince the presenters of projects of the pitfalls of the projects when it came to implement them, and to provide continuous financial support and experienced qualified manpower to carry the project through to what may be called a 60 to 70 per cent rate of success. Philip was often taken aback with a gasp of bewilderment and lean back in his chair when the presenter pressed hard to secure the approval of the Board for an obviously flawed project. He would contemplate for a few minutes and then pounce with a clear, calculated and a logical question or solution to see if the project could, in any way, be improved or implemented.

When the time came to roll up the work of the Board of Trustees, I noticed a note of sadness in his voice and a withdrawn face showing his disappointment. After all, he was the architect of the BASED-UK and had dedicated himself for several years to its consolidation, proper functioning and advancement. Hassan Sabrí and myself shared in this sadness and disappointment because the Board of Trustees of BASED-UK had, after several years of hard work, finally developed into an entity that could easily implement future Bahá'í social and economic development projects to the highest standards.'

LEGAL INCORPORATION OF LOCAL SPIRITUAL ASSEMBLIES

Another aspect of his post-National Spiritual Assembly work was concerned with the legal incorporation of local spiritual assemblies, which was of considerable importance for the development of the Faith in this country. Kian Golestani, a lawyer who deals with the legal aspects of incorporation, has described his work in this connection.

What could I say that has not already been said more fully and eloquently by those who had the real honour to know Philip longer and more closely, as well as the privilege to have worked with him over the course of many years? I sincerely hope that these few paragraphs will add a little, however small, to the cherished memory of one whose like one rarely witnesses.

My earliest memories of Philip date back to my childhood, having come to the UK from Iran in August 1972 as a nine-year-old boy with a very limited knowledge of English. I nevertheless recall the spiritual colossus who was Philip Hainsworth. If a speaker were needed, Philip's name would be the first on everyone's lips. Even at that time one could say that his reputation preceded him. He was the man with the gravitas and knowledge to charm even the most important or difficult dignitary. His presence was such that one would be galvanised by the energy exuded by him. His enthusiasm was infectious and filled the room, bridging the linguistic divide.

These initial recollections of Philip gained through the eyes of a child and youth were very much of an individual occupying a station far above that of mere mortals and certainly well above anything I could aspire to. It was only the passage of more than 20 years and my involvement in the process of the incorporation of Spiritual Assemblies in accordance with the wishes of the beloved Guardian that I was fortunate enough to get to know him on a closer and more personal level.

Philip has left his indelible mark on so many spheres of Bahá'í activity that it will not come as a surprise to anyone that his boundless energy and commitment also came to be focused on the incorporation process. Indeed Philip, together with Oliver Christopherson, had been engaged in the task of drafting a new model constitution for incorporated assemblies when I came on the scene and was requested by the National Spiritual Assembly to deal with the topping and tailing of the document.

However, Philip's contribution did not end here. The task of rolling out the incorporation process to roughly 150 Assemblies throughout England and Wales was a monumental and daunting one, which was not only logistically demanding, but which was made more difficult by the essential requirement to educate a community unfamiliar with and often intimidated by the legal red tape on the one hand, and the need to respond to and convince certain sceptical individuals of the benefits of the process on the other. Who should the National Spiritual Assembly call upon at this hour to assist with the process but Philip? He not only played a significant role in the drafting of the article published in the *Bahá'í Journal* back in 1997 explaining the incorporation process to the UK Bahá'í community (an article which continues to serve as the initial source of guidance for each Assembly and individual on each particular incorporation) but he also volunteered with his typical indefatigable energy to take part in the demanding and time consuming tour of meeting with individual Assemblies to explain the incorporation process in detail and to deal with the execution of the requisite documentation. It was at one of these such meetings, which I attended together with Philip, that I witnessed for myself at close quarters Philip's ability to manage even the most difficult individuals and questions. It was only as a result of his knees finally failing him, thus preventing him from driving and necessitating surgery that he reluctantly had to step back from such visits.

One enduring memory of this period is the story of the faulty overhead projector, which Philip had taken to a meeting with him. The projector had malfunctioned and filled the room with acrid and unpleasant fumes. Characteristically, this proved no obstacle to Philip who continued with the meeting unfazed.

It was during this period of working closely with Philip and certain other individuals such as Hugh Adamson and Fuad Rizai that I experienced the truly high regard in which Philip was held and with which I could not but be compelled to agree. Oftentimes I recall the words of the late Fuad Rizai, who now resides with Philip in the Abhá Kingdom. Fuad's reverence for Philip knew no bounds. He always recalled with deep appreciation the kindness and support shown to him by Philip at a time when he had been experiencing many difficulties. It had been Philip who had ridden to the rescue and had helped him out of his predicament.

My most cherished memory of Philip dates back to the relatively recent Sidcot summer school of August 2000. I sat genuinely spellbound, as did the rest of the audience, by Philip's touching personal recollections of his days as a British officer in the Holy Land and of his first meetings with the Guardian. It was then that the true gentleness, simplicity and above all the dedication of this great man to the Cause of Bahá'u'lláh struck me in a way I had never felt before. His recollections seemed to bring the events of those many years ago back to life.

In my mind's eye, the picture I will always carry with me of Philip is not that of an old man with failing health, but rather of a young and dashing army officer dressed in shorts and sitting with his legs crossed in the mandar at the Haifa Pilgrim House in the presence of the Guardian and before an audience of besuited and shocked Oriental gentlemen, totally unaware of the social *faux pas* he was committing. I am sure that this would bring a smile to his face. I cannot help but to smile when I think of it.

I sincerely hope that these few paragraphs will add a little, however small, to the cherished memory of a man whose like one rarely witnesses.'

The tributes of these three distinguished Bahá'ís give an insight into aspects of Philip's work of which I have only a scanty knowledge, and I am truly grateful to the contributors.

TRAVELS

In addition to a great deal of travelling around the United Kingdom, Philip made two spectacular visits to the Falkland Islands, where his wisdom, kindness and jocular personality were much appreciated, and he was able to contribute to their public relations work through radio and press interviews. He also made visits to Malta and Canada in addition to those mentioned elsewhere in this chapter, and together we went to Gibraltar and Cyprus. Wherever he went, he gave the same wisdom and guidance and told of his visits to the beloved Guardian, always stressing the need to turn to the Supreme Body, the Universal House of Justice.

His last years were marred by intense pain and decreasing mobility – in 1996 we travelled to Madrid for the celebration of the fiftieth anniversary of the Faith's arrival in Spain, where he represented the British National Assembly. Very reluctantly, he agreed that I could arrange for him to have wheelchair assistance at the airports. This was the last time he was to see 'Amatu'l-Bahá Rúḥíyyih Khánum, whom he met in 1946 when he went to meet Shoghi Effendi – a friendship which lasted for over half a century.

At the International Convention in 1998, Richard was asked by some of the Ugandan Bahá'ís whether we could make a visit to their country, in which Philip had done so much successful teaching from 1951 to 1966, and where we had served as chairman and secretary of the committee which had built the Mashriqu'l-Adhkár – very important parts of both our lives. Eventually this was arranged for the summer of 1999 and he was lionised, as his name is so highly respected by the community in Uganda. He was immensely happy to see old Bahá'ís to whom he had introduced the Faith, with their children and grandchildren. The visit was also memorable for the number of Uganda government ministers with whom appointments were made for us, giving real opportunities for more teaching, with radio and television interviews. We were also able to renew our acquaintance with Princess Dorothy, the daughter of Kabaka Mutesa and Nabagereka Damali.

The Golden Jubilee of the introduction of the Faith to Uganda was held in August 2001 and this wonderful occasion was our last visit together. He had already been diagnosed with cancer of the bone and could walk only slowly, but was so invigorated by the obvious growth of the Faith during these 50 years and the love that was showered upon him that it gave him strength. A further joy was that Zarin and her family – her husband Soroush and children Iman, Anisa, Erfan and Iqan, as well as Richard and his wife, Corinne, also attended this tremendous celebration. We missed Richard's children, Arwyn, Reissa and Melissa, and Michael and his newly married wife, Katherine (née Lee). Richard had hired a car, which was a real blessing and for which Philip was deeply grateful as it made travelling in the town and the long journeys away from Kampala much easier for him, and the support of Richard and Corinne at this time gave him real joy.

After our return, although in great pain, he continued to accept requests to speak on the Faith although long journeys became insupportable.

HIS PASSING

He died quite suddenly on the evening of 16 December. The cancer had been diagnosed the previous June as a result of a visit to the doctor to see a swollen leg, which was caused by a pulmonary embolism. He had been given at least two years to live.

We had talked together quite normally on the day before, discussing the possibility of a pilgrimage. We were also making plans for Sunday when Michael and Katherine, Zarin, Soroush and their family would be coming to help us to take seven large boxes of historic papers to be stored at the Afnán Library. On Sunday morning he appeared to be sleeping quite peacefully when I got up to prepare lunch for the family. I went upstairs at about 9.30 am to find him comatose and he never properly recovered consciousness. I telephoned Michael, who came over immediately with Katherine and from that time, Philip was never alone. The doctor was called and gave him only hours to live as the blood clot had moved to his lungs, and she ordered visits from the MacMillan Nurses. They were wonderfully kind and told us what to expect. They also told us that although he appeared not to respond, the last sense to go is that of hearing and that we should continue to talk to him. I telephoned Richard in Moscow and Philip's old friend in Haifa, 'Alí Nakhjavání: both spoke with him while I held the telephone to his ear and I am convinced he heard them as he gripped my hand and his eyelids moved.

Zarin and her family arrived a little later and her children were able to speak to him before they returned home with Soroush. Zarin, Michael and Katherine stayed with us all night, saying prayers continuously, and the girls were chanting a prayer at the time he died. Devastating though it was for us, that he should go so quickly, it was a bounty that he was spared the slow and painful death usual with bone cancer – perhaps a gift for the incredibly devoted service he had given to the Faith over his entire adult life.

There are many whose lives he touched, many whom he helped in a myriad different ways, and this was borne home to me when I began to receive the six hundred or so messages from all over the world after his passing. It was also evident from the very large number of people from many parts of this country, from the United States, Europe, Israel, Dubai and who knows where else, who attended his funeral on a cold, cold day, some filling the chapel at the New Southgate Cemetery, but most waiting in the freezing cold outside. He must have been happy to look down and see that 'Alí Nakhjavání had come to say, 'goodbye' as, indeed, was I.

He is buried just opposite the grave of the beloved Guardian and close to our old friend Hassan Sabrí who had died shortly before him and who had served with us on the Temple Committee and with Philip on the Central and East African Regional Spiritual Assembly.

He was enormously proud of our three children, all of whom have already given outstanding service, and was continually delighted at the teaching activities of our seven grandchildren.

As if confirmed by Bahá'u'lláh Himself, Philip's death became a teaching event. His obituary in the Daily Telegraph – where the passing of the Great is recorded – mentioned specifically his contributions to the Bahá'í Faith.

Though other Bahá'ís have been so honoured, yet always their achievements were described as if their Faith was some personal affectation, not central to their lives and deeds. Philip's obituary marks a stage in the perception of the British nation, a recognition that the Bahá'í Faith was indeed something to which a Great person would be willing dedicate his life. Such perception shifts occur ever so gradually, barely noticeably, until one day it appears in the public record. And we can identify the perception and label the time. Such was Philip's obituary.

He was a legend in his own lifetime – someone at his funeral said, 'We shall never see his like again'.

Of life's inevitable transitions, death is normally accompanied by a rite of passage full of grief and loss. The family wanted Philip's funeral to reflect the things he truly valued: inspiring others and making them smile. We asked the friends and family who spoke at the reception which followed the funeral to mention the things he did to make them laugh, that had inspired them, that had touched them. For Philip's spirit is not buried beneath black earth and stone, it is not lost and gone forever. It remains with us, who knew him, and with anyone who turns the pages of this book and recognises a soul who just tried to be a good Bahá'í.

Lois Hainsworth

APPENDIX 1: *UNFOLDING DESTINY*

THE LAST COMMAND OF THE MASTER

> After the passing away of this wronged one, it is incumbent upon … the loved ones of the Abha Beauty to turn unto Shoghi Effendi … as he is the sign of God, the chosen branch, the guardian of the Cause of God, he unto whom all the Aghsan, the Afnan, the Hands of the Cause of God and His loved ones must turn.[252]

Only a handful of the believers appreciated the implications of this final command of 'Abdu'l-Bahá when His Will and Testament was published in 1922. It was not until about half way through the first British Six Year Plan (about 1947) that the hundred or so Bahá'ís then enrolled began to catch a glimpse of what these vital words really meant.

A study of the words of Shoghi Effendi in *The Unfolding Destiny of the British Bahá'í Community,* written to the English Bahá'ís, in the first 200 pages of that volume (Scotland, Ireland and Wales were virtually unopened), the preface by David Hofman and the introduction will reveal how lovingly and with deep affection the Guardian, from his first letter of 16 December 1922, encouraged the believers in these Islands to arise and serve the Faith they had espoused. After almost 22 years of this gentle and sympathetic support, he seized with startling enthusiasm the decision of the 1944 convention to adopt a Six Year Plan that asked him to set its goals.

The few believers gathered in a blacked-out basement room at N°. 1 Victoria Street, London, representing fewer than 100 registered Bahá'ís, and daily expecting to hear news of the invasion by Allied troops of the European continent, were so filled with excitement at the news they received of the successful completion of the first American Seven Year Plan and their decision to ask the Guardian for his blessing on their Six Year Plan, that they did not even record it in their convention resolutions!

None present suspected that the goals set would include Spiritual Assemblies in Wales, Scotland, Northern Ireland, and Eire. After 45 years of the Faith in England, London, Manchester and Bradford were the only firm Assemblies; Torquay had just managed to re-form and Bournemouth had lapsed, yet a total of 24 Assemblies had to be established covering the whole British Isles within six years.

[252] Abdu'l-Bahá (1971). The Will and Testament of Abdu'l-Bahá. Wilmette, Ill., Bahá'í Publishing Trust., p. 11.

In the first two years virtually nothing was done, three pioneers had set out and had returned home, yet on the 27 March 1945 the Guardian wrote:[253]

> *Dear and valued co-workers,*
>
> The Six Year Plan which the English believers have conceived and are now energetically prosecuting constitutes a landmark in the history of the Faith in the British Isles. It is the first collective enterprise undertaken by them for the spread of the Faith and the consolidation of its divinely appointed institutions.

By August he was writing:[254]

> *Dear and valued co-workers,*
>
> I grieve to learn of the slow progress of the Six Year Plan which the English believers have so nobly conceived, and which, I pray and hope, will be triumphantly consummated. The Plan constitutes a direct and grave challenge to the English Bahá'í community in its entirety. It should be regarded as the greatest collective enterprise ever launched by the followers of the Faith of Bahá'u'lláh in the British Isles. It is thus far one of the most significant undertakings embarked upon by the members of Bahá'í National Assemblies during the opening years of the second Bahá'í century. To it, as already observed, the immediate destinies of the community of the English believers are linked, and on it must depend the future orientation and evolution of the institutions which the members of that community are labouring to erect for the diffusion of the principles and the establishment of the Faith of Bahá'u'lláh in their country. It must not, it cannot, fail.

Even such strong words were not understood by the majority of the believers and no extra efforts were made – they had not learned the implications of the Master's words – 'turn to Shoghi Effendi'.[255] Within a year, however, a change began to be observed which was brought about because of several influences:

Marion Holley, a most dedicated and experienced Bahá'í teacher and administrator with the vast background of knowledge of being on the Teaching Committee which had spearheaded the triumph of the

[253] Effendi, S. (1981). The Unfolding Destiny of the British Bahá'í Community: The Messages from the Guardian of the Bahá'í Faith to the Bahá'ís of the British Isles. London, Bahá'í Publishing Trust., p. 173.
[254] Ibid., p. 178.
[255] Abdu'l-Bahá (1971). The Will and Testament of Abdu'l-Bahá. Wilmette, Ill., Bahá'í Publishing Trust., p. 11.

American Seven Year Plan, had come to England to marry David Hofman. She and David had been inspired with an abounding love for the Guardian by their Bahá'í teacher – May Maxwell, the mother of 'Amatu'l-Bahá Rúḥíyyih Khánum, and together they began spread this love among the English believers.

Hassan Sabrí, aflame with that same love and understanding of the station of the Guardian from his father, chairman of the Egyptian National Spiritual Assembly, had come to study in England and began to travel teach in his free time.

Philip Hainsworth, on release from the Army, had arrived back home after spending some 14 hours with Shoghi Effendi in the Holy Land and was called upon to travel and share his experiences with the believers. In his last interview with the Guardian, he had answered questions about the way the teaching work was conducted in England and the Guardian had said that he would write to the National Spiritual Assembly to call on them to organise their work on a new basis and this letter was being written as Philip left Haifa. This letter was dated the 29th of May 1946 and when received caused the National Spiritual Assembly to adopt an entirely different approach to the use of teachers and pioneers.

The small community in England then began to 'turn to Shoghi Effendi'. The National Spiritual Assembly would immediately send out mimeographed copies of all messages received from the Guardian rather than await the next *Bahá'í Journal.* Believers began to write him personal letters and when they received a reply, they would usually share them with the National Spiritual Assembly or the National Teaching Committee and with their friends by carbon copy. Frequently these messages would be read aloud and discussed to explore every nuance of the letter. As the months went by the spate of messages increased – more than 40 were received by the National Spiritual Assembly and its committees in the following two years in addition to the many passed around by individual Bahá'ís.

As this 'turning' increased the capacity of the believers, the Guardian was able to call on them for ever-greater services and their appreciation of their 'beloved Guardian' grew in proportion. They seemed to live for the moment when another message would come. By the end of the Six Year Plan their dedication to their Guardian was universal; they reached all their goals and their reward was his cable to the 1950 Convention which opened with these thrilling words, 'heart flooded joy'.[256]

THE DESTINY OF THE BRITISH BELIEVERS BEGINS TO UNFOLD

To 'Awaken the masses':[257]

29 May, 1946: 'The present Plan is but a stepping stone that must lead eventually the English believers to execute so tremendous and meritorious an undertaking'.

However, the whole section in the Guardian's handwriting should be studied carefully.

1946 a 'pivotal year':[258]

6 July 1946: 'establish . . . nucleus future Assembly both Scotland, Ireland . . . nation-wide expansion progressive consolidation'.

'Opening of a new era':[259]

16 October 1946: 'The consummation of their present task will . . . signalise the inauguration of a great epoch in the history of the Faith in their land – an epoch that must witness the universal recognition of their Cause . . . throughout the British Isles'.

The first mention of their overseas rôle:[260]

26 February 1947: 'Upon the success of the Plan . . . must depend the scope and effectiveness of their two-fold task of proclaiming the verities of their Faith to their fellow countrymen at home, and of implanting its banner abroad amidst the peoples and races of a far-flung Empire'.

Also repeated in his handwriting on 8 May 1947.[261]

'Safeguard Prizes Won':[262]

29 April 1947: On successful completion of the goals set for that year, the Guardian cabled, 'Confident all members community,

[256] Effendi, S. (1981). The Unfolding Destiny of the British Bahá'í Community: The Messages from the Guardian of the Bahá'í Faith to the Bahá'ís of the British Isles. London, Bahá'í Publishing Trust., p. 245.
[257] Ibid., p. 187
[258] Ibid., p. 189.
[259] Ibid., p. 191.
[260] Ibid., p. 196.
[261] Ibid., Para., two, p. 201.
[262] Ibid., p. 198.

young, old, teachers, pioneers, administrators, will resolutely safeguard prizes won'.

Repeated 10 October 1947: 'Newly formed Assemblies must be maintained at all costs'.[263]

Basis for progress: [264]

9 October 1947: Written on his behalf by his secretary to the Assembly Development Committee. 'The unity, love, harmony and proper understanding of the administration of the Cause which exists in a community are the measure of its progress, and on them depend directly the expansion of the Faith'.

An Assembly in every county essential for proclamation to the masses 24 October 1947: 'A Bahá'í administrative centre in every county . . . an essential prelude to the effective proclamation of the Faith to the masses'.[265]

The formation of Assemblies of Cardiff, Dublin, Edinburgh applauded:[266]

25 April 1948: 'Unprecedented British Bahá'í history, constitutes landmark annals world Bahá'í community, signalises commencement significant phase spiritual history Irish, Scottish, Welsh peoples. . . . Concourse on High applauds brilliant feat unitedly achieved British followers Faith…'

Also applauded in letter 29 April 1948.[267]

The best way to help our fellow-men: [268]

9 April 1949: 'All humanity is disturbed and suffering and confused; we cannot expect to not be disturbed and not to suffer - but we don't have to be confused. On the contrary, confidence and assurance, hope and optimism are our prerogative. The successful carrying out of our various Plans is the greatest sign we can give of our faith and inner assurance, and the best way we can help our fellow-men out of their confusion and difficulties'.

'A glimpse of the future glory of their destiny'[269]: The whole of the section in the Guardian's handwriting of the letter on pages 226 – 7 should be read aloud and deeply studied. The final paragraph reflects the Guardian's love and experience of mountain climbing.

[263] Ibid., pp. 206, 209.
[264] Ibid., p. 205.
[265] Ibid., p. 209.
[266] Ibid., p. 211.
[267] Ibid., p. 215.
[268] Ibid., p. 225.
[269] Ibid., p. 227.

As the community entered the final year of its Plan the appeals from the Guardian became even more intense and compelling until almost every Bahá'í was seeking a way to pioneer or introduce the Faith to a new seeker. This feeling may be gained from a study of his cables of 19 April[270] and 27 April,[271] and 8 July 1949,[272] the final paragraph of his letter of 6 September 1949[273] and every word of that same letter in his own handwriting. His cable to the Teaching Conference at the close of 1949 raised everyone to an even higher level of excitement.[274] The National Teaching Committee, centred in Oxford, was meeting almost weekly and then daily as the end of the Plan approached and his message to them, written by his secretary on his behalf, of 28 March 1950 contained the pregnant words: 'to do something for God 100 per cent has an attractive power, and brings future Divine confirmations'.[275]

Finally, sent only two days later his cable made the astounding offer, 'total success Plan now hanging balance for my part utmost can do is stretch period Plan to July 9th.'[276]

The Committee would have none of this and set in motion its final arrangements for confirmation of new believers and settlement pioneers and the National Spiritual Assembly was able to cable him on 10 April, 'Joyfully transmit Teaching Committee report arrangements made complete Plan by Ridván earnestly entreat prayers Bahá'u'lláh seal victory'.[277] This was followed by a cable on 17 April,[278] 'Total victory assured loving gratitude bounties beloved Guardian assistance whole Bahá'í world' to which he responded on 19 April: 'Overjoyed deeply grateful immensely proud signal victory achieved Bahá'í Community British Isles shedding lustre opening years second Bahá'í Century'.[279]

The National Spiritual Assembly immediately responded, 'Joyous Ridván greetings beloved Guardian from National Assembly and twenty-four local Spiritual Assemblies British Isles'[280] to which he

[270] Ibid., p. 228.
[271] Ibid.
[272] Ibid., p. 229.
[273] Ibid., p. 231.
[274] Ibid., p. 237.
[275] Ibid., p. 239.
[276] Ibid., p. 240.
[277] Unpublished report (personal archives).
[278] Unpublished cable (personal archives).
[279] Effendi, S. (1981). The Unfolding Destiny of the British Bahá'í Community: The Messages from the Guardian of the Bahá'í Faith to the Bahá'ís of the British Isles. London, Bahá'í Publishing Trust., p. 240.
[280] Unpublished cable (personal archives).

answered, on 21 April:[281]

> Share joy reciprocate noble sentiments heartily congratulate national elected representatives, triumphant community, indefatigable National Teaching Committee, all subsidiary agencies particularly self-sacrificing pioneers who so outstandingly contributed signal victory reverberating Bahá'í world.
>
> *Shoghi.*

At the Convention that followed, the cable from the Guardian was read in faltering voice by National Spiritual Assembly Chairman, Ḥasan Balyúzí and hardly a dry eye was to be seen as the past achievements were reviewed and the challenging future was revealed.[282]

The Two Year (Africa) Plan (1951 – 53) was started ahead of time and more than achieved all its goals. (See *Bahá'í Journal* May 2001 "It All Began Fifty Years Ago"). The Guardian changed his plans for a third American Seven Year Plan and launched the Global Crusade (Ten Year Plan) in 1953 and the British Bahá'í Community made a distinctive contribution. A careful study of the messages from the Guardian which followed right up to his untimely passing are given in Unfolding Destiny and amply confirm the principle which forms the basis of this article – which is that in turning to the Centre of the Covenant, not only do those who turn develop ever-increasing capacity, but that Centre is able to shower more and more powerful guidance. It was true in those days – it is equally true today. Referring to this unique collection of messages from the Guardian, the Universal House of Justice wrote on 2 April 1981:[283]

> The House of Justice hopes that it will be constantly drawn to the attention of the friends, many of whom are new and have entered the Faith since the Guardian's passing. If study classes and other occasions are devoted to it and if it is prominent in the programmes of summer schools and institutes its message must surely have a galvanising effect upon the spirits of the believers.

It is with this Divine guidance of twenty years ago in mind that I commend this study to you.

Philip Hainsworth

[281] Effendi, S. (1981). The Unfolding Destiny of the British Bahá'í Community: The Messages from the Guardian of the Bahá'í Faith to the Bahá'ís of the British Isles. London, Bahá'í Publishing Trust., p. 240.
[282] Ibid., pp. 245 – 6.
[283] Unpublished letter (personal archives).

APPENDIX 2: PUBLICATIONS

Books

Beyond Disarmament	Bahá'í Publishing Trust	1984
Bahá'í Focus on Human Rights	Bahá'í Publishing Trust	1985
Bahá'í Focus on Peace	Bahá'í Publishing Trust	1986
The Bahá'í Faith[284]	Ward Lock International	1980
Historical Dictionary of the Bahá'í Faith: Historical Dictionaries of Religions, Philosophies, and Movements, N°. 17[285]	The Scarecrow Press, Inc.	1998
The United Nations – A Bahá'í Obligation	UNA World Religion Series	1998

The section on the Bahá'í Faith in

World Religions – a Handbook for Teachers	SHAP	1972
Living Faiths – Initiation Rites	Butterworth Educational	1978
Living Faiths – Death	Butterworth Educational	1980
Living Faiths – Marriage and the Family	Butterworth Educational	1985
I believe	CEM	1978
Festivals in World Religions	Longmans	1986

Editor

The Unfolding Destiny[286]	Bahá'í Publishing Trust	1981

Pamphlets translated into numerous African languages from 1948 including

Swahili Chinyanza Hausa Luganda

Magazines

Contributed many articles on different aspects of the Bahá'í Faith over a period of fifty years

[284] Co-authored with Mary Perkins; A Textbook used in many countries, translated into five languages
[285] Co-authored with Hugh Adamson
[286] A 550 page volume of annotated letters from Shoghi Effendi.

APPENDIX 3: THE BAHÁ'Í FAITH

Sweeping across the globe in the twentieth century, the Bahá'í Faith is the personally chosen religious profession of independently minded individuals from every walk of life, cultural background and ethnic group. Despite their diversity, which they celebrate, cultivate and promote, Bahá'ís are remarkably united when it comes to the fundamentals of their belief.

There is only one administrative structure in the Bahá'í Faith, with an elected collegiate institution at the very top, and elected and appointed bodies at every geographical region. Despite the diversity of its membership, the Bahá'í community has not splintered as have all religions in the past, and a remarkably high proportion of Bahá'ís, especially those who are active and enthusiastic, are involved in the daily administration of the community. In every town and village across the entire world, wherever there are more than nine adult believers, the community elects a local Spiritual Assembly (LSA). By giving control over the spiritual, social and religious aspects of a Bahá'í community to the ordinary believers, there is no need for a specialised priesthood.

The Founder of the Bahá'í Faith, Bahá'u'lláh, was born in Persia in the early part of the nineteenth century. One way of translating 'bahá' is 'glory', so Bahá'u'lláh is the 'Glory of God', and 'Bahá'ís' are followers of that glory. For Bahá'ís, Bahá'u'lláh is a 'manifestation of God'. The concept is fundamental to their theology and belief system. Rather than being merely representatives, or apostles or, at the other extreme, incarnations, of God, the Founders of the world's major religions are 'Manifestations of God'. They manifest the attributes of God, provide a body of knowledge and understanding to humanity that mankind might grow and develop. In Bahá'í eyes, all the Founders of the major religions are Manifestations, eg., Krishna, Buddha, Christ, Muhammad, and the latest (not the last) of this line is Bahá'u'lláh.

Moreover, the Manifestation must always constrain the knowledge He outpours to the abilities of humanity at the time. Just as a child growing up is able to understand more of what a teacher is able to transmit, so humanity's capacity to understand is increasing. In one way, there is nothing inherently different between any of these Manifestations. Bahá'ís do not revere Bahá'u'lláh above other Manifestations. Yet in another way, the body of teachings he has given is more relevant and abundant for people today. Since all religions are founded by Manifestations of a single God, they all have one source. Whatever differences may be observed between individual religions can only be the product of the interpretations made by those who chose to emphasise differences rather than celebrate common understandings.

The effect of this view of religion – recognising they are all from a single source – means that Bahá'ís have no inherent antipathy to any other religious confession. Moreover, Bahá'ís see acceptance of a new believer of the Faith as a confirmation of their faith in all other religions.

Yet the direction of Bahá'u'lláh's revelation is not just religious harmony, nor even peace on earth, but the complete transformation of the way society is constructed and the way human beings interact. Humanity covers the face of the globe – the effects of industrialisation in one part will lead to ecological catastrophes in others. We compass continents in less than a day. Political structures that have evolved to co-ordinate countries and clans are inadequate for the world today. The divisions of functions between male and female now generate injustices no longer tolerable in a technological society. The desperate straits of the world's poorest when set against the wealth of the middle class in the wealthiest states are unconscionable to any reasonable and sensitive person.

It is to bring an alternative into a working reality that is the goal of the Bahá'í community. As Bahá'ís we know humanity does not compromise the potential of all its members and accept outmoded ways of life. This is what we work for, a vision of a better world, and one that is already demonstrably practical.

Richard Hainsworth

BIBLIOGRAPHY

Abdu'l-Bahá (1971). The Will and Testament of Abdu'l-Bahá. Wilmette, Ill., Bahá'í Publishing Trust.

Bahá'í Year Book (1939). Bahá'í World (1936-1938) Vol. VII An International Record. New York, Bahá'í Publishing Committee.

Bahá'u'lláh (1992). Kitáb-i-Aqdas - The Most Holy Book. Haifa, Bahá'í World Centre.

Compilation (1988). Lights of Guidance: A Bahá'í Reference File. New Delhi, India, Bahá'í Publishing Trust.

Effendi, S. (1965). Messages to Canada (1923-1957). Toronto, Ont., National Spiritual Assembly of the Bahá'ís of Canada.

Effendi, S. (1971). Messages to the Bahá'í World 1950-1957. Wilmette, Ill., Bahá'í Publishing Trust.

Effendi, S. (1979). God Passes By. Wilmette, Ill., Bahá'í Publishing Trust.

Effendi, S. (1981). The Unfolding Destiny of the British Bahá'í Community: The Messages from the Guardian of the Bahá'í Faith to the Bahá'ís of the British Isles. London, Bahá'í Publishing Trust.

Effendi, S. (1984). The Advent of Divine Justice. Wilmette, Ill., Bahá'í Publishing Trust.

Hands of the Cause of God, l. (1992). The Ministry of the Custodians 1957-1963 - An Account of the Stewardship of the Hands of the Cause - With an Introduction by the Hand of the Cause Amatu'l-Bahá Rúhíyyih Khánum. Haifa, Israel, Bahá'í World Centre.

Rabbani, R. (1969). The Priceless Pearl. London, Bahá'í Publishing Trust.

Rabbani, R. (1988). The Guardian of the Bahá'í Faith. London, Bahá'í Publishing Trust.